MODERN MEAT

MODERN
MEAT

ORVILLE SCHELL

VINTAGE BOOKS
A DIVISION OF RANDOM HOUSE
NEW YORK

First Vintage Books Edition, July 1985

Copyright © 1978, 1980, 1983, 1984 by Orville Schell

All rights reserved under International and Pan-American Copyright Conventions. Published in the United States by Random House, Inc., New York, and simultaneously in Canada by Random House of Canada Limited, Toronto. Originally published by Random House, Inc., in 1984.

Portions of this work have previously appeared in the following publications: *Country Journal, Los Angeles Times, Mother Jones, The New Yorker* and *Rolling Stone.*

Library of Congress Cataloging in Publication Data

Schell, Orville.
Modern meat.

Includes index.
1. Antibiotics in animal nutrition.
2. Hormones in animal nutrition.
3. Feed additive residues—Hygienic aspects.
4. Meat—Contamination.
I. Title.
[SF98.A5S34 1985]   636.08′83′0289   84-40543
ISBN 0-394-72919-6 (pbk.)

Manufactured in the United States of America

FOR MY FATHER

ACKNOWLEDGMENTS

I would like to thank Meredith Tromble, Burr Heneman and Amey Urdang for their editorial help in preparing this manuscript, and Liz Tuomi, Debbie Perrin and Jennifer Meyer for their stenographic help.

I would also like to thank Dr. Richard Novick, Dr. Jere Goyan and Dr. Stuart Levy for giving so much of their time to explain the scientific research they have undertaken and to check various drafts of this work for errors.

The patience of Rob Cowley and other editors at Random House during the years this book was in progress will not easily be forgotten.

Finally, I would like to express my appreciation to the Alicia Patterson Foundation for their fellowship which enabled me to undertake much of the research and travel that went into this book.

Orville Schell
Bolinas, California
August 1983

PROLOGUE

Number 9 is a pure-bred Hampshire sow, one of the breeding animals on our California hog and cattle ranch. Her name comes from a small white plastic tag that hangs from one bristly ear. Tonight she is about to give birth to a litter of piglets.

It is well after sunset when she finally eases her large and distended body down onto the floor of her farrowing pen to await labor. The evening is chilly, and the cold renders the usual squadron of buzzing flies that plague the pigs by day immobile on the underside of the farrowing barn's tin roof. I sit and wait under a heat lamp in the creep, a small warm sanctuary into which the newborn piglets will be able to retreat after nursing so as to minimize the risk of being crushed by their elephantine mother.

In the neighboring pens the sows and their litters sleep soundly, lost in porcine reveries, punctuating the still night with occasional contented sighs and a seemingly inexhaustible basso continuo of crepitations.

Just as I am dozing off, one of the largest sows awakens for a drink at her watering device. The soup noises she makes as she loudly slakes her thirst arouse the entire barn. Like a jungle suddenly coming to life as a prowler passes through, all the sows and piglets awake and begin a chorus of grunting and squealing.

Number 9 is, however, oblivious to all the commotion. She is stretched out now, eyes closed, her large body racked by contractions. I reach over and give her a scratch behind one leathery ear. For a moment she opens her eyes, looks at me with an eerie humanness, oinks sotto voce, and then returns to her concentration of labor.

As the other litters begin to nurse, the barn quiets down, and I again fall asleep. When I awake several hours later, Number 9 has not yet given birth, although she is straining and struggling.

Two hours later, at 3:00 A.M., she has still not produced any of her progeny. Fearing a breeched piglet, I give her a shot of penicillin to guard against infection, wash up and then, covering my right hand and forearm with surgical lubricant, I lean down behind her and reach up into her vagina.

When my arm has disappeared almost to the elbow, I suddenly feel two tiny back hooves. Cautiously grabbing the breeched piglet by its delicate hindquarters, I coax it slowly down Number 9's birth canal, pausing for each contraction until at last it slithers out onto the floor.

As I clean the mucus out of its nose with a towel, the newborn piglet, sounding like an engine trying to start on a cold morning, gives its first spluttering breaths. After clipping its umbilical cord, swabbing the end with iodine and removing the remains of the damp, cold embryonic sack from its body, I place the piglet beside one of Number 9's teats, already dribbling colostrum. Milking one of the nipples, I fire it right into the snuffling piglet's mouth. Driven by its own instincts, it burrows forward, making desperate smacking noises with its lips until finally it captures the teat in its mouth.

Once more I doze off under the heat lamp. When I awake anew, Number 9 still has not produced any more piglets. She tries to stand, but cannot. Her breathing is heavy, and her contractions seem to have stopped.

Walking to the supply room, I pick up another syringe and a bottle of Butocin (a synthetic oxytocin, a hormone produced by the pituitary gland that induces uterine contractions and has milk-releasing action). Back in the farrowing barn, I give Number 9 her second shot of the evening. Within moments, she begins having strong contractions once again. And before the sun rises, she has given birth to eight more healthy piglets.

Living and working on a ranch, one is constantly made aware of the growing number of drugs, chemicals and new technologies—such as the two injections with which I have just simplified Number 9's labor—that have become a regular part of livestock production over the past few decades.

Hardly a day goes by that the mail does not bring promotional literature advertising some new agricultural technology such as oral larvicides, which are designed to kill fly larvae in manure after being eaten by cattle, barn paint that contains insecticides which will kill insects on contact, new vaccines to prevent disease, injectable worming agents to control internal parasites, feed additives and subcutaneous implants to promote faster growth, mold inhibitors to preserve feed, gadgets that can tell if an animal is pregnant, electronic ejaculators to collect semen for artificial insemination, machines that tenderize meat by electrically stimulating the muscle tissue of carcasses and even small battery-powered radio transmitters designed to be swallowed by cows as alternative means of identification to branding.

The ingenuity of these scientific discoveries and new inventions attests to the creative genius and spirit of innovation that continue to make American agriculture the most productive in the world. But there are aspects of this revolution in livestock production, such as the increasing reliance on drugs and chemicals, that are unsettling. Compounds that are closely regulated for human use can easily be bought in any quantity for animal use without prescription. Frequently, through carelessness, ignorance or both, they are also grievously misused. It is not surprising, then, that many consumers have a vague but fearful sense that modern meat may somehow be unsafe to eat.

Wanting to know whether or not such fears were ill founded, I set off across the country to write this book. In it, I have concentrated on three aspects of modern meat production: antibiotic feed additives that are used on a "subtherapeutic" or daily basis to control disease and promote growth in almost all commercially raised meat animals, several new animal-feed technologies to increase the efficiency of feedstuffs, and hormonal compounds that are widely used either to enhance the growth of cattle or to manipulate their reproductive systems.

I

ANTIBIOTICS

1

"Indiana Loves Pork—Welcome APC" proclaims a political campaign-style button on the lapel of a bus driver waiting just outside the baggage-claim area at Indianapolis International Airport. The initials APC stand for American Pork Congress —an organization that is holding its 1982 gathering this spring at the Indiana Convention Center, in downtown Indianapolis. The bus driver has been hired by the Elanco Products Company (a division of Eli Lilly & Company, one of the nation's largest manufacturers of antibiotic feed additives for livestock) to shuttle arriving hog farmers from the airport to the city.

By the time I arrive at the convention center, the registration area is jammed. Before this three-day event ends, some nine thousand pork producers (a term that the sponsoring National Pork Producers' Council would like to see replace traditional appellations, such as pig farmer and hog farmer) and "Porkettes" (the APC's ladies' auxiliary) will have participated in a crowded schedule of lectures and seminars, ranging in topic from "How to Avoid Financial Disaster in a Recession" and "Purchasing Pork on Carcass" to "Does Testes Size Influence Reproduction?" The Pork Congress not only provides American hog farmers (who in 1982 produced 82,197,000 hogs worth $10.94 billion) and their families with a welcome occasion for leaving their farms and socializing with friends and acquaintances, but also enables them to keep abreast of the multitude of new techniques, drugs, chemicals and kinds of equipment that have made the raising of swine one of the most rapidly modernized sectors of American agriculture. At the annual banquet, on the closing night, this year's Pork All-Americans—model hog farmers chosen from each of the thirty-three major pork-producing states—will be announced, and the 1982 Pork Queen will be selected, crowned and presented with a three-thousand-dollar scholarship check from the American Cyanamid Co., another large manufacturer of pharmaceuticals for animal use.

Of all the activities at the Pork Congress, by far the best attended is the trade show in the convention center's Main Hall—a vast indoor exhibition area. Here some 370 companies have erected several acres of commercial displays spread out along carpeted corridors on the open floor. Surrounded by booths and a crush of farmers in shovel-bill caps with labels advertising swine-related products, it is as if one had stumbled into a surreal theme park for people who loved pigs; where the steeds on the merry-go-round are pigs instead of horses, the arcades along the midway all have porcine themes, and even the food concessions (here serving the "Official American Pork Congress Sandwich") have been mysteriously transformed to correspond to the prevailing motif.

There are pig posters, pig statues, silhouettes of pigs, slide shows and video cassettes of pigs, displays of feed for pigs, medicine for pigs and paraphernalia for pigs. DeKalb Swine Breeders, Inc., has erected a display that consists simply of a large glass meat cooler with the carefully dissected remains of two pigs propped up inside. Only the back halves of the two demonstration pigs are left. Their hindquarters have been fastidiously sawed diagonally from the middle of the backbone to just under the anus, so that one can peer right into the middle of the hams. These amputated pigs, which still wear their skin, give the unsettling appearance of being neither alive nor dead—of being animals who are trying without success to make the metaphysical transition from beast to meat.

Apparently, the object of the display is to illustrate the superior musculature of the genetically improved pig on the left, which is identified as the DeKalb strain, while the considerably thinner pig on the right is identified simply as "other."

Rising up over most of the exhibits is the American Hoechst Corporation's display, a seventeen-foot-high stack of fifty-pound sacks of Flavomycin—a feed additive containing the antibiotic bambermycin—which lists slightly, like the Tower of Pisa. Below this precarious promotional edifice is a sign proclaiming, "Feed Saved with Flavomycin Over Other Antibiotics Really Adds Up." Toward the center of the hall, a salesman from the Continental Animal Health company wades through the crowd passing out badges that depict a cheerful pink pig pressing a set of barbells, above the slogan "Gleptocil Double Strength Iron."

Every imaginable hog-farming accoutrement is on display, including feed grinders and mixers, manure separators, irrigation systems, a trailer-size portable hog barn, livestock prods, ear tags, automatic watering nipples and a wide panoply of drugs. Like hikers accumulating clusters of burrs on their woolens as they walk through brush, many of the hog farmers roaming the Main Hall floor soon become festooned with promotional badges, buttons and stickers:

"Pork Producers Have Personality Plus."

"Have You Hugged Your Hogs Today?"

"I'm a Pushover for Pork."

The displays of the smaller firms are little more than counters with banners as backdrops and piles of free literature. The large firms, however, have created elaborate indoor environments, which sit on the hall's floor like re-created decors in a department-store showroom.

Across the densely packed floor, thickets of placards rise above the various booths like gas-station and motel signs at interstate cloverleafs. It is, however, almost impossible to overlook one particularly prominent sign—a large, revolving semicircle of Masonite emblazoned with the white profile of a pig and the words "Aureo SP 250, Granule Premium." This marks the booth of American Cyanamid, the maker of Aureo SP 250, which is a granulated antimicrobial feed additive for swine, composed of tetracycline, penicillin and sulfamethazine; Aureo S 700, which is a feed additive for cattle, containing tetracycline and sulfamethazine; and a host of other livestock drugs. It is one of the largest booths, and in fact cannot really be called a booth at all, since it occupies the entire end of one block of the hall and is completely furnished, with a red rug, coffee tables, lamps, plants, and a stylish living-room set of white Naugahyde and chrome. The display might be mistaken for any doctor's office or a corporate lounge were it not that the room has no walls. And American Cyanamid occupies a choice piece of the hall's real estate. Bounded on three sides by aisles and situated near the front of the hall, the display is one that the crowds flowing through the entranceway are likely to encounter before they fan out to remoter regions and the booths of smaller and less prosperous companies.

The prominence of American Cyanamid—the nation's largest manufacturer of tetracycline for use as a livestock-feed additive—at the American Pork Congress is fitting. And, in view of the increasingly important connection between animal husbandry and the pharmaceutical industry, it is hardly surprising to find that many of the largest displays at the Pork Congress are those of the agricultural divisions of such drug companies as Eli Lilly & Co., Pfizer Inc., Upjohn Co., American Hoechst Corp., Diamond Shamrock Corp. and Smith Kline Beckman Corp., all of which manufacture antibiotic feed additives, part of the two-billion-dollar-a-year animal-health business.

American Cyanamid's sales staff has set up a small white plastic table outside its lounge, with a poster proclaiming to passersby, "Prizes! Prizes! Prizes! Win one of the valuable Cyanamid premiums!" The premiums include key chains, pens and plastic coffee cups, all embossed with the American Cyanamid logo; American Cyanamid caps; and bright-yellow T-shirts decorated with a pig profile and the legend, in green and red letters, "Aureo SP 250. Totally Granulated. Each Granule a Complete Pre-mix." A number of people have gathered around the table and are studying a color poster of the booty that can be "won." (Since Cyanamid wishes everyone to win a trinket and thus become a walking advertisement, anyone who fills out a name card is sent a gift.)

As I pause at the table, a white canister that looks like a large industrial vacuum cleaner with a plastic fishbowl affixed to its top rolls across the Cyanamid lounge and lurches to a halt in front of a woman inspecting the poster. Making a series of preliminary bleeps, it suddenly begins to speak. "I can tell you're a winner," it says, addressing the surprised woman, who recoils into the aisle as if she had been bitten. "Just fill out a card, honey, and you'll be a winner for sure," proclaims the voice from the canister, sounding like a broadcast from a very inexpensive radio. The woman's expression reflects a mixture of curiosity and embarrassment, but the canister is undaunted. "What's your name, you sweet thing, you?" it continues relentlessly. The woman is now grinning foolishly but remains mute. "Oh, come on, now! How's about a name," it insists. The woman looks around at the growing crowd of hog farmers, who, stopping to stare at the unlikely spectacle of a small mobile machine trying to engage a woman in conversation, have gridlocked the aisle. "Don't you have a name?" asks the canister.

"Yes. It's Mabel," the flustered woman says reluctantly.

The garrulous white canister is Big Cy, a robot hired by American Cyanamid to liven up its display and publicize its drugs at the Congress. Covered with American Cynamid decals, this contrivance is radio-controlled by a roboteer behind a rattan screen at one end of Cyanamid's make-believe lounge and is capable not only of talking and rolling about on casters but also of bleeping, blinking, moving its arms of corrugated plastic tubing, and twirling its spheroid head.

Leaving Mabel to collect her wits, Big Cy turns and glides over to another young woman, who is eating an ice-cream cone while she watches the fun. "Hey, sweetheart, how ya doin'?" he asks provocatively as he rolls to a stop in front of her. "Big Cy's the name, and Aureo SP 250's the game. And remember, my dear, 'Once on the lips, forever on the hips.'"

The young woman stops licking her ice-cream cone and blushes crimson.

"Hey! Maybe I can invite you over for a quick pork chop after work," Big Cy continues proffering one of his skinny plastic arms to the nonplussed woman, as if he expected her to take it and escort him through the crowd and out of the exhibition hall to a trysting place. A long silence ensues, broken only by titters from the crowd of onlookers.

"Hey, waddya say, good-lookin'? Just you and me and a nice big pork chop?" insists Big Cy, with a hint of salaciousness in his tinny voice.

"Uh, well . . . I have to . . . the thing of it is, I'm busy," the young woman says, as if she felt she needed an excuse for turning down an assignation with a robot.

* "Oh, no! You mean I'll have to eat that pork chop all by myself?" Big Cy groans despondently, to the amusement of the crowd. "Well, how about at least giving my head a scratch?" he asks plaintively.

Gathering courage and beginning to appreciate the comedy of her situation, the girl suddenly leans over and plants a single smooch on the robot's plastic cranium.

"Ohhh, nooo!" moans Big Cy, blinking and bleeping in apparent ecstasy, his head whirling around. "That did it! You just blew out all my circuits!"

Apparently seeing how embarrassed the young woman is by the laughter of the crowd, which has paid rapt attention to her every response, Big Cy backs off, turns around and scuttles off to find new prey. The next thing I know, Cy is heading right toward where I am standing taking notes. "What's up, big boy? You from the CIA or something?" he asks.

Like the two women, I am confounded by the absurdity of engaging in conversation with a machine. Trying to turn the encounter to my advantage, I decide to attempt an interview with Big Cy about his company's products. "Well," I begin, not unaware that dozens of eyes are fixed on me, "I'm a journalist writing about antibiotics in animal feed. Maybe you can give me some information."

"Antibiotics in feed—that's me," says Big Cy confidently. "Give Aureo SP 250 to your pigs, and it'll make 'em perky as hell."

"How does it work?"

"Oh, it just gives those little piggies all the high-energy factors they need to grow," replies Cy cheerfully.

"But how does it actually work?" I repeat.

The audience grows silent at such a seriously insistent question.

"OK, partner. Now you're getting just a little technical on me here," Big Cy says, his voice suddenly losing some of its jocularity. He turns and rolls toward a white Naugahyde couch where two Cyanamid representatives sit talking.

"Hey, B.T. Come here a sec," says Big Cy, coming to a halt just short of a coffee table and addressing one of the men.

As if he were responding to another member of the sales staff, the man called B.T. walks over to talk with Big Cy. For several unlikely moments, they confer in lowered voices, as if they were two human beings making an important policy decision. Then Big Cy slides away toward the other side of the display, and B.T. walks over to where I stand.

B.T. introduces himself as Booker T. Alford, a technical-service consultant from the Animal Industry Department of Cyanamid's Agricultural Division. On the lapel of his red-

white-and-blue-checked sports jacket he wears an official
American Pork Congress badge, inscribed with this year's
slogan: "America Is Leaning on Pork"—a play on words suggesting that this year America will both rely on pork and
become thinner by eating it. He greets me cordially, with a
firm handshake. When I explain to Alford that I am interested
in the subtherapeutic use of antibiotics in animal feed, and in
American Cyanamid's role in this aspect of the animal-health
industry, he suggests we retire to the couch to chat.

"What can you tell me about Aureo SP 250?" I ask.

"Well, sir, our Aureo SP 250 is a feed additive combining
Aureomycin—chlortetracycline—with penicillin and sulfamethazine, which we recommend that farmers use for young
pigs up to one hundred pounds," Alford begins, as if he were
giving a briefing. "After animals reach one hundred pounds,
most of your producers will switch over and use our straight
Aureomycin up until slaughter. We feel that this gives the
producer the best shot at growing a healthy pig."

"What is the point of feeding these drugs to animals if they
are not sick?" I ask.

Alford seems a little startled by being asked such a primitive question. He uncrosses his legs, shifts his weight and
emits a barely audible sigh. "What you are asking me, sir, is
'What do these drugs do?'" he finally responds. "Well, it's
hard to say—but there are theories," he goes on. "One theory
is that these antibiotics make pigs and other animals grow
faster and more efficiently by limiting subclinical disease.
Another theory is that somehow the drugs increase the animals' metabolism. A third theory is that antibiotics increase
the absorption rate of nutrients in the animals' guts. Frankly,
we don't quite know how or why they work. But I can tell
you that if you took these drugs away from the farmer, you
would be costing the consumer over half a billion dollars in
increased meat prices."

Alford reaches across to the coffee table and approvingly

pats the top of a stack of brochures. I open one up. Inside is a photograph of a small pink pig asleep in the arms of a farmer. "Healthy and happy. You and Aureo SP 250 will keep him that way," reads the caption.

"We're the largest producer of tetracycline for animal use in the country," Alford continues, with pride. "We were the ones who originally developed the drug, although now that the patent has lapsed, other companies have started to manufacture it as well."

"How many pounds of tetracycline does Cyanamid manufacture each year?" I ask, even though every other official at Cyanamid to whom I have put this question has declined to answer it.

"Well, frankly, you'd have to get those figures from someone else," Alford replies. "All I can say is that we produce tons and tons and tons of the stuff." (While the exact tonnage is still a mystery, F. Eberstadt & Company, a New York firm of securities analysts, issues an annual report entitled "The Animal Health Products Market," which gives sales figures for the industry. In 1981 American Cyanamid produced and sold approximately $120 million worth of antibiotics for animal use in this country and $265 million worth abroad. About half of these sales are of tetracycline-based products.)

"What's your attitude toward those scientists who believe that antibiotics in animal feed are creating transferable drug resistance in livestock bacteria that is showing up later in human bacteria?" I ask.

"All right. You want to talk about resistance." Alford pauses for a moment, reflectively cradling his chin between forefinger and thumb. "Well, it's an unproved theory," he announces finally, his voice tinged with irritation over being assaulted with this controversial subject. "If you feed antibiotics to anything, some resistant bacteria will result. They're the ones that survive. But if you're asking whether resistance can be transferred from one type of bacteria to another, or from animals to men—well, that's another question. I don't think that any cases of transferable drug resistance have been documented. That is, nothing has ever really been proved." Alford eyes my notebook with increasing distress, as if it were a weapon pointed at him. I am beginning to feel that my insistent questioning is a little unfair to him, since he is, after all, neither a researcher nor a policymaker at American Cyanamid but simply a member of the sales staff. "Listen, this whole business about antibiotic resistance really isn't my field," he says, as if he were reading my thoughts. "It's a very heated issue, and I'd rather not say anything about it. I think you ought to talk to Bud Loats." He rises from the couch and walks over to the white plastic table, where a tall, solid man is helping people fill out name cards.

E. F. "Bud" Loats, central-regional manager of Cyanamid's Animal Industry Department, also greets me with a firm handshake. His lapel is adorned with a yellow sticker saying, "Surprise 'em with Ground Pork." Lowering his large frame onto the couch beside me, he gives a preparatory smile, but before he has a chance to say anything, Alford begins a summary of our conversation.

"All right, Bud. Just for the record, I want to run through what I've been talking about with this gentleman. I've gone through the three theories of growth-promoting effects of Aureomycin as a feed additive, and we were just starting to brush on the question of resistance. I told him that it was, of course, a timely issue, but that as far as I knew, we had never—"

Loats appears uninterested in Alford's efforts at summation and at this point takes charge of the discussion himself. "Now. This resistance thing. It's not a question that your farming people ask about much," he tells me. "We don't usually sell to the farmers direct. We sell our product through feed companies. It's a very competitive business, because, as you know, there are many other companies who manufacture antibiotic feed additives. Now, the thing to remember is—"

"How do you view the findings of those researchers who are now cautioning us that the indiscriminate use of antibiotics in animals as well as in human health may be destroying their effectiveness?" I put in, bringing Loats's exposition to a halt.

Loats purses his lips. "All right, let's talk about what Aureo SP 250 does. Let's face it, hog farming, like cattle feeding, has become almost completely confined. The pigs are indoors together in barns their whole lives. The situation is sort of like kids at school. You know, one kid gets sick with the sniffles, and then all of 'em get it." He gives a little chuckle and continues, "Now, what we want for our farmers is for them to get their young pigs through that early period of their lives when they get sick easily. We want the pigs to start healthy, stay healthy, and gain as much weight as they can. But don't get me wrong." He raised his hand from his lap in a cautionary gesture. "I'm not saying that our drugs are a substitute for good management or a solution to crowded, unsanitary conditions in the barn."

"No way!" cries Alford antiphonally. "The antibiotics help farmers raise well-fed, well-cared-for animals more efficiently."

"But what about the theory that levels of antibiotic resistance are climbing and that organisms are capable of transferring this resistance from animals to humans? What are your views on this, as someone involved in the sale of antibiotic feed additives?" I persist.

"Who's ever proved that bacteria transfer their resistance?" retorts Loats, probably not because he thinks that no one has proved it, but because he is fairly sure that no one in the present company is knowledgeable enough about the matter to cite chapter and verse of the research literature.

"Well, there have been a number of studies that seem to suggest that—"

"I don't think transferable resistance has been proved yet," interjects Alford.

"Well, we do have some studies that show some level of antibiotic resistance, but the drugs are still working," says Loats.

"What I think Bud, here, is trying to say is that we have been doing tests all along," Alford says. "All we know is that the stuff still works."

"Do you mean that you assume that the resistance levels couldn't be significant, or otherwise the antibiotics would have no growth-promoting effect?" I ask.

"Let me just put it this way—your average American farmer today is pretty smart," Loats replies (although not to the question), wagging an admonishing forefinger in my direction, as if he thought I was insinuating that farmers were being duped. "Why would these farmers pay money to us if they weren't getting results? Our Aureo SP 250 costs about two dollars and fifty cents a pound, and about eighty-five percent of all hog farmers are using some sort of subtherapeutic antibiotic like Aureo SP 250. You tell me why these guys would be putting out all this money if they weren't getting any returns. We think that with our product farmers are looking at a ratio of four to one. We calculate that for every dollar they put out on drugs they get four dollars back. That speaks for itself."

Still hoping to elicit a response on the controversial subject of drug resistance, I probe Loats again for his own views.

"I'm not sure what all the ruckus over drug resistance is about," he replies. "I mean, you've got these animals on drugs in their feed. Then, five months after they're weaned, they're on a truck. Then they arrive at the packing plant and—boom! —they're gone. That's the end of that." He sweeps both hands upward, describing a mushroom cloud in the air.

2

Millions of years ago, certain single-celled organisms dwelling in the soil developed the ability to produce within themselves compounds that could either inhibit the growth of or kill competing microorganisms. This ability, which was acquired through random genetic mutation, was an extraordinary evolutionary development. The microorganisms that could produce these compounds, which have come to be known as *antibiotics*—a term derived from the Latin and meaning literally "against life"—gained an immense advantage in the struggle for survival. But, as if in illustration of the Newtonian principle that to every action there is always an equal and opposite reaction, another group of microorganisms developed a defense. Once the ability to produce antibiotics had given the first group of microorganisms an initial advantage, nature's evolutionary one-upmanship endowed this second group with the capacity to resist the effects of the antibiotics.

There was a wide variety of antibiotic-producing organisms, each able to elaborate a different bacteriostatic or bactericidal compound, and the surrounding bacteria responded by developing a wide variety of resistance strategies. For instance, resistance to penicillin, which kills a bacterium by disintegrating its cell wall, takes several forms. Some bacteria are able to produce a powerful degrading enzyme called penicillinase, which chemically breaks down the antibiotic so that it can do no harm. In others, a mechanism prevents the drug from reaching its target in the cell, the target being certain binding proteins, essential in cell-wall synthesis. In order for penicillin to be effective, it must adhere to these proteins, but still other penicillin-resistant bacteria modify the proteins so that the penicillin can no longer attach itself to them. The mechanism for resistance to tetracycline, another common antibiotic, is completely different. Instead of breaking down the invading bactericide with degrading enzymes or denying it access or accommodation, tetracycline-resistant bacteria use an efflux system that operates something like a ship's automatic bilge pump, to expel the substance from the interior of the cell as fast as it comes in. Because tetracycline is not actually destroyed by this efflux system (as penicillin is by penicillinase) and is a relatively stable compound, some researchers fear that it is accumulating in the environment and that this growing reservoir of released tetracycline may be exerting more and more pressure on the bacterial pool to "select for" resistant organisms; meaning that those bacteria that are not resistant to tetracycline will die, while those that are will flourish.

When the various resistance mechanisms first evolved, they were of relative insignificance in the big biological picture, for, besides soil and a few other places where antibiotic-producing microorganisms lived, there were no other ecological niches where it behooved a bacterium to acquire these traits. The competition between microorganisms occupied an obscure corner of the ecological battlefield, having no impact on human beings or other animals until modern times. Although two thousand years ago the Chinese noted that the application of moldy bean curd to carbuncles and boils had a healing effect, it was not until the 1940s, almost two decades after Sir Alexander Fleming's accidental discovery of penicillin in 1928, that antibiotics began to be mass-produced—a process that disrupted the balance between naturally produced antibiotics and resistant bacteria. As the biologist Marc Lappé pointed out in his book *Germs That Won't Die*, there were only 29 pounds of manufactured penicillin in existence in

1943. By 1953, 860,000 pounds had been produced. Between 1967 and 1971, domestic U.S. production increased 30 percent while the American population only increased by 5 percent. By the beginning of the 1980s, antibiotics had become a $1.5 billion business.

As these new drugs were manufactured in even greater quantities, they began to deluge first the human and then the animal bacterial pools, killing vast numbers of those bacteria that were sensitive—that is, vulnerable—and leaving to reproduce their kind only those insensitive bacteria whose genes carried resistance factors. As the antibiotic era proceeded into the 1950s and '60s, doctors started to encounter pathogenic, or disease-causing, bacteria that would not respond to "the drug of choice"—the commonly accepted, first-line therapy for a given illness. In some cases, patients died before anyone discovered that the bacteria they harbored were resistant. By the end of the sixties, less than twenty years after antibiotics began to be widely used both as human medicine and as feed additives for livestock, epidemics caused by antibiotic-resistant bacteria were being reported around the world.

In 1968, for instance, an extremely virulent form of dysentery broke out in Guatemala. Three years later, the offending microorganism—*Shigella dysenteriae*—was still not under control. It had spread throughout Central America, infecting hundreds of thousands, and, according to a paper given at the proceedings of the 1971 International Epidemiological Association, had killed tens of thousands of people. Perplexed when patients did not respond to the normal drugs of choice (chloramphenicol, tetracycline, streptomycin, and sulfonamide), doctors presumed that they were faced with an epidemic of amoebic dysentery. It was only some time later that they discovered they were dealing with resistant dysentery bacteria. As the World Health Organization noted in a 1978 report on antibiotic-resistant intestinal bacteria, "this delay in diagnosis contributed greatly to the formidable mortality."

In 1972, a prolonged typhoid epidemic broke out in Mexico, where a strain of *Salmonella typhi* infected tens of thousands of people. Even though most were treated, thousands died, because the bacteria were resistant to chloramphenicol, which was the first-line drug for this disease. Not until samples of the *S. typhi* were finally subjected to antibiotic-susceptibility tests did doctors discover why they had been administering chloramphenicol in vain. (Susceptibility tests are not a normal procedure in remote regions of Third World countries, because they are costly, and pathology labs are not always available.) The 1978 WHO report noted that "the case-fatality rate early in this epidemic was similar to that experienced before the antibiotic era." After the tests revealed the typhoid bacteria to be resistant to chloramphenicol, doctors switched to ampicillin, and the death rate declined dramatically.

Even in the industrialized countries, epidemiological studies began showing alarming increases in antibiotic-resistant organisms. A 1982 article in the British medical journal *The Lancet* reported that in England 90 percent of all strains of *Staphylococcus aureus* (bacteria that are a major cause of infection in sutured surgical incisions) were resistant to penicillin, and 35 percent of *Escherichia coli* (common and relatively harmless intestinal bacteria) were resistant to ampicillin, a member of the penicillin family. In its 1978 report, WHO noted ominously,

> Outbreaks of infection due to drug-resistant organisms are an increasing problem in both the developing and developed countries. This problem has been brought into prominence by the recent widespread outbreaks of enteric disease caused by drug-resistant organisms; delayed recognition of drug resistance has, on several occasions, caused unnecessary suffering and loss of life. . . . The problem is global and is the result of the widespread and indiscriminate use of antimicrobial drugs in man and animals.

While by the 1960s many members of the medical profession were alert to the obviously increasing levels of antibiotic resistance in both pathogenic and nonpathogenic bacteria, the common assumption was that the problem was simply one of overuse and misuse of antibiotics in human medicine. After all, it was known that in many Third World countries antibiotics could be bought without prescription and that some times ill-informed people even took them for headaches.

Biologists and clinicians concerned about the problem were aware that the practice of feeding antibiotics to livestock "subtherapeutically"—that is, at dose levels below those required to treat an actual disease—was widespread by the late sixties, both in this country and elsewhere in the industrialized world. Initially, believing that the reservoirs of animal and human bacteria were essentially separate, they were little worried by this procedure; though resistance levels in animal bacteria were high and rising higher, the rise seemed to have little possible consequence for human beings. There were certain species of pathogenic bacteria—such as various strains of *Salmonella*—that could migrate from animals to infect people, but such well-traveled microbial species were few. Then, as research on the subject blossomed in the sixties and seventies, the notion that the bacterial universes of animals and humans were relatively discrete began to come into serious question.

The practice of feeding antibiotics subtherapeutically to livestock was adopted by farmers in the early fifties, not only to prevent and treat "subclinical" diseases—those which may not cause evident symptoms but are nonetheless taxing to the animal—but also to promote growth (as Alford and Loats had explained). According to the Animal Health Institute—the Washington lobby for companies manufacturing pharmaceuticals for animal use—American farmers spent more than $242 million on antibiotic feed additives in 1980. A report issued by the National Academy of Sciences that year, entitled "The Effects on Human Health of Subtherapeutic Use of Antimicrobials in Animal Feed," stated that almost half the antibiotics manufactured in the United States were fed to animals. The Office of Technology Assessment, a research arm of the United States Congress, issued a report in 1979 noting that virtually all the commercially raised poultry, 70 percent of the beef cattle and veal calves and 90 percent of the swine reared in this country consumed such additives as part of their daily feed regimen. This practice has been responsible for changing the way livestock is raised in the United States; it has also alarmed a growing number of scientists, who worry about the effects of introducing such large amounts of antimicrobial drugs into the environment.

In 1948, chlortetracycline (Aureomycin) was discovered at Lederle Laboratories, a division of the American Cyanamid Corporation, completing the initial quartet of antibiotic "wonder drugs" (penicillin, streptomycin, chloramphenicol and tetracycline), which subsequently transformed the face of modern medicine. With the advent of these drugs, doctors had available inexpensive and effective remedies, with few harmful side effects, for previously incurable bacterial diseases. In 1949, Dr. Thomas Jukes, Lederle's director of nutrition and physiology research, was searching for a microorganism that could produce substantial quantities of B-12, a vitamin largely absent from the usual soybean-based livestock diet. One of the organisms he was experimenting with was *Streptomyces aureofaciens*—the organism that elaborated the newly discovered antibiotic chlortetracycline. Discovering relatively high concentrations of vitamin B-12 in the wastes from the fermentation process that produced the tetracycline, Jukes and his colleagues decided to feed some baby chicks the mash and see what happened. They were surprised and elated to find that the chicks quickly showed weight gains of anywhere from 10 to 20 percent above normal. They surmised that the weight

gain was due to the increased level of vitamin B-12. But Jukes
wondered if there might not also be some relationship between the weight gain and the antibiotic residues in the mash.
Since the mass production of antibiotics was still in its infancy
and there was a shortage of tetracycline for human use, Jukes
was forced to scavenge for more fermentation wastes—or
"odds an' ends," as he described them—to continue his testing, this time on pigs.

"The effects were even more spectacular with piglets than
with the chicks," Jukes, who is now a professor-in-residence
at the Department of Medical Physics of the University of
California at Berkeley, told me when I visited him at his office.
"We still don't know exactly how the weight gain came about,"
he continued. "The only interpretation I can give you is that
the antibiotic must have caused a depression of harmful bacteria in the animals' intestines, and this helped to control
subclinical diseases that we otherwise might not have noticed.
In any case, the growth-promoting effect clearly had something to do with the antibiotic, because we later discovered
the same effect in animals that were given ordinary feed but
were grown under germ-free conditions. Keep the bugs out,
and animals grow faster than they would in a normal environment. In our experiments, it didn't really seem to matter what
antibiotic we used. The growth-promoting effect was not specific to any one drug. While antibiotics are all different chemically, they have the common characteristic of antimicrobial
activity, and the animals responded remarkably to all of them."

Antibiotic feed additives appeared to be particularly useful
in promoting weight gains in animals that suffered from stress
as a result of crowded conditions—a finding that influenced
the livestock industry in the most profound way. "It was the
discovery of the effectiveness of the drugs as feed additives in
these conditions that led to the concentration of the meat
industry," Jukes told me, with a touch of pride in his voice.
"For the first time, farmers could confine a large number of

animals and still keep them healthy." In the past, livestock
had been raised for the most part on relatively small family
farms; now it was possible to run huge intensive operations,
for diseases that would often have been caused by crowding
could be efficiently controlled with drugs.

Even in the early years of antibiotics, researchers like
Thomas Jukes were familiar with the problem of resistance.
They knew that once an antibiotic had been used for a while,
it would kill all sensitive microorganisms in an animal's gut,
leaving those microorganisms that were resistant to the drug
to survive and multiply. "At first we didn't think antibiotics'
growth effect would last very long," Jukes recalled. "We of
course assumed that once the bacteria in the animal became
largely resistant, the animal would cease to benefit from the
drug. But this did not happen. Although we still don't know
why, the animals continued to gain more weight, on less feed,
year after year, even after their bacterial flora showed very
high levels of resistance."

Jukes and his colleagues were perplexed. How could a drug
work if bacteria were resistant to it? "What we were not prepared for was the fact that the changed and resistant flora
were in some way beneficial. And it took us some time to
adjust to such a concept. Indeed the growth effect is so
illogical that I recommended others trying the experiment,"
Jukes later wrote in the *Journal of Applied Microbiology*.
When I asked Jukes if he still believes in the efficacy of antibiotic feed additives, he replied, "I think the continuing usefulness of subtherapeutic antibiotics has been amply demonstrated. The usefulness of antibiotic feeding can be measured
in the marketplace. If too many resistant pathogens develop,
the economic advantage will disappear, and so will the use of
antibiotic additives. In the meantime, I don't think we have
that many cattle, pigs and chickens that we can afford to stop
feeding them by the most economical means."

Calling the discovery of the growth-promoting effect of antibiotics on livestock "a unique phenomenon, perhaps without precedent in medical history," Jukes and his colleagues began publishing their results, which attracted considerable attention in both the scientific and the agricultural communities. In March 1950, *The New York Times* ran a front-page story on Jukes's findings. So widespread did word of Jukes's work become that the New York *Daily News* ran a political cartoon that showed Harry Truman administering a growth-promoting dose of tetracycline to a pig—a symbolic representation of the President's presumed complicity in the ballooning of the national debt.

The country's leading pharmaceutical firms sensed a great business opportunity, and soon began building plants to manufacture antibiotics for feed-additive use. By 1954, six years after the discovery of tetracycline's growth-enhancing effects, American farmers were using 490,000 pounds (245 tons) of antibiotic feed additives a year in livestock feed. In a 1977 article entitled "The History of the Antibiotic Growth Effect," Jukes euphorically noted of his experiments: "The results produced on the farms were so spectacular, especially with pigs, that we could not begin to supply the demand." By 1960, 1.2 million pounds were used annually. The present figure is some 9 million pounds, and it is now the exception rather than the rule to find a farmer who does not use antibiotic feed additives on his livestock.

As the use of antibiotic feed additives has increased, so has the concern of many clinicians and researchers, who fear that bacterial genes that code for resistance are being developed in dangerously large numbers through the use of such additives. (Bacteria, which reproduce by simple cell division, proliferate extremely rapidly. Under optimal conditions, certain species can produce a billion copies of themselves within a twelve-hour period.) Animal bacteria resistant to antibiotics may colonize human beings directly; or they may transfer their capacity for resistance to other species of bacteria within the animal, which may then colonize human beings; or resistant animal bacteria that end up in the intestinal tracts of human beings may transfer their capacity for resistance to indigenous human bacteria. The pathways are numerous and nefarious. Confusion over the various ways that drug resistances are transmitted has in no small measure been responsible for the misunderstandings that have plagued the growing dispute over the use of antibiotics in animal feed.

In 1955, a Japanese woman returned to Tokyo from Hong Kong with a case of dysentery caused by S. *dysenteriae*, the same pathogen that was to cause the 1968 Guatemalan epidemic. When doctors tried to treat her, they found, to their surprise—as the doctors in Guatemala did later—that the causative bacteria were resistant to all four drugs of choice: streptomycin, tetracycline, chloramphenicol and sulfonamide. Perplexed by this finding, Dr. Tomoichiro Akiba, at Tokyo University, decided to investigate the phenomenon of multiple resistance. Conducting susceptibility studies on a variety of bacteria isolated from hospital patients, Akiba found that some intestinal *E. coli* in these patients were resistant to the same four drugs. He wondered how it was possible that two such different bacteria as *E. coli* and *S. dysenteriae* should suddenly acquire genes coding for multiple resistances to exactly the same set of drugs. Was it conceivable that multiple spontaneous mutations had occurred in the chromosomes of both species of bacteria, making them simultaneously resistant to those four drugs?

Akiba thought not. He knew that the mutation of a drug-sensitivity gene in a bacterium's single chromosome could occur only once in anything from 10 million to a billion cell divisions, and when it did occur, it could alter that bacterium's sensitivity to only one drug at a time. But here were two different species of bacteria that had simultaneously acquired not one but four resistance traits. Such a phenomenon was as likely as two writers sitting down simultaneously in different rooms and writing the complete text of Lady Murasaki's *Tale of Genji* word for word. Where did these duplicated patterns of resistance come from? Was it possible that resistance itself was transferable from one species of bacteria to another like an infectious disease?

In the next few years, several more epidemics of intractable bacillary dysentery broke out in Japan. Each time, the disease organism revealed resistance to the same quartet of drugs, and again *E. coli* from the intestines of the patients showed the same resistance patterns. Trying to unravel the reasons for this phenomenon, a research team headed by Dr. Kunitaro Ochai of the Nagoya City Higashi Hospital began mixing liquid cultures of drug-resistant *E. coli* with cultures of drug-sensitive *S. dysenteriae*. The researchers found, to their amazement, that the resistance from the former was being transferred to the latter—just how, they could not immediately determine. It remained for another Japanese microbiologist, Dr. Tsutomo Watanabe, of Keio University's School of Medicine, to probe the mystery further. Watanabe soon confirmed that drug resistance was indeed being transferred from one cell to another, via what he termed *R factors* (*R* standing for resistance), which were tiny pieces of DNA—deoxyribonucleic acid, the material of which genes are made—that resided within a bacterial cell but outside its chromosome.

Dr. Stuart Levy, a microbiologist at the Tufts University School of Medicine, worked with Watanabe for a short period in Tokyo during the early 1960s and recalled for me the research climate there. "It was one of indescribable excitement," he said. "We were dealing with a concept—Watanabe called it infectious drug-resistance—that seemed almost unimaginable to us, since it flew in the face of so much accepted biology and genetics. It was completely new territory. Whenever we had an idea, there was nothing to do but go right to the lab and test it. We were never sure what we were going to find."

Watanabe's work (which was quickly confirmed by other researchers) concentrated on a whole new fund of bacterial genes, which were called plasmids. These genes, which drifted around in the cytoplasm of the bacterium, replicating and carrying on a life of their own, owed no fealty to the chromosome. One type, the F (fertility) plasmid, was capable of causing the host bacterium to conjugate, or mate, with a bacterium of a different species, not a reproductive act, but one that resulted in the transfer of plasmids that carried a number of traits, including antibiotic resistance.

These errant pieces of DNA presaged a fundamental reevaluation of evolutionary theory. Formerly scientists had assumed that evolutionary changes came about slowly, as a result of a species' taking advantage of infrequent random mutations of chromosomal genes, but Watanabe and other plasmid biologists showed that—at least in bacterial genetics —free-floating genes, unconnected to the chromosome, could drift from one microorganism to another with great speed and substantially alter the genetic makeup of their new host. Geneticists, who had been used to thinking of evolutionary changes in terms of millennia, were now confronted with evidence that at least some traits could be acquired by bacterial cells in a matter of moments.

Watanabe's discovery of R (resistance) plasmids caused a few members of the scientific community to begin making another reevaluation; namely, of the advisability of continuing to use large quantities of those antibiotics that were important in human therapy as animal-feed additives. For the first time, they faced the possibility that resistance generated in animals could transfer itself, by means of plasmids, to bacteria that cause human disease, and vice versa as well. Battle lines were soon drawn between those who believed in the advisability of curbing nonessential uses of such antibiotics as tetracycline and penicillin in livestock feed and those who felt that credible evidence of significant animal-to-man plasmid transfer was still lacking and that the benefits of anti-biotics should not be denied to farmers, who presumably passed those benefits on to consumers in the form of lower meat prices.

Watanabe himself was troubled enough by what he called the "ominous phenomenon" of infectious drug-resistance to write in the December 1967 issue of *Scientific American*, "Unless we put a halt to the prodigal use of antibiotics and synthetic drugs, we may soon be forced back into a pre-antibiotic era."

3

When it comes to discussing the potential dangers of the overuse of antibiotics, one of the most outspoken members of the American scientific community is Richard P. Novick, M.D., a plasmid biologist and the director of the Public Health Research Institute of the City of New York, an independent nonprofit research corporation supported by grants and contracts from such organizations as the American Cancer Society, the National Institutes of Health, the National Science Foundation and the Food and Drug Administration.

I became aware of Dr. Novick's concern over the use of antibiotics as feed additives when he wrote a letter to *The New York Times* in November 1977, in support of efforts that the FDA was making under Donald Kennedy, then its commissioner, to regulate the unrestricted use of penicillin and tetracycline in animal feeds by making their sale and use contingent on veterinary prescription. (The effort ultimately failed, and feed mills and livestock-supply houses continue to market these drugs today in any quantity to anyone who wishes to buy them.) "Recent years have witnessed massive increases in the use of antibiotics for livestock as well as for human medicine," Novick wrote the *Times*. "These practices have caused the development of vast populations of disease-bearing bacteria that are simultaneously resistant to many different antibiotics and are becoming a greater and greater threat to human as well as animal health."

Novick's name appears repeatedly in the literature on the

subject of antibiotic resistance. In a 1979 article in *The Sciences*, he wrote,

> Antibiotics have been (and still are) given for everything
> from headaches to ingrown toenails; they are swallowed,
> sucked, injected, and smeared; they are painted on cuts,
> dumped into wounds, fed to the chickens and pigs, and
> sprayed on the floors of hospital wards . . . Through a char-
> acteristically human combination of greed and ignorance, we
> are now well on the way to negating totally the usefulness of
> antibiotics.

The offices and laboratories of the Public Health Research
Institute are in a modern high rise at First Avenue and
Twenty-sixth Street, across from the Bellevue Hospital Center.
Novick's office is lined with shelves of scientific texts and
scholarly journals; there is a scattering of plants and a mish-
mash of unmatched furniture. He is a tall, mustachioed man
in his early fifties, whose energy and youthfulness belie the
strands of gray that radiate up from his temples through his
bushy head of hair. Like the room in which he works, Richard
Novick evinces little attraction to the formalities and grand
effects of his executive position. He is clad, the day of my visit,
in an open-necked shirt and blue jeans.

When I ask his views on the hazards of modern antibiotic
use, I find him plainspoken, almost shocking, in the bluntness
of his assessment. "I think that the evidence is overwhelming
that what we have been doing with antibiotics in both animal
and human use is very dangerous and entirely self-defeating,"
he begins without hesitation, speaking in rapid-fire bursts of
words, as if what he wanted to say were both so urgent and
so self-evident that punctuation was a waste of time. "I think
our experience in this age of chemicals has made it abundantly
clear that we can't keep spewing biologically active substances into the environment without paying a high price in
undesirable modifications of the biosphere. What is happen-

ing to animals on antibiotic feed is having an effect on levels
of resistance in human beings, because of the plasmid trade-
around. And I myself am far from convinced that these antibiotic additives are all that effective in promoting growth
anyway. Basically, I think, the farmers have been sold a bill
of goods and are squandering an extremely important human
resource. As far as I'm concerned, the drug companies are
responsible.

"The discovery of plasmids did unlock some extraordinary
mysteries," he continues, when I ask him what a plasmid is.
"However, we still have a hard time classifying them. In
many ways, they're like parasites, in the sense that they are
totally dependent upon the cells within which they live, although they do not actually harm them. And they are ubiqui-
tous among both pathogenic and nonpathogenic bacteria in
plants and in animals, including human beings."

Although a single plasmid usually accounts for only 2 to 4
percent of the total genetic material stored in a bacterium,
Novick estimates that certain common *E. coli* can harbor fifteen to twenty different types of plasmids, which together are
capable of introducing several hundred different genetic traits
into another bacterial cell. In certain bacteria, the plasmid-
borne genetic material may be equal to, or may even surpass,
the entire DNA content of the organism's chromosome.

New kinds of plasmids besides those that carry antibiotic
resistance or initiate conjugation have only recently come to
light. They are responsible for an interesting collection of
accessory characteristics—functions that are not specified by
the chromosome—such as resistance to the toxicity of heavy
metals (lead, cadmium, arsenic, mercury), the ability to de-
grade insecticides and other petroleum products, and the ability to cause certain diseases, such as traveler's diarrhea,
staphylococcal impetigo and possibly tetanus.

"Some bacteria are just jammed with plasmids," Novick
continues. "There's theoretically no limit to how many a cell

can harbor. Moreover, the vast majority carry unidentified genes. There are many plasmid-determined functions yet to be discovered besides the ones—like antibiotic resistance— that we know about." As he speaks, Novick picks up my note-book, draws an oblong shape and writes the word *Cell* above it. At one end of the cell, he draws a single asterisk and labels it *Chromosome*. Then, still speaking, he draws a whole galaxy of small *x*s at the other end of the cell and scrawls an arrow into their midst connecting to the word *Plasmids*.

"The thing about plasmids is that they are so beautifully specific to their task," Novick says, his expression brightening, like that of a salesman who finally arrives at the moment when he can make a pitch for the most positive aspect of his company's product. "Take a bacterium that happens to ac-quire resistance to a particular antibiotic through a mutation affecting the antibiotic's target. If the chromosome is modified even in this theoretically beneficial way, it almost always compromises the vital cellular function that has been mu-tated, inhibiting growth and reproduction. Mutations often end up making a cell an evolutionary cripple. On the other hand, if a cell acquires that same new trait from a plasmid, its overall health and adaptability will be only minimally—if at all—compromised, and thus its capacity for survival is not really impaired."

While adding *x*s inside the cell he has drawn, he goes on to say, "Plasmids are also capable of making numerous copies of themselves. This is an area in which we have done some work here at the lab, and we have found that a plasmid can sometimes replicate two thousand times inside a single cell. But oddly, the cell doesn't seem to mind these copies very much and keeps on growing just about as well as it does without the plasmids."

I ask Novick how plasmid-borne resistance factors actually leave one cell and take up residence in another, as Watanabe discovered. Novick reaches over to a shelf, pulls out a biology text and opens it to a section on bacterial conjugation. A photograph shows two microorganisms in a cellular embrace, their fuzzy caterpillarlike bodies docked close to one another and connected by a filamentous appendage called a pilus. The pilus, Novick tells me, provides an avenue through which plasmids of all types can be transferred from one bacterium to another. Moving his pencil point from the body of one of the cells across the pilus to the other, he explains that since F plasmids are responsible for initiating conjugation, and since bacteria containing these plasmids mate not only with partners of their own species or genus but with other bacteria as well, the potential for spreading plasmid-borne genetic material far and wide in the bacterial world is great.

Once inside the gut of a pig or a cow, for instance, an R plasmid carrying antibiotic resistance may move from its original home in a harmless *E. coli* into an adjacent dysentery-causing microorganism. Or it may trade up from bacteria that live exclusively in animals to some that can colonize human beings. Like cowbirds, laying their eggs in the nests of other birds—one in this nest, one in that—these R plasmids are capable of insinuating their DNA through the act of bacterial conjugation into a limitless number of alien cells. There they wait until the animal or the human being in which their host bacteria reside is prescribed antibiotics. Then, suddenly, their hour arrives.

"What happens is actually quite simple," Novick says. "When an antibiotic is introduced, it immediately starts killing off the sensitive bacteria. But it can't kill those bacteria that have acquired R plasmids. Cells with these plasmids are the ones that survive and multiply when their competition has been wiped out. This is why we say that antibiotics 'select for' resistant organisms. Once the sensitive organisms have been destroyed, the antibiotic serves merely to maintain a favorable environment for the resistant ones."

I ask Novick to explain how bacteria can acquire multiple resistance traits from plasmids.

He turns, rummages through a file in a bottom desk drawer and extracts a sheaf of eight-by-ten glossy black-and-white photographs. "These are electron micrographs of plasmids magnified—oh, let's see." He flips one of the pictures over and reads a notation on the back. "This one is magnified thirty-two thousand times."

The plasmids in Novick's micrographs appear as loopy strings of minute beads. "These plasmids include segments of DNA called transposons, which are able to detach themselves from one plasmid and hop over, or 'transpose,' themselves onto another plasmid, or even onto the bacterial chromosome," Novick says, tracing the outline of one plasmid to a place where it loops over on itself. "Let's say you have an *E. coli* that happens to harbor plasmids with genes that code for tetracycline resistance. Then along comes another *E. coli* harboring genes for chloramphenicol resistance. The cells conjugate and trade R plasmids through the pilus, so that each cell now has both R factors. Through transposition, the gene for tetracycline resistance can now hop off its plasmid as a transposon and climb onto the plasmid that previously contained only chloramphenicol resistance. Presto! In both *E. coli* cells you've got a plasmid that codes for resistance to both drugs at once. In this way, you can get genes for resistance to a number of antibiotics all on one R plasmid. Then, as I have explained, that plasmid can replicate itself and transfer a copy to a new bacterial cell during conjugation, and in that way these multiple resistances can spread like wildfire."

Next, as if the gymnastic feats of plasmids and transposons that he has been describing were not enough to create a legend of biological agility, Novick describes another, involving bacteriophages—viruses that have a specific affinity with bacteria. "Viruses are the tiniest of organisms, existing as simple submicroscopic particles in which the genetic material is encapsulated within a protective shell, usually made up of proteins," he explains. "A virus is the ultimate parasite, since outside a suitable host cell it becomes totally inert. But once it's inside a host cell, it sheds its protein capsule and begins to reproduce its DNA, commandeering the host cell's metabolic energy for its own purposes. After manufacturing a few hundred new copies of its DNA, it encapsulates them in new protective protein shells, which it also manufactures, and then causes the cell to lyse, or dissolve, releasing the new virus particles to repeat the process when other suitable cells are encountered. This basic reproductive strategy is the same for all viruses, whether they infect human cells—causing, for instance, polio, yellow fever or rabies—or plant cells or bacterial cells, except that bacterial viruses sometimes make mistakes in the encapsulation process. When this happens, they may encapsulate some particles containing DNA from the host cell instead of viral DNA. Since each infected cell yields a few hundred new phage particles in less than an hour, the phage can afford to be somewhat sloppy in its encapsulation process. As a result, about one particle in a hundred contains host DNA rather than phage DNA. This particle can itself enter a suitable new host cell after lysis, where its DNA—perhaps including a transposon with an antibiotic-resistance gene, or even an entire R plasmid—may be incorporated into the genetic makeup of the new cell. We call this phenomenon transduction. We're not quite sure how often this particular delivery system works in nature, but we know that it can happen, and that it provides another avenue of genetic exchange by which antibiotic resistance can be spread."

Still another means that cells have of exchanging genetic material, Novick continues, is known as transformation. When cells lyse, like bursting piñatas, they splatter their plasmids, transposons, and chromosomal genes around their microenvironment. Other cells in the neighborhood may acquire R factors simply by incorporating through their walls bits of this free-floating DNA, so that their own genetic endowment is altered. In the pre-antibiotic world, a cell that had to maintain several R factors it did not need might have had difficulty surviving the competition, because of a slight increase in its metabolic load. To be resistant to an antibiotic that is not present is not an asset; in fact, it can be a liability, because the maintenance of an unnecessary genetic trait may tax and weaken a cell, even though the degree of debilitation may be slight. If, however, antibiotics are suddenly added to the equation, the cell's investment in resistance proves well spent. Whatever price it may have paid to maintain the plasmid is suddenly negligible compared with its ability to survive in an antibacterial environment.

"All this genetic trading must sound as if it takes place quite without inhibition," says Novick, smiling. "But there are natural limits. Some cells will defend themselves against accepting these newly arrived genes. For instance, a cell may sometimes mobilize to destroy a plasmid because the new addition somehow stresses or unbalances it by increasing its genetic burden. But before it is able to get rid of the new plasmid, a transposon may hop off and attach itself to an indigenous plasmid and thus preserve itself while the alien plasmid perishes. Stanley Falkow, a molecular biologist at Stanford, has shown good evidence that this is what happened in penicillin-resistant strains of *Neisseria gonorrheae*, which suddenly appeared a few years ago. We think that the R factor may have been transferred from an ordinary *E. coli* via a plasmid that came across during conjugation and couldn't survive, but left a gene for penicillin resistance behind in the form of a transposon. Then, under the selective pressure of all the penicillin that was being thrown at the disease, the new resistant organism obviously had a tremendous selective advantage and multiplied like crazy. When you look at the transposons in *N. gonorrheae* that carry the penicillin-resistance factors, you can see that they are very similar to the ones we usually find in *E. coli* plasmids. But when we compare the sequential arrangement of transposons on the plasmids themselves, we find the sequences are not the same. That's what makes us think that a plasmid was the vector, and it perished, but not until the transposon carrying penicillin resistance jumped ship. All this is corroborated by some other evidence that Falkow uncovered; namely, that this same transposon that codes for penicillin resistance in *N. gonorrheae* has gotten into plasmids carried by *Haemophilus influenzae* bacteria, which cause meningitis in small children."

In our conversations, Novick has told me about a study that his institute is doing for the Food and Drug Administration with the College of Veterinary Medicine at Cornell University in Ithaca, New York, on the possibility of infectious drug resistance being transferred from animals to humans.

The Cornell study is unique, he tells me, because unlike the gram-negative bacteria, such as *S. dysenteriae* and *E. coli*, that Watanabe and others have studied, this research project is concentrating on gram-positive bacteria, such as streptococci and staphylococci, which have not been widely investigated as vectors, or carriers, of R plasmids. The animal-test phase of this $220,000 contract will end in a few days. Thereafter Novick and Dr. Gary Dunny, an assistant professor of veterinary microbiology at Cornell, will be working with bacterial cultures taken from their test pigs and their handlers and will be comparing them with a collection of other bacterial cultures of human-borne staphylococci and streptococci gathered from around the country by the FDA. They will be analyzing the plasmids of each for similarities to determine the extent to which the different species of bacteria in different hosts appear to be changing R factors.

Anxious to visit the test pigs before they go to their ultimate reward—there is a barbecue planned to mark the end of this phase of the project—I head up to Ithaca.

"What we have been doing is isolating bacteria from our pigs that are being fed Tylosin [a popular animal antibiotic manufactured by Eli Lilly & Company with annual worldwide sales of approximately $150 million] and comparing them to isolates from their handlers," Dunny tells me when I meet him in his campus office. "Then we will take the plasmids from these resistant bugs and compare them with plasmids from bacteria gathered around the country to determine if any of the plasmids that are turning up in human infections have farm origins.

"Antibiotics are so widely used in livestock production to-day that we had a hell of a time simply getting clean pigs without previously existing high levels of resistant organisms." As we leave the Cornell campus and drive out toward where the test hogs are kept, Dunny continues, "There are so many resistant organisms floating around that almost every pig or cow is loaded with them, whether they're on feed additives or not. We went to the Cornell swine barn to see about buying pigs, but because they're all on antibiotics, eighty percent of their bacteria were resistant. Everywhere we looked, we found animals with large numbers of resistant organisms. Clean ones just don't exist anymore. The whole bacterial pool has been affected. Finally we found this small farmer who had never used drugs. He had a few pigs." Dunny laughs wryly. "Even his pigs tested out with about twenty percent resistant organisms. But that was the best we could do."

Dunny also had trouble finding an acceptable environment in which to house the animals. "We were looking for virgin territory, a farm that had no antibiotic history," he says. "We couldn't find a suitable place until one of my graduate students offered to let us put up some pens on his organic farm, where there hadn't been any other animals for a long time."

After we have driven for about twenty minutes, Dunny slows down in front of a ramshackle wood-frame house and turns in the driveway. The farm, like so many others in upstate New York, suggests an agricultural era whose heyday has long since gone. The farmhouse is in disrepair; an old wooden barn, surrounded by rusting farm equipment, is on the verge of collapse.

Dunny and I walk down a grassy lane past these ruins of an agricultural America where a farm meant a family, a barn, a few milk cows, pigs and chickens pecking around the barnyard and some field crops. The lush green grass and thriving weeds glisten with the first melting frost of autumn. Above us, maples are fiery red and orange. Nearing a clump of bushes, we hear the distant oinking of unseen pigs. Drawing closer, we approach a muddy pen surrounded by a hog-wire fence, which shows signs of having been battered for some time by probing pigs. Broken wires, unseemly bulges and fence posts pushed out of plumb by the dense bodies of the pigs inside all suggest that the impending barbecue may be scheduled none too soon if a great escape is to be avoided.

Suddenly, eight Yorkshire pigs—characteristically pink, with upright ears—tumble out of a crate that serves as a shelter. Tripping over the tank of a water heater that has been cut in half for use as a feed trough, they mob the fence in front of us, probing the hog wire with their round salami-like noses as they inspect us.

"The minute we started these pigs on Tylosin, the levels of antibiotic resistance of their indigenous staphylococci and streptococci just shot up," says Dunny, raising his right thumb up like a hitchhiker and elevating it into the air over his head. "Now the levels are up around eighty percent, more than three times higher than the control group, which just gets straight feed.

"What really bothers me is that farmers and drug companies treat antibiotics as if they were vitamins," continues Dunny.

"What these people fail to grasp is that the dangers of antibiotics are not visual. You can't readily see the effect in large
animals. You have to look at the smaller animals—the microorganisms. It's among the plasmids of these little bugs that
we're really bollixing things up. That's where all this multiple
resistance is developing, and that's what future generations
will be paying for."

Like lodestones gathering iron filings around them, plasmids
appear to have an unlimited capacity for incorporating new
transposons into their genetic sequences. It is the unique
ability of plasmids to introduce new genetic material into
bacterial cells without significantly compromising the cell's
existence that first attracted the attention of researchers interested in genetic engineering. In many ways, the plasmid was
the gene splicer's dream come true: Here was an example of
nature already doing exactly the kind of recombining of DNA
that scientists were trying to do—inserting new genes into a
bacterial cell to reprogram it in a specific new way. Since
plasmids had already proved themselves to be prodigious
vectors for genetic change on their own, researchers began
eagerly working with them. Plasmids were marvelously con-
venient genetic units to manipulate, being infinitely less complex than chromosomes. And, in fact, it was a plasmid that
scientists first used as the vehicle to introduce foreign genes
successfully into a bacterial cell—a significant scientific breakthrough in recombinant-DNA research.

Breakthroughs such as these also led to much discussion
among scientists about the dangers of unregulated meddling
with the genetic determinants of life. After several years of
debate, guidelines for recombinant-DNA research were set by
the National Institutes of Health. But, ironically, while the
regulators concerned themselves with the potential dangers of
gene-splicing research, genetic trading caused by the widespread use of antibiotics went on unabated, in the form of
R-plasmid transfer.

Stanley Falkow, chairman of the Department of Medical Molecular Biology at Stanford University, is one of the pioneers of R-plasmid research. In a 1977 article in *The Sciences*, entitled "Genetic Loose Change," Falkow and a colleague, Lynn Elwell, noted that "while committees of scientists and laymen banter about recombinant DNA around conference tables, nature, in introducing *R* plasmids in *H. influenzae* and *N. gonorrheae*, has been conducting experiments prohibited under the National Institutes of Health guidelines for recombinant-DNA research."

Refusing to stay within the confines of one bacterial cell, like the monogamous chromosome, free-spirited transposons circulate throughout their bacterial microenvironments, congregating with whomever they please, riding on viral phages like hitchhikers, hopping from one plasmid to another and moving from cell to cell as if they were insects pollinating blossoms, and generally evincing little respect for the frontiers separating the bacterial pools of different animals, and of animals from humans.

"We used to see only one or two resistance factors on a plasmid at a time," Novick comments when I talk to him after my trip to Cornell. "Now we're getting as many as twelve. That has all happened in the last thirty years. What's frightening is that there seems to be no limit to the number of multiple resistances that these R plasmids can carry. Why it is that people in the drug industry cannot see the obvious danger here is beyond my comprehension. There is very clearly an interactive worldwide pool of bacteria and plasmids, and I think that by this point it should be quite obvious that the selective pressure of all the antibiotics used in human medicine and on farms is speeding up the spread of drug resistance. Even if doctors stopped the imprudent use of antibiotics in their practice tomorrow, I don't think we would see a profound effect on resistance levels unless we also stopped the subtherapeutic use of antibiotics in animals.

"If I had any reason to believe that subtherapeutic drugs were effective, I think I would have second thoughts about pushing for an absolute ban on routine feed-additive use. But the voluminous data on the emergence of resistance indicates beyond the shadow of a doubt that antibiotic prophylaxis is a total waste of time and money when it is aimed against the kinds of organisms that usually cause disease and threaten herds of livestock. I do not deny that there are a few bacterial pathogens that have not yet become resistant, and I have no objection to using antibiotics against these. However, the only hope of maintaining the usefulness of antibiotics is to use them for specific purposes in a limited and carefully controlled manner, and only against organisms that are known to be sensitive to them.

"The pools of animal and human bacteria are like two huge tanks connected by a thin pipe at the bottom," Novick continues. "Although their interrelationship may not be immediately evident, the level in one tank is inevitably influenced by the level in the other. And while I think that doctors are beginning to appreciate more and more the importance of using these drugs sparingly, so as to protect them, I see little evidence that the drug companies and the farmers are willing to make a similar effort."

4

The sun has just dropped below the horizon as I near Normal, Illinois. I am heading west, bound for American Cyanamid's tetracycline plant just south of Palmyra, Missouri, on the banks of the Mississippi River. I am also hungry.

About a year after I first began traveling around the country to learn about drugs and meat, I decided that wherever possible, I would try to dine on the specific animal that I was investigating at the time.

Until I made this decision, I had generally not looked forward to mealtime on the road with much gusto. The food was rarely very good.

But now, armed with my pad and pen, any roadside restaurant became an object of interest, if not for its fine gastronomy, then for what it revealed about the state of meat as an end product.

Since over the last few weeks I have been investigating antibiotics as they are used in swine, lately I have been sampling a lot of pork. And thus tonight, when I suddenly spot a huge red-and-yellow plastic sign embossed with the name Bob Evans' Restaurant and advertising "Farm Fresh Sausage," I decide to stop.

Bob Evans' Restaurant sits, illuminated with bright spotlights, in the middle of an expansive asphalt parking lot. Its fire-engine-red walls and white gingerbread decorations make it look like a cross between a Mississippi riverboat and an old-fashioned barn.

Getting out of the car, I walk toward the front door. From close up, the building's affected nineteenth-century styling clashes jarringly with its actual construction. Far from being made with rustic barn-wood planking, its exterior is sheathed in a substance that gives off such an unearthly sheen that it is hard to know whether it is made out of painted wood, tin, some new kind of epoxied cardboard, or if the whole building might possibly have been simply extruded from a pug mill like a child's plastic toy.

Walking inside is like stepping onto a brightly lit stage set. A U-shaped counter situated in the middle of a large room is surrounded on three sides by tables and booths of eating people. The place is humming with activity. Waitresses in matching uniforms that combine aspects of a cowgirl ensemble with those of an oral hygienist's garb are industriously criss-crossing back and forth carrying trays of food and dirty dishes. Like a Pavlovian dog, my salivary glands begin to secrete in anticipation of a meal.

As I am surveying the scene, a uniformed hostess comes up, greets me, hands me a large menu laminated in plastic and squires me to a stool at the counter opposite a stainless-steel display case filled with presliced pieces of Day-Glo–yellow lemon chiffon pie.

Almost as soon as I have settled on the stool, a pert waitress named Cindi arrives to take my order. On her recommendation I order pork ribs.

I have only half-eaten my salad when I spot Cindi coming down the counter with a steaming dish. When she sets it down in front of me with a smile, I recognize nothing on the plate but a baked potato, which sits beside a pool of red sauce with a few lumps in it.

"Where are my ribs?" I ask Cindi, having imagined a rack of succulent barbecued ribs with crisp bones that I can gnaw on.

"There," says Cindi, pointing to several submerged objects in the runny red sauce.

"But where are the bones?" I ask with incredulity.

"No bones," replies Cindi sweetly. "We take them out for you. You just get the meat."

I poke at my ribs with a fork. They have the consistency of wet chicken skin. "Do you cook these ribs here?" I ask Cindi with disappointment.

"I think so," she replies.

"I mean, is there an actual grill, you know, with a fire and . . ." I continue.

"Well, I think it's more like a pot. We just heat 'em up," she says, smiling, and then departing.

I spear one of the "ribs" with my fork and begin to chew it. It is so drenched in barbecue sauce that the meat has absolutely no taste of its own. I turn to the baked potato. Beside it is a pale-yellow blob the texture of hydrolyzed Brylcream, evidently some kind of whipped butter substitute. I am about to apply it to my baked potato when I spot a young man with a manager's badge patrolling among the tables with his hands clasped behind his back, like a constable on his beat. I summon him over to my stool and ask him to tell me a little about Bob Evans' Restaurant.

"Well, we now have eighty-five Bob Evans' Restaurants in seven states," says Gene Ritter, sounding a little like a Chinese cadre reciting the number of bushels of millet his commune has extracted from each hectare of land. "Bob Evans' Farm Fresh Sausage owns three packing plants in Michigan, Illinois and Ohio as well. We get all our meat from them. Our sausage comes already boxed in four- and six-ounce patties right from the packing plant. At this one outlet, we sell about eight hundred pounds of sausage and five hundred pounds of ribs a week."

"Does that five hundred pounds of ribs include the bones?" I ask.

Ritter pauses for a moment before answering, not quite sure what I am driving at. "People don't like the bones," he finally replies. "They're too messy. This way they get more meat and don't have to go through all that trouble chewing it off the bone." He points to the ribs on my plate.

"How are these ribs prepared?" I ask.

"Well, first they are steamed in a big pressure cooker, and then they're cooked in barbecue sauce."

"Are people generally pretty enthusiastic about them?" I ask.

"Oh, yeah. They're real popular. I think it's the convenience of them that people like."

"But don't people ever miss having real barbecued ribs? You know, that crispy charcoal flavor you get around the bone when they're done on a grill?", I find myself saying, suddenly feeling as if I had involuntarily become part of a commercial for a rival product.

"Well, I don't know. It's just the way we do it here," replies Ritter with a shrug, but without any sense of combativeness in his voice.

"Have any of your customers ever expressed concern about the various drugs and chemicals used to grow pork?" I ask Ritter, realizing before I have even finished my question that the leap I have made from the pork on my plate to the hog barn is too precipitous.

"Well, I'm not sure I get your drift," he replies, with a perplexed look on his face.

I do not pursue the question, feeling somewhat ridiculous for having asked it in the first place. After all, how many restaurant managers are besieged by customers worried about how the meat they are eating is raised? It is a subject most people would rather not think about, particularly while dining. I thank Ritter for his time, pick through my dinner, leaving most of it uneaten, and then depart Bob Evans'.

Later on, I run across an article in *Pig American* magazine entitled, "On Boneless Ribs and Hams What Ain't." In it, writer Steve Marberry discusses the problems of "restructured meat products" with University of Nebraska meat scientist Dr. Robert Mandigo. "What we have is an animal with a head, four legs and a tail," notes Mandigo. "Somewhere in between is the edible portion. But even all of that edible portion is not considered a high value desired product. It isn't in a form today's consumer really desires."

Through the alchemy of "restructuring," however, these cuts that aren't "in a form today's consumer really desires" can be transformed into something new. They can now be made, in Marberry's words, to "look, taste and feel better than the lesser-valued whole muscle cuts from whence they came—and without the bother of those pesky bones."

It would appear that pork eaters are entering a *fin de siècle* period when old-style cuts of meats with bone, fat and gristle are rapidly fading into oblivion.

"Refinement in processing technology, coupled with rising demand for new 'value added' products by meat merchandisers striving to maintain profit margins, could spell obsolescence for the pork chop, as we know it," writes Marberry.

The ribless ribs at Bob Evans' Restaurant on the outskirts of Normal, Illinois, are only one manifestation of this trend. McDonald's has also begun to market a restructured "McRib" pork sandwich, which is composed of miscellaneous pieces of pork that have been rent apart and then resculpted in a meat press to simulate an actual rack of ribs, albeit a diminutive one that will fit into a bun.

Bonanza, another large restaurant food chain, has introduced a boneless pork product of its own called Hearty Ribs, and a frozen take-home entree called Johnny Rib.

Webber Farms in Cynthiana, Kentucky, has announced a new frozen boneless pork dinner, also shaped like a rack of ribs, which will (according to the company's promotional literature) convey to housewives the traditional appeal of "southern quality."

Some restructured meat products designed for easy microwave cooking are even packaged with imitation grill marks preapplied for that extra touch of authenticity.

In his *Pig American* article, Marberry goes on to note that restructured meat is still in its infant stages, and that there remain many unsolved technical problems, such as "consumer appeal, product image, color, shelf life, binding characteristics, product texture, and establishing a method for conveying the product in a fresh form that appeals to consumers at the retail level."

But if the customers here at Bob Evans' Restaurant are any indication of the future of restructured meat products, Steve Marberry need not worry. On the Tuesday night I dined there, the restaurant was so full that an almost constant crowd of people was backed up around the cash register waiting to be seated.

5

It is a brisk fall morning as I drive north along the Mississippi River on Route 168, heading for Palmyra, Missouri. Coming around a sweeping curve in the road, I suddenly see clouds of white steam rising over stubbled cornfields into the cobalt-blue sky. This marks the home of American Cyanamid's Agricultural Products Plant—one of three plants that make Cyanamid the nation's largest producer of the antibiotic tetracycline for use in livestock feed. The particular form of tetracycline that Cyanamid produces is chlortetracycline, which is marketed as Aureomycin; it was the first of the tetracycline drugs to be discovered, its successors being oxytetracycline—marketed now as Terramycin by Pfizer Inc. for animal use. As these and other antibiotics began to be manufactured in great quantities during the early fifties by American Cyanamid and other companies—both for human therapy and for use as a livestock-feed additive to promote growth and control subclinical disease—the bacterial world was assaulted with a new and withering barrage of antibiotic compounds. It was faced with an evolutionary challenge to respond or succumb. Becoming resistant in increasing numbers by the transfer of R plasmids, it responded as if it were an outdated army refitting itself for modern warfare.

While I wait in the plant's reception room for my arrival to be announced to the plant manager, I leaf through a copy of *The National Hog Farmer*, a hog-farming trade journal, and come upon a two-page advertisement for one of American

Cyanamid's tetracycline products. On the first page, the words "ASK YOURSELF: Can I afford to finish my hogs with Aureomycin tetracycline during a tight year?" stand out in bold red lettering against a plain white background. On the opposing page, in the same red lettering, are the words "THEN ASK YOURSELF: Can I afford slow growth, poor feed efficiency, cervical abscesses, bacterial enteritis, and the drag of atrophic rhinitis during any year?" Below this, in black, is the statement "Aureomycin doesn't cost, it pays."

Actually, as I look through the magazine, I am a little surprised to find myself sitting in this lobby at all. Getting corporate permission to visit Cyanamid's Missouri plant has not been an easy undertaking. When it comes to publicity that cannot be orchestrated or controlled by their own staff or advertising firms, most large drug companies would rather do without. In preparation, I had put in a call some weeks earlier to Cyanamid headquarters, in Wayne, New Jersey, and was referred to Richard Gustafson, at the company's research facility in Princeton, who, I was told, has a Ph.D. in microbiology from Rutgers and is an associate research fellow in charge of "antibiotic defense" in Cyanamid's Agricultural Research Division. "He defends the product when it is attacked," his secretary told me when I inquired about the meaning of this title.

Gustafson began his defense cheerfully enough. "I think the most significant question to ask in all this is, Are antibiotics useful in livestock production?" he said. "Now, I'd have to answer, Yes, they sure are. Very useful. It's important to control animal disease and produce food efficiently. So I think for us to reject technology like antibiotics on the chance that their use in animals is imprudent is . . . Well, I don't think any practice should be regarded as imprudent if it's an important technological device for the production of food. I think that we should require some evidence of its harm before we give it up."

"Do you feel that the evidence so far suggests that there might be such harm from the use of large amounts of antibiotics in animal feed?" I asked.

"As you probably know, a number of organizations, such as the National Academy of Sciences, have been studying this question," Gustafson replied. "None of them have been able to come up with any conclusive data for or against the hypothesis that livestock resistance to antibiotics is being passed from livestock to human beings." There was a weariness in his voice, suggesting that this was not the first time he had been asked to discuss the subject. "My view as a microbiologist is that animal bacteria provide an insignificant source of antibiotic resistance in man," he continued. "I think the evidence shows that the increase in human resistance to antibiotics we are witnessing results from the medical treatment of human beings rather than from the use of animal-feed additives. I don't doubt that a person who is in contact with antibiotic-resistant bacteria from animals is occasionally going to consume some of those bacteria—particularly if he is working in an environment where he might get feces on his hands. We all consume things we don't know about, whether we're working in a chickenhouse or preparing food. But the question is whether or not this represents a significant source of antibiotic resistance. I don't think it does."

After a pause, he continued, "The evidence that *we* have seen doesn't support the assumption that it's all that easy for animal bacteria to establish themselves in a human being. You may have heard about the experiments that H. W. Smith did in the late sixties at the Houston Poultry Research Station in England. He cultured up a bunch of *E. coli* from chickens and drank them. He wanted to find out how well animal bacteria could survive in a person. What he found after monitoring the levels of these bugs in his own gut by taking periodic fecal samples is that they disappeared fairly rapidly."

"But couldn't a substantial number of R plasmids have been

transferred to his own bacteria during that interim period?" I asked.

"Well . . . I just don't know the answer to that question," Gustafson replied. "I guess it's not implausible to think that it could happen. But you need contact. Bacteria have to conjugate before that can happen."

"Why wouldn't they conjugate?"

"This may happen *in vitro*, in lab studies, where you can arrange it so that a hundred percent of the bacteria are potential R-factor donors because you have made sure they all have the right plasmid. But it has never been demonstrated *in vivo*—in the guts of living animals—where there may be very few bacterial cells carrying R factors."

"What about Mr. Smith? Did he show any sign of R-plasmid transfer to his own intestinal bacteria?"

"Under circumstances like that, where Smith was introducing trillions of organisms into his system, I would say that there was a very good chance of transfer to his own resident gut flora. But we don't know, because he wasn't checking for plasmids, only for bacteria. There haven't been very many studies of this nature, because plasmids are devilishly hard to follow in real life."

"So you're not saying that it isn't happening—just that we aren't sure of the degree to which it is happening?"

"I think that finally we have to admit that this is a very elusive subject," Gustafson said amicably. "There are so many facets to this problem that dealing with it is a little like grappling with smoke."

Anton F. Nagy, the manager of American Cyanamid's plant, turns out to be a tall, fatherly-looking man with a thick dark mustache. He left his native Hungary in 1946 to immigrate to the United States and study engineering, and he still speaks English with a slight accent. In his office, we sit across from each other on chrome-tubed, executive-style furniture set in a grove of potted rubber plants and ficus trees. Nagy asks his secretary to bring us each a cup of coffee, and, leaning back in his chair, he fills me in on information about the plant. As manager, Nagy is in charge not only of chlortetracycline production—like B. T. Alford, of Cyanamid's sales staff, he refuses to give statistics about how much chlortetracycline Cyanamid manufactures each year—but also of the production of Prowl (an agricultural herbicide), Thimet (a soil and systemic insecticide for control of several agricultural pests) and ammonium nitrate (used in the production of chemical fertilizer).

After this brief introduction, Nagy hands me a hard hat and a pair of protective plastic goggles. Thus armored, we head out to the parking lot. For ten minutes or so, Nagy and I drive around the plant while he explains the functions of the various buildings, cooling towers, steam vents, tanks, ducts, storage bins, freight areas and incinerators for the burning of hazardous wastes. Nagy finally pulls up in front of a large silvery building with a corrugated metal roof. Inside, we enter a laboratory, where he introduces me to an owlish-looking man in a white smock and very round glasses. This is P. R. Joshi, a microbiologist originally from India in charge of the plant's Animal Feed Ingredients Laboratory.

"Our job is to make sure that the plant always has a good supply of seed microorganisms to keep the chlortetracycline production line moving," says Joshi, standing in the midst of an array of bottles, scales, coolers, sterilizers, microscopes, centrifuges and other tools of his trade. "You might say that our lab is like a nursery," he continues, his Indian accent giving his voice a cheerful lilt. "This is where we raise the bugs that will actually produce the chlortetracycline."

What Joshi refers to as "the bugs" are the Actinomyces class of microorganism called *Streptomyces aureofaciens.* "What is unique about *Streptomyces aureofaciens* bacteria is that they are able to reproduce through cellular fission—simple division of the cell—as well as by means of spores, like a mold.

They are a bridge in the evolutionary chain between bacteria and molds," Joshi says. "They are quite prolific reproducers," he adds, speaking of his tiny wards proudly, the way the principal of a school for gifted children might speak of his pupils.

"Let's have a look here," he says, turning toward a microscope on a counter behind him. He squeezes a single tear of liquid from an eyedropper onto a slide, places it on the microscope tray and peers down at it through the eyepiece. "Ah, yes. Have a look for yourselves." He adjusts the focus and beckons Nagy and me closer. Looking down through the eyepiece into the warm yellow light, I see a spiderweb-like growth of gray vegetable matter magnified on the slide. "What you are seeing are the mycelia, the moldlike filaments of which the culture is composed," says Joshi.

The production of the chlortetracycline itself takes place in an adjacent building, inside huge tanks known as fermenters, similar to those used in beer production. Joshi's responsibility is to grow breeding stock and have it on hand each time a fermenter has been emptied and is ready to be restocked.

From a Cold Spot refrigerator, he removes a glass flask and shakes it up as if it were a bottle of salad dressing. "This is part of the master culture," he says. "One cc contains nine hundred million bugs. If we run out of this stuff—well . . ." He rolls his eyes, looks at Nagy and then gives a little chirrup of laughter. "Well, too bad! Thirty-seven years of research down the drain!" Nagy, who has been standing respectfully to one side while Joshi explains the lab, smiles wanly at the thought. "Actually, the strain of bugs itself is not as important anymore as the process for making the chlortetracycline," Joshi continues quickly, apparently not wanting to leave his commander-in-chief with such a dark thought. "We can always get more bugs from our master culture, which is kept elsewhere," he murmurs reassuringly. "To produce our seed microorganisms, we take some of our inoculant stock from our master culture here, and put it in an incubator at an exactly controlled temperature. We've used the same strain of inoculant bugs since the beginning," he says, making me think of the owner of a sourdough-bread company in San Francisco who used to boast that his family used the same, or "mother," yeast culture in its bakery for three generations.

Before Joshi's bugs can graduate from his lab and proceed to the fermenters in the next building, he tells me, they must be tested. "We put them into this miniature fermenter with a slurry of food," he says, pointing to a small cylindrical machine standing on a countertop at the far end of the lab. "After they have been warmed and agitated awhile, I will extract a sample and culture it. We must keep our seed culture absolutely clean. By culturing the bugs, we can see if any other microorganisms have been mixed in with them. If that happened, it would throw off production in the large fermenters. And then we'd have a problem." As Joshi speaks, he picks up a glass petri dish, which contains a peach-fuzz growth of mold on a gelatinous surface, and examines it carefully.

After a tour of the lab, Nagy and I once again don our goggles and hard hats and step outside into the din of the plant. As we cross the road, Nagy stops to point out three large silos along a railroad spur, which contain raw materials used as food for the *Streptomyces aureofaciens* during the fermentation process. A little farther down the tracks, in back of the Fermentation Building, is a huge, overhead storage bin capable of holding 150,000 pounds of feed material and chlortetracycline, part of some 9 million pounds of antibiotics for animal-feed additives currently shipped each year in the United States. I am accustomed to thinking of antibiotics in terms of a few small capsules or several cc's of an injectable solution in a rubber-tipped bottle; the idea of the thousands of tons of raw chlortetracycline feed additives that have passed through this plant on their way to the farmers of America is just barely comprehensible.

Nagy leads me up a steel staircase on the outside of the

Fermentation Building and, opening a door at the top, ushers me into a noisy, windowless space, filled with immense round tanks that rise up through the building's three floors like intercontinental ballistic missiles. Nagy surveys the scene before us for a moment and then, cupping his hands between his mouth and my ear, yells over the industrial roar, "These little tanks over here are seed tanks, where we grow bugs in volume from Joshi's culture before pumping them into the fermenters!" He is pointing to three relatively small tanks standing to one side of the large fermenters. Then, pointing toward a corner of the room, he shouts, "Over there is the cook tank, where we sterilize all the food for the bugs after it comes in from the outside silos! And there are our thirty-eight-thousand-gallon fermenters." With an outstretched arm, Nagy makes a sweeping arc across the rest of the room, where the fermentation tanks are grinding away, each with a large electric motor perched on top driving an internal agitator. They look like giant ice-cream makers. "Since the fermentation process is an aerobic one, requiring a supply of oxygen, we must constantly inject the slurry inside the tanks with air," he continues, pointing out compressed-air lines leading past clusters of gauges and valves into the tanks. "Another problem is that fermentation generates heat, and if the bugs become too hot, they stop producing and can even die," he says. "So we also have to pump cold water through coils inside the fermenters to cool the slurry."

In the midst of all this machinery it is hard to imagine that these leviathan industrial tanks are filled with life. But as we stand watching, it occurs to me that this production line for S. aureofaciens is quite similar to the hog-confinement barns, cattle feedlots and poultry factories to which the tetracycline will ultimately go. Here Nagy and Joshi are overseeing the husbanding, fattening, slaughter and sale of microorganisms just as the proprietors of farms oversee the husbanding, fattening, slaughter and sale of meat animals. There may be no

roping, branding or sitting on the corral fence with a bag of
Bull Durham here at American Cyanamid's Agricultural Products Plant, but the principle is the same.

"Sometimes it all seems more like an art than a science,"
remarks Nagy after a moment of silence. "We're really at the
mercy of these little devils. They need such a delicately balanced environment. If they don't like the temperature, the
food, the pH level or the oxygen content, they rebel and die."
He smiles and shakes his head.

After the bugs have been eating, reproducing and secreting
chlortetracycline for about a week, a sample is bled out of
each fermenter and tested. If technicians feel that an optimal
level of production has been reached, the bugs are pumped
from the congenial environment of the fermenters into two
large vacuum filters, where unwanted liquid is separated out.
Then the brown gooey mash of microorganisms (which are
rich in protein and thus left in the feed additive) and their
antibiotic excrescence is dropped on a conveyor belt and
whisked away to a dryer, where all the bugs are killed, soon
to be loaded into trucks and boxcars for shipment across the
country to feed-additive formulators. Much of it will go to
Cyanamid's own plants, where it will be mixed with other
drugs and processed into Aureo SP 250 for pigs.

"Our plant is right in the middle of the Corn Belt," Nagy
says with satisfaction at the end of our tour, as we stand on a
steel catwalk and watch the raw chlortetracycline disappear
down the production line through a hole in the wall to the
dryers. "We're right here where we belong, within five hundred miles of the major hog-producing areas of America."

6

The hog farm of Arthur Lehman, outside the small town of Strawn, Illinois, is some 180 miles from American Cyanamid's fermentation tanks—well within the radius described by Anton Nagy. Lehman Farms is acknowledged by many Midwestern hog farmers to be a well-run operation, and last year Arthur Lehman was chosen Illinois Pork All-American—an honor bestowed by the National Pork Producers' Council in conjunction with the Illinois Pork Producers' Association.

Built on a slight knoll elevated above the otherwise flat prairie, Lehman Farms is visible from some distance away, its long, low steel hog barns looking more like industrial warehouses than places of animal husbandry, and its two cylindrical corncribs silhouetted like the turrets of a castle against the early-morning sky.

I turn in at a long driveway, passing an RFD letter box with a tin pig perched on top, and drive up through fields white with frost toward a green-shingled house. As I pull to a stop beside a huge John Deere combine, a man emerges from the back door of the house and walks to my car. He appears to be in his late thirties, and he wears a cap with the words "Lehman Farms" embroidered just above a patch that shows two smiling pigs nuzzling each other, a bright-orange parka embossed with the American Cyanamid logo for Aureo SP 250, Levi's and manure-encrusted galoshes.

"Hello, I'm Art—Art Lehman," he says, removing his work gloves so we can shake hands. "I'm just on my way to the barns to do the morning chores." When I suggest accompanying him, so that we can talk, he appears slightly hesitant, like someone who suddenly realizes just as a guest arrives that the bed isn't made and there are unwashed dishes in the sink. "Well . . . suit yourself," he replies. "I haven't really had a chance to tidy up."

In fact, there is nothing untidy about the farm, which he runs with his brother Ken, Art caring for some six thousand hogs while Ken looks after the surrounding eight hundred acres of corn and beans, much of which is fed to the livestock. As we head for one of the barns, I ask Lehman how he came to be a Pork All-American.

"Well, it'll damn near kill you," he replies, with a laugh. "First you got to fill out all these applications. Then the state Pork Producers' Association takes them. Then, if they like what they see, they come out and pay you a visit. Then either you get it or you don't."

Other than our voices and the hiss of the wind as it blows unobstructed across the miles of flat cropland, there is no sound. But when we reach the hog barn and Lehman opens the door, the solitude is broken by a thunderous burst of squealing, oinking and trumpeting.

Lehman's arrival signals breakfast. Two hundred and sixty-five sows and fifteen boars shriek in anticipation of food, and, like prisoners beating their cell bars with tin cups, they rattle the steel gates of their individual stalls with their snouts. As if we were superstars walking onstage as a sold-out house explodes into a delirious accolade, Lehman and I step across the threshold into the full volume of this pig pandemonium. Although the noise is deafening, there is another sensation that is even more overpowering—the smell. The moment Lehman opens the door, a tropical zephyr of ammonia-saturated air comes billowing out into our faces.

This is Art Lehman's gestation-and-breeding building—an example of what is known among hog farmers as a confinement

barn. Animals live within such barns "from farrow to finish,"
or from birth to the last stages of growth. Confinement systems rely heavily on modern technology to deliver feed and
water to each stall, to remove manure and to farrow and care
for the young piglets. While this new technology has revolutionized hog farming during the last twenty years and made it
possible for one man, with a minimum of outside assistance,
to maintain a herd of some three hundred sows, which annually produces approximately six thousand piglets, it has also
created some new problems. The crowding of so many animals within such close indoor quarters renders them highly
susceptible to disease, so a heavy reliance on drugs has become an integral part of modern livestock production.

Lehman's barn reeks of ammonia because it is constructed
over a large pit, into which the feces and urine of the animals
fall through a slatted floor. In the 1960s and early '70s, such
buildings were considered state of the art, and farmers built
thousands of them. It soon became apparent, however, that
serious health problems could be caused by the toxic gases—
ammonia, methane and hydrogen sulfide—that the excreta
produce, which rise from the pits and become trapped inside
the barns. Recognition of the problem—particularly in the
Midwestern states, where farmers are forced to close all barn
windows during the cold winter months—brought about a
new design. Instead of barns built over pits, farmers began
building confinement systems equipped with flush gutters,
which remove the animal wastes outside to storage lagoons
several times a day. But, like many other farmers, Lehman—
who, as he puts it, "modernized too soon"—still has several
barns over pits. Because his fields are covered by mud and
snow during the winter and by crops during the summer, he is
unable to pump out the pits and spread the manure more than
twice a year; he has had to work around his problem by adding
various ventilation systems, which apparently have not completely solved it.

Although Lehman Farms is in truth a "family" farm, it is far from the bucolic scene of years ago when each farm had a few sows in an outdoor sty and a family milk cow in the barn. Like most other aspects of American agriculture, hog farming has become an industry, and men like Art Lehman have had to modernize to stay in the running. "Some people think raising hogs in these small indoor stalls is inhumane," Lehman says defensively, looking out across the rows of steel-barred enclosures—four rows of seventy stalls each—which stretch to the end of the two-hundred-foot-long building, creating an eerie Op Art effect. "We're getting a whole lot of flak from the animal-rights people about having hogs in confinement. But look at this huge pig." He walks over to a nearby stall and strokes the bristly back of a blimplike pink Yorkshire sow. "OK. Let's just say that I'm not for confinement, either—that I want to keep all my pigs outside on dirt lots, like in the old days. So I put this big old lady out there with a bunch of gilts [young females that have not been bred]—and do you know what will happen? This old sow will probably kill every last one of them." Lehman pauses for a moment and looks directly at me, like a minister who has just warned of damnation in the most extreme form and is watching to see how his congregation will respond. "Well, if she doesn't end up killing them, at least she won't let them get any feed," he adds, relenting a little when all I do is nod. "Pigs are real social. They get into a pecking order under a boss sow at the top, and woe to the ones at the bottom! Those boss sows can really kick ass!"

From where Lehman and I are standing at the front of the barn, all we can see of the rows of confined pigs is a chorus line of moving extremities—a snout or an ear that will momentarily bob up above the top of a stall, or a trotter thrust for a moment through the bars of a front panel as the animals continue their prefeeding frenzy. Then Lehman turns, reaches up and grabs an overhead lever at the end of one of the aisles. Giving it several strong yanks, he triggers a mechanism that drops measured portions of feed into individual feeders bolted to the front of the stalls along that aisle. In a single instant, the clamorous row of pigs falls into ghostlike silence. Lehman releases the morning ration into the dump feeders of each row in turn, and soon all that can be heard is the sound of masticating pigs.

"Sure, it might be nice to let your hogs out every now and then for a run," Lehman says as he returns from the last aisle. (I try to imagine his six thousand pigs released from their barns like so many furloughed prisoners to jog across the fields surrounding his farm.) "But in January it will be twenty degrees below zero. All the waterers will freeze up. The feed troughs will freeze up. You wouldn't even be able to get in with a tractor to feed the animals. You're going to have pigs with frostbitten ears and feet climbing over snowdrifts and ice trying to find shelter. Or in August the temperature hits one hundred, and if your pigs don't have shade, they're going to die fast, because pigs can't sweat to cool themselves. All the pigs will be thinking about then is survival. To heck with being comfortable and gaining weight fast!"

For a moment, it appears that Lehman's argument in favor of confinement barns has come to an end. But one more point occurs to him. "And then you've got to think about how expensive land around here has become recently. Good cropland costs four thousand dollars an acre. So how can you afford to let pigs run around on it?"

The barn door opens. A momentary gust of welcome fresh air sweeps in as a young blond man enters. Lehman introduces him as Bob Frase, who became herdsman at Lehman Farms a year ago, after graduating from Western Illinois University's swine-management program.

"What effect does the ammonia in the air have on the pigs?" I ask Frase as Lehman strolls down an aisle to check on the feeding sows.

"These barns built over manure pits aren't so hot, if you

ask me," Frase replies, somewhat apologetically. "The ammonia really chews up the animals' lungs. They get listless
and don't want to eat. They start losing weight, and the next
thing you know you've got a real respiratory problem—
pneumonia or something. Then you'll see them huddled down
real low against one another trying to get warm, and you'll
hear them coughing and gasping. The bad air's a problem.
After I've been working in here awhile, I can feel it in my
own lungs. But at least I get out of here at night. The pigs
don't, so we have to keep them on tetracycline, which really
does help control the problem." As Frase says this, he points
upward to the feed-delivery system, which brings ground
corn and soy, mixed with the proper subtherapeutic levels of
drugs, into the barns from a feed mill outside.

Respiratory diseases are not the only problems that Art Lehman and Bob Frase have to be on the lookout for in these
barns. Bacteria that cause animal diseases like scours (bloody
diarrhea) and atrophic rhinitis (a highly contagious disease
that atrophies the bones and tissue of a pig's snout) can spread
very quickly in close confinement and can knock the profit out
of an operation or, worse, jeopardize a whole herd. When the
piglets are born (about four months after conception) in one
of Lehman's two windowless farrowing houses, they are almost immediately given their first treatment of antibiotics—a
prophylactic injection of TUCO, Upjohn's Lincomycin, an
antibiotic named after its parent microorganism, *Streptomyces
lincolnensis*; it was first isolated from a soil sample found near
Lincoln, Nebraska. ("It helps the little fellas through the first
few days, when they might pick up something around the
barn," Lehman explains.)

The piglets spend the first four weeks of their lives with
their mothers, kept in stocklike steel structures called farrowing crates, which permit the sows either to stand or to lie
down but not to walk or even to turn around. The object
of this seeming cruelty to the sow is to protect her piglets

from being rolled on by her heavy, bulky body as she lies down to nurse. ("If a sow has a litter of twelve and rolls on three, right there you've lost about a hundred dollars," Lehman says.)

Inside the warm, low-ceilinged farrowing houses, banks of sows lie virtually immobilized in the farrowing crates, with their piglets squeaking like bats as they scamper around at the teats. (Weighing an average of only 2.2 pounds at birth, these piglets will double their weight in the first week, triple it by the end of the second week, and weigh 15 pounds by the end of the third week.) Like patients in an intensive-care ward, the sows are kept alive by life-support systems that minister to most of their needs. Automatic devices provide water to each crate. A system of augers brings in feed containing fifty grams of tetracycline per ton. (Such a sub-therapeutic dose is approximately ten times lower than that required as therapy for an actual disease.) The two farrowing houses, unlike the gestation and breeding barn, have gutters that automatically flush away the manure and urine. Wires bring electricity for heat lamps to warm the piglets during the cold months. Underground plastic ducts pipe cool air onto the sows' faces during the warm months. At the end of each crate is a chart, like a clipboard hanging at the foot of a hospital bed, that details the sow's farrowing record and medical history.

To wean his piglets, Lehman moves them into a climate-controlled nursery. This is a critical stage in their lives, because, stressed from weaning and deprived of the antibodies in their mother's milk, they are particularly susceptible to disease. So in the nursery Lehman begins feeding them a 21-percent-protein "starter" ration with fifty grams of Mecadox per ton. (Mecadox is a synthetic chemical antibacterial manufactured by Pfizer and used in controlling swine dysentery and promoting growth.)

When the young pigs reach forty pounds, they are moved from the nursery to the growing barn, and there they are put

in pens by litter to minimize stress. Now Lehman feeds them
a 16-percent-protein "grower" ration of corn and soy, laced
with a hundred grams of tetracycline per ton. When the young
pigs reach seventy pounds, they are cut back to a 15-percent-
protein feed containing fifty grams of tetracycline per ton.

After the animals on this pig assembly line reach 120
pounds—about four months after birth—they make their last
big move on Lehman Farms: They go into the finishing barn,
a vast building that has been partitioned into scores of small
pens. Here the animals may eat as much as they wish of a
14-percent-protein feed, which may or may not contain fifty
grams of tetracycline per ton, depending on Lehman's assessment of their health. His pigs will gain approximately 1 pound
for every 3.5 pounds of food they eat. By the time the pigs
finally leave this building and Lehman Farms for the slaughterhouse, each of them will have gained, over a period of six to
seven months, up to 220 pounds on approximately 600 pounds
of feed and antibiotic feed additives, mixed in Lehman's own
feed mill. There is no withdrawal time for chlortetracycline-
supplemented feed; regulations of the Food and Drug Administration allow pigs to consume this particular antibiotic
additive right up to the day they are slaughtered, as long as
the dose remains at or below fifty grams per ton.

Lehman asks me if I would like to have a look at the feed
mill, which he built himself. As we emerge from the warm,
ammoniated air of the gestation-and-breeding barn into the
clear cold air outside, I feel as if I were surfacing from a
subway station after a long ride on a hot, crowded train. My
parka and my hair are permeated with the barn's odor.
(Several weeks later, my parka still emits an acrid smell.)
Even though a chill wind is blowing and my teeth are soon
chattering, I am relieved to be out in the fresh air.

The feed mill stands in front of Lehman's gestation barn,
near the two tall, cylindrical corn bins. It is here that the corn
and soy raised by Ken Lehman are cracked, ground and mixed

with feed additives—antibiotics, sulfa drugs, worming agents, vitamins, minerals. Then, like blood pumped by the heart to the organs of the body, the mixed feed is sent by auger through an intricate network of conveyor tubes to the various barns. Behind the milling-and-mixing apparatus is a small padlocked room, where Lehman keeps his arsenal of drugs: fifty-pound sacks of American Cyanamid's Aureo SP 250, Pfizer's Terramycin (oxytetracycline) and Upjohn's Lincomycin.

Unlike antibiotics for human use, which can be bought only with a doctor's prescription, these agricultural drugs are readily available to a farmer in any amount he wishes. Recommended dose levels and required withdrawal times before slaughter, which have been established by law, are printed on containers, but it is difficult for government regulators to monitor for compliance with these instructions. Although farmers like Art Lehman take great pride in their operations and strive to administer these drugs with intelligence and caution, there exist numerous other livestock operations where proper dose levels and withdrawal times are frequently ignored. Some farmers heavily overdose their animals with antibiotics to control diseases brought on by filthy and poorly heated barns. Others, desperate to get weak, or even sick, animals to market, will continue to administer a variety of drugs to their stock right up to the day they are shipped to the slaughterhouse. Still others will use illegal or banned drugs. More often than not, these violations will go undetected by the Department of Agriculture's meat inspectors, who must examine hundreds, and sometimes thousands, of carcasses a day in busy packing plants.

It must be said, however, that most farmers do not deliberately misuse the drugs and chemicals at their disposal. But farms and ranches are rough-and-tumble places, where mistakes and accidents are not infrequent. Every herdsman, hired hand or cowboy in effect becomes a veterinarian when he ad-

ministers drugs, and not all are graduates of agricultural-
college programs, as is Bob Frase. The constant presence of
these drugs on the farm can breed a dangerous sense of fa-
miliarity. They become so much a part of the daily routine
that it is easy to lose respect for the hazards their continued
use poses.

Like everything else around Art Lehman's feed mill, his
drug room is covered with a film of dust. Although most of
it is doubtless ground feed that has sifted out of the milling
machinery, there is also, mixed in with this fallout of corn
and soy, a modicum of each of the drugs neatly stacked in
their paper sacks. As Lehman explains the design of his mill
and how he built it, he leans with one hand on the V-shaped
hopper that funnels the mixed feed into the auger system.
Then, standing upright, he scratches his face with his dusty
hand, leaving a powdery blotch on his upper lip. As he continues his explanation, I am unable to take my eyes off this
smudge, which bobs up and down as he talks. Then, uncon-
sciously sweeping his tongue around his mouth to wet his
lips, he licks off part of the dusty smudge. I find myself
thinking about resistant microorganisms and wondering what
goes on among the flora of Arthur Lehman's gut.

I ask him if he is ever concerned about working around so
many drugs and toxic chemicals on the farm. (His pigs are
dipped in lindane, a carcinogenic and extremely toxic compound, to control lice, and Ken uses herbicides for weed
control on all the cropland surrounding the farm.)

"Well, I'm not so worried about the stuff," he replies. "We're
pretty careful here. Actually, I'm trying to cut down a lot on
antibiotics. I know it's something that people are getting concerned about. What I would like to do is to make our management so good that we won't need any drugs."

Then, after pausing to consider what he has just said, he
adds, "Of course, I don't know if we could actually attain that
state. Anyway, more and more of the smart farm money is

going into vaccines to make animals immune to diseases, so we won't end up having to treat them." He walks over to a dusty refrigerator standing against one wall and opens the door to reveal scores of rubber-tipped bottles, full of vaccines and other injectable drugs. "Sure, there are a lot of guys using drugs instead of cleaning up their barns, as a substitute for good management and sanitation," Lehman continues. "They get a problem and they just throw drugs at it, hoping they can get by. I don't go for that technique. I use drugs, but I'd like to get the pigs off them as much as possible."

I ask Lehman if he relies on antibiotic feed additives for their purported growth-promoting qualities as well as for disease control.

"I never bought all that stuff about these drugs promoting growth and increasing profits," he replies without hesitation. "I think you end up paying as much for antibiotics as what you get out of them. My sense of the situation is that if you don't overuse them, then you get a much better response when you really need them, because you haven't built up all those resistance problems."

I ask him why so many other farmers seem convinced of their efficacy.

"Maybe they've had success, or maybe they choose to believe the claims of the drug companies," he replies diffidently. "Everybody's just trying to make a living."

Whether or not drug company claims of increased profits from antibiotic feed additives are accurate (and there is disagreement on this point, even in veterinary circles), a farmer is constantly confronted with what can only be described as a propaganda barrage on their behalf. Trade journals such as *The National Hog Farmer, Pig American* and *Hog Farm Management* are filled with articles extolling subtherapeutic drugs and with glossy full-page color advertisements singing their praises. "I've looked at these trade journals, and I must say I have found that there is a great deal of misinformation

being disseminated in them," comments Stanley Falkow, of
Stanford University, who is very much concerned about increased bacterial resistance to antibiotics. "And I think that
this misinformation has been fueled in part by people from
some of the pharmaceutical houses. These drugs are the source
of a lot of revenue, and of course their manufacturers want to
defend them. It's hard to know if antibiotics really contribute
to growth promotion, because most of the research the drug
companies have done has been aimed at justifying their claims
rather than understanding the actual mechanisms of what happens when these drugs are used."

At every national livestock and feedstuffs convention, like
the American Pork Congress or the National Cattlemen's Association Annual Convention and Trade Show, and at regional
and state gatherings for industry people, the companies that
manufacture antibiotic feed additives have display booths and
sales staffs. Lest livestock producers grow skeptical of the
glowing encomiums, drug companies sponsor numerous and
costly field trials, which measure weight gains of animals fed
their products. According to Helen M. Maddock, the swine-
program manager at American Cyanamid, a 1981 test on the
Iowa farm of D. D. Johnson showed that hogs on Aureo SP
250 (fifty grams per ton of feed) gained weight 10 percent
faster on about 5 percent less feed than those without the
additive. In a test the same year at a research farm of the
Cargill Company, a Minnesota manufacturer of livestock feed,
Dr. Kent Elkstrom, a swine-research nutritionist at Cargill,
reported that in general for every dollar invested in antibiotic
feed additives farmers could expect to get a two-dollar return
at the marketplace. However, in an independent study carried
out by Vaughn Speer, a swine nutritionist at Iowa State University, results were less conclusive. After comparing the
growth of thousands of hogs on subtherapeutic antibiotics,
Speer concluded that, while piglets seemed to show faster
weight gains from antibiotics right after weaning, "improve-

ment in gain . . . as a result of antibiotic feeding begins to diminish" as pigs grow older. Suffice it to say that data on weight gains in trials involving subtherapeutic antibiotic feed additives is conflicting. Nonetheless, for a struggling cattleman or hog farmer, the prospect of increasing profit margins even a few percentage points simply by using a feed additive is almost irresistible. Many farmers will admit that they are not eager to use subtherapeutic drugs but that they feel they must do so as an insurance policy.

Although Art Lehman is not an uncritical defender of the use of antibiotics in animal feed, when I ask him what he knows about transferable antibiotic resistance, he replies with uncharacteristic irritation. "Sure, I've read some articles about it, but I'm bothered when I hear people in the cities, who don't know anything about animals, criticizing farmers for contaminating their meat with drugs. City people use cleansers, sanitizers, bug bombs, weed killers and solvents, and half the kids are on dope," he continues as we walk together back toward the gestation barn, where he has five sows to breed today. "The parents are on tranquilizers and all kinds of other stuff. The way I see it, these things are just as dangerous as the drugs we give our animals and the chemicals we put on our fields."

As we reach the door and return to the suffocating atmosphere of the barn, he adds, "I don't think we could feed all the people in this country at a reasonable price if we abandoned these new methods of raising food." He opens a steel gate and lets a boar, frothing at the mouth, into a breeding pen to mount a sow. "I say that before all the city people criticize what we're doing, they ought to stop and compare what the Japanese, the Germans and the Russians are paying for their food. Then I think they'd realize how cheaply they're getting off.

"We've made some amazing advances in animal health in the last twenty-five years. Before we give them up, I want to see all those people who criticize us riding a horse or a bicycle to work and giving up their garbage compactors and automatic garage-door openers. Why should farmers go back to a peasant way of life and let everyone else live in the twentieth century?"

When Lehman has finished breeding his sows, he suggests that we take a tour outside. As we set off around the farm, we come to several small outdoor pens, where a few pigs, stretched out in the sun, doze blissfully on the ground, their nostrils making little puffs of dust each time they exhale. Compared with the interior of the gestation-and-breeding barn, where row upon row of sows stand in their steel stalls all facing in the same direction like parked cars in a lot, this haphazard assemblage of pigs sprawled in the open air next to an antiquated feed trough seems like something out of a time warp.

"You could say that this is my hog sanatorium," Lehman remarks, as we stop for a moment to survey the unlikely scene. "I bring sows and gilts out here when they fail to cycle—come into heat—and give them one more chance before I get rid of them." He shakes his head and laughs in seeming embarrassment at the primitive pens, as if he were a renowned scientist caught consulting a fortune-teller. In these makeshift enclosures, where the animals sleep on straw bedding in rough wooden shelters, none of the sophisticated technology—and none of the drugs—employed on the rest of the farm is in evidence. Here in this "hog sanatorium," the only curative powers are the sun and the fresh air, as well as the change of night to day, the progression of the seasons, and the waxing and waning of the moon—all the normal rhythms of life that the hogs in confinement are only dimly aware of.

"I don't know what it is about putting a pig out here in the dirt," Lehman continues meditatively. "All I know is that after an animal gets out here, she often shapes right up and comes into heat. I've saved quite a few that way." He smiles and shrugs, acknowledging that there are still a few ineffable aspects to modern hog raising.

7

Although the majority of cars that gush out of the Lincoln Tunnel on the western side of the Hudson River heading toward Secaucus carry license plates that proclaim New Jersey to be the Garden State, the surroundings hardly suggest agriculture. The tangle of roadways, the refineries, factories, warehouses and urban blight littering the landscape do not conjure up images of farms, much less gardens.

However, it was not so many years ago that Secaucus (which lies only six miles from downtown Manhattan) played host to one of the most important agricultural operations in the East. In an area of just a few square miles, sixty-odd New Jersey farmers raised more than 350,000 pigs.

Reminiscent of the kind of marine colonies that are found flourishing at the end of sewage outfall pipes, the multitude of pigs living outside Secaucus on the Jersey side of the Lincoln Tunnel thrived on New York's garbage. Like the Cloaca Maxima, which drained ancient Rome of its waste, the tunnel served as a conduit for convoys of garbage trucks, which left Secaucus each night to make their midnight rounds of restaurants, bakeries, schools, hospitals and jails. What was unwanted waste to the citizens of New York City was treasure to the New Jersey hog farmers.

"We were hauling garbage from everywhere, from some of the city's finest restaurants. We even done the '21' Club," remembers Mike Rozansky, whose family had a farm in Secaucus and who still hauls garbage from the Americana and Statler hotels, Mount Sinai Hospital and the Riker's Island Prison in New York to his present hog operation outside Trenton, New Jersey.

The unusual symbiosis of pigs and urban people came to an end when construction on the New Jersey Turnpike began in the 1950s. The new highway was aimed like a harpoon across the Secaucus mud flats, right through the hog farms.

"You couldn't fight it," Mike Rozansky remembers dolefully. "The government had rights to condemn land, so what could you do? The pigs had to go, and the farms closed."

By 1957, there was not a hog farm left in Secaucus. Like aborigines driven into the jungle by the advancing modern world, those "garbage" feeders who did not give up entirely were forced to retreat deeper into New Jersey.

Today on the very turnpike that was the hog farmers' undoing, I look out across the bleak mud flats in vain for any remaining sign of their presence. None is visible. No historical marker. No turnout where a pilgrim such as myself might pause and make a quick genuflection. The traffic whizzes along with such unnerving speed that following the green highway signs demands every bit of attention.

My destination is Lafferty Farms in Deptford, one of New Jersey's remaining garbage feeders. Bill Lafferty is director of a hog farmers' association called National FACTS, which stands for Food and Conservation Through Swine. Composed of more than five hundred garbage-feeding pork producers all across the nation, National FACTS is dedicated to the defense of what its members have discreetly renamel PFW, or Processed Food Waste (in other words, garbage), as a livestock feed. "PFW," says their brochure, "is a valuable recycling process that produces protein for human consumption . . . [which] saves untold amounts of taxpayers' dollars for garbage disposal by reducing the amount of solids going into sewage plants, dumps, lakes, and landfills. PFW feeders assist . . . in producing wholesome quality pork from a potential pollutant."

Bill Lafferty has surprised me by agreeing to a tour of his farm. Getting permission to visit a garbage-fed hog farm in New Jersey is no easy task, even if you are a hog farmer yourself. As one irritated PFW farmer warned on the phone just before hanging up, "We haven't had it so good from the press. So I doubt there is anyone who'll let a reporter on his place. And if you want to know why, I'll tell you. It's three words, 'garbage,' 'mud' and 'pigs.'"

A letter to the National FACTS headquarters in Sewell, New Jersey, elicited no reply. Like inquiries to the embassies of some Communist countries, calls to the FACTS office requesting an opportunity to visit a member farm brought chilly demurrals about the inconvenience of such a tour.

But when I called Bill Lafferty, who runs a three-thousand-hog, garbage-fed operation, he surprised me with his politeness and willingness to receive me. In fact, he not only agreed to my visiting Lafferty Farms, but promised to try and convince the current president of National FACTS to stop by (he only lives a short distance away) and chat.

It is nine o'clock when I finally pull off the New Jersey Turnpike at Bellmawr. After a quick cup of coffee and a doughnut at the Club Diner, I call Lafferty Farms for instructions on how to get the rest of the way.

"Oh, my gosh!" exclaims Vicki Lafferty, Bill's wife, when I explain who I am over the phone. "You're that fellow who was so interested in seeing our place. Well, Bill's out with the hogs and . . ." Her voice trails off. I get the distinct feeling that they have forgotten about my impending visit, or worse, have received a directive from the National FACTS central committee to cancel my tour.

"I can find my own way if you will just give me rough directions," I offer, hoping to head off a reversal.

"Now, I'll tell you what," she begins again after a pause, her voice becoming decidedly more buoyant. "Why don't you just wait at your diner, and I'll come along down and bring you back here. I'll be driving a blue Sedan de Ville Cadillac."

A half hour later Vicki Lafferty's Sedan de Ville pulls into the Club Diner parking lot. Vicki looks like a pilot sitting in the cockpit of a massive 747; her face, which peers over the steering wheel, is dwarfed by the scale of the vehicle she is driving.

"Why don't you just follow me out," she says, as the push-button window on the driver's side of the car slides noiselessly down to reveal a pleasant-looking woman who appears to be in her late fifties.

As I fall in behind Vicki in my subcompact car, I feel as if I were a small dinghy caught in the wake of a huge cabin cruiser. Just past a sagging Colonial-style house and an abandoned farm, Vicki turns into a long driveway. She pulls her Sedan de Ville up next to a pickup truck displaying a bumper sticker that reads, "Recycle It Again, Sam."

Two green garbage trucks with "Lafferty Farms" neatly lettered on their doors are parked across the parking area next to an equipment shed. From behind one of them emerges a man wearing a brown corduroy cap, a green coat, baggy gray trousers and leather boots with white socks.

"Honey! This is Mr. Schell," yells Vicki, poking her head out of the car window. "Why don't you take him out to see the farm and then come on in together for some breakfast."

Bill Lafferty is a shy, graying man. As he walks across the parking area, he extends his right arm in anticipation of shaking hands twenty paces before reaching the spot where I stand. Once his greeting has been accomplished, he immediately thrusts his hands into his trouser pockets as if he were uncertain what to do with them next. For a moment we both stand awkwardly together, our breath making little jets of exhaust in the raw morning air.

Eager to break the ice, I ask Bill if he would mind showing me around. He agrees, and we get into his pickup and drive down the dirt road that connects his house to the five-acre area where his hog pens are located.

Bill brings his truck to a halt in a bleak farmyard surrounded by graying barns, disheveled sheds and more garbage trucks. Broad dirt lots of pigs are arrayed around the central barnyard like airport runways around a passenger terminal. The colorless expanse of dirt, mud and puddles, which have swollen in the recent rains to the size of small ponds, are broken only by cross fencing, a few old truck bodies that afford shelter for animals, and an ever-changing kaleidoscopic pattern of moving pigs.

In the distance there is a roaring sound. Looking northward just above a thicket of brush, I can see the tops of cars and trucks speeding past on the highway, a reminder that even here in Deptford the great retreat before progress that began several decades ago in Secaucus, scattering pigs and farmers westward as if they were the Cherokee Nation, may not yet be over.

"It used to be that a fella could get all the garbage he wanted," begins Bill Lafferty, his voice tinged with nostalgia. "But they stopped separating the garbage and the trash when they went to dumpsters and compactors. That made it hard for us garbage feeders. And oh, my God, what a mess! They leave that stuff in the compactors for a week or more instead of picking it up daily. It starts to rot, and all the juice starts leaking out all over the place." As Bill launches into this narrative of the history of garbology, he begins to lose much of his earlier reserve.

"People just started getting spoiled. All they wanted to do was to chuck everything in bins and forget it," he continues volubly. "All that good garbage just started being taken away to the landfills!" He shakes his head with regret.

"Then everyone started installing those kitchen grinders, and people started putting all their garbage down the drain. In them days nobody thought one thing about recycling. That word hadn't even come out yet. Actually, that was *our* word." He stabs a stiff index finger at his chest. "It was us garbage-feeding hog farmers in National FACTS that brought that word out. Until then, it was just something we'd been doing all along without thinking about it."

He pauses a moment and stares out his truck window across his pens of hogs. Then, as if he were quoting Confucius, he adds, "When people start giving up the garbage can, then we're in trouble.

"My family was always into trash and garbage," Bill continues, turning the engine of the truck back on to start the heater. "Our people began feeding hogs this way back when there was no welfare. People had to work or else! My dad had a tallow-rendering plant, so we were into fat, meat scraps and bones. They used to raise pigs up fat for lard in those days. Everyone cooked with lard, and they made soap out of it. But when they started using synthetic oils after World War II, that killed the tallow industry.

"Maybe you don't know, but there is a difference between 'rubbish,' 'trash' and 'garbage,'" Bill says, as if he were a social scientist at a seminar trying to establish a rigorous definition of terms before proceeding with the formal discussion. Rubbish is just junk, trash is your paper, tin cans and bottles, and garbage is your edibles, what FACTS people have renamed 'processed food waste' because it sounds better than 'garbage.'" Bill gives a sheepish grin as if he felt he might have too casually exposed an intimate FACTS secret.

Even though the word *garbage* accurately connotes the substance that is the life's blood of these farms, it is a term that society has so supercharged with stigma that these farmers (particularly when talking with strangers) seem to avoid using whenever possible. One of Bill Lafferty's favorite euphemisms for *garbage* is *plate waste*. But often after using *plate waste* two or three times, he will suddenly grow careless and lapse back to the vernacular, calling garbage *garbage*.

"The only way we could keep getting plate waste after they went to the compactors was to go into the hauling business ourselves and get people to separate the trash from the garbage again," Bill continues, letting his vigilance slide. "So that puts us in the trash business, which is OK because that's a paying business.

"I'd say we haul about a hundred and fifty yards of trash out of Philadelphia to the landfill each day, and bring about fifteen to twenty tons of garbage here for the pigs. We got four trash trucks and two garbage trucks." He gestures over to a fleet of trucks parked by one of the pigpens.

"Some farmers work the districts picking up household garbage," he continues. "The city pays them for taking it away. It's a good deal for the farmer and the city. The farmer gets out there with a couple of men on a truck and goes to town. He wants to get home and feed his pigs, so he really gets the job done fast. If the city had to do it, they'd have to hire three trucks and nine men, because their men just sit around and drink coffee all day."

Just then a young man in a brown cowboy hat drives up in a red four-wheel-drive pickup, gets out and walks over. Bill rolls down his window and introduces me to his son Tom. "Tom here handles the trash. My other son, William the Third, hauls the garbage," Bill says with fatherly pride. "That leaves me with the pigs." He laughs.

Leaving the warm cab of the truck, we walk over to a weathered wooden barn. Inside is an aging truck with a massive steel-plated tank on the bed. The entire truck is splattered with a patina of pureed garbage that has built up over the years on its exterior surfaces like plaque on a set of unbrushed dentures.

The vehicle is of a species not likely ever to be seen on a highway. It is a garbage-cooking truck. The reason Bill must cook his garbage before feeding it is not to make it more palatable, but to kill disease organisms. New Jersey state law requires him to cook it for thirty minutes at 212 degrees F to kill parasites and hog cholera, a virus that is transmitted to pigs through feeding uncooked pork scraps back to pigs. Causing a highly contagious and deadly disease, the hog cholera virus was responsible for decimating American swine herds in the late sixties and early seventies, when eight hundred thousand infected hogs worth $25 million had to be destroyed.

Since the last major outbreak of hog cholera, which was traced back to a garbage-feeding farm in New Jersey in 1972 and ultimately led to the declaration of a national emergency by the U.S. Department of Agriculture, states like New Jersey have adopted strict laws requiring inspection of all farms like Bill Lafferty's. Since 1978, the United States has been declared hog-cholera free.

Nonetheless, currently sixteen states with more than 50 percent of the hog population continue to prohibit garbage feeding. In 1982, only 1.4 percent of the hog farmers in the United States fed food wastes to their herds.

"The garbage goes in through the hatch in the top," says Bill, standing beside his truck. "Then we fire up a fifty-horse diesel boiler and inject steam into the bottom of the tank through these fittings." He points to a network of pipes that girdles the truck. "Then we turn on the agitator inside, which stirs the garbage around while it cooks."

To the side of the truck is a loading chute that enables full garbage trucks to back up to the cooker and dump their cargo directly through the open hatch into the steam truck.

Bill and I walk over to the chute. Gazing down into the bowels of this huge garbage-filled vat is as awesome in its way as peering into the core of a nuclear reactor. Below is a boiling stew of every imaginable foodstuff, resembling a casserole concocted on a scale so grand as to deserve a place in the *Guinness Book of World Records.*

Looking down on what will soon be meals for Bill's pigs, I find it hard to visualize this maelstrom of rejected human food as the orderly series of meals, divided up into neat courses of soup, salad, entree and dessert it once was. As if I were looking through a city that had been bombed and was searching the wreckage for familiar remains—a once-frequented building, a particular street or the skeleton of a great cathedral—I find myself carefully examining the effluvia before me for recognizable pieces of food.

Amidst the tons of partially pureed vegetables and fruits are peelings, bones, hunks of fat, crusts of bread, globs of rice, colonies of soggy french fries, tattered grapefruit rinds and snarls of old spaghetti, all mixed in with an inedible garnishing of Styrofoam cups, paper plates, tin cans, napkins and plastic tableware. The feast below us looks as if a vengeful spirit had sucked up ten thousand dinners (table settings and all) with a powerful vacuum cleaner and dumped them all here in Bill Lafferty's steam truck.

I would enjoy tarrying longer over this unusual archaeological midden, but I am suddenly aware of Bill's hovering presence. When I turn around, the expression on his face suggests an eagerness to move on, as if he were unnerved by my apparent fascination with his hog feed.

We leave the garbage area and walk over to a large gray barn with an open front, which houses what Bill refers to as "the baked goods." On approaching, what one sees first is a large disorderly mound of pale-yellow crusts and crumbs that looks as if someone has attacked a supernaturally large pound cake (fully wrapped) with a powerful outboard motor.

From a distance, it is hard to identify all the goods that have gone into forming this miniature Alp of bakery products. Only upon drawing nearer does one begin to be able to discern the outlines of familiar shapes. Mangled English muffins, caved-in pies, crushed cakes, deformed slices of bread and squashed hot-dog buns lie in a matrix of crumbs, aluminum trays and tattered plastic wrappers. In fact, all around Bill Lafferty's farmyard, shredded pieces of plastic blow in the wind and then eddy into small drifts against fences and buildings, creating an effect somewhere between that of fallen autumn leaves and driven winter snow.

"The nice thing about baked goods is that they don't have to be cooked. Along with the garbage, they provide a good balanced diet for the pigs so that we don't have to feed any mineral or vitamin supplements," Bill says authoritatively.

"We have one garbage truck that does a bakery route. We do Acme, Mrs. Smith's Pies, and we used to do the A&P bakery before it closed. We get all their cripples, their return stuff, waste dough. But some of the bakeries are grinding up their own old bread and either putting it back in their dough or using it to make packaged stuffing," laments Bill.

"These baked goods take the place of grain for us, but they're getting harder and harder to come by. They're not free. We got to bid on them with other guys who want to use the stuff for dog food or sell it to mink farms, something like that. Just recently we lost a contract to an outfit that outbid us by offering five thousand dollars for a month's worth, stuff that we used to pay no more than one hundred dollars a month for.

"Sometimes I think it might be better if we threw away all our garbage trucks and the boiler and just brought in grain for the pigs like those other farmers do in the Midwest," Bill adds wearily.

For a moment, I think back to Lehman Farms in Strawn, Illinois. From the midst of Bill Lafferty's hog operation it seems far away indeed.

As we head back to the Laffertys' house, the ruts in the dirt road made by the garbage trucks are beginning to freeze. A plastic bread wrapper scuds across one of the dirt lots in the wind like a tumbleweed and flies right into the midst of a milling throng of pigs. But inside the Laffertys' house it is warm. Vicki has set a tray of doughnuts and Danish pastry out on the kitchen table.

"I just called Norman and told him to come right over," Vicki announces as we enter. "He said he was too busy to talk. But I told him we were about to eat breakfast. He said he'd be right over." She laughs and shakes her head indulgently.

Norman is Norman Lichtman, the current president of National FACTS. Although he has given up raising hogs, his company, Del Valley Enterprises, still deals in livestock. Hardly five minutes elapse before Norman Lichtman suddenly appears in the doorway. He greets the Laffertys with great affection, sits down and immediately asks Vicki for a weak glass of whisky and water.

Norman wears a red shirt and vest, baggy pants that have long since had the corduroy ridges eroded away on the seat and muddy black oxfords with worn heels. He is balding and has a lugubrious, drooping face, which, when he laughs (often), looks as if the frowning and smiling masks of Tragedy and Comedy had been superimposed on one another.

"Sure, us garbage feeders have a tough image problem," Norman says, reaching for a glazed doughnut and beginning to talk as if he had already been sitting in discussion with the three of us for hours. "We're into garbage. What do you expect? Our people raise pigs! We're not the Avon Lady." He laughs through a mouthful of doughnut with a mirth that betrays no defensiveness.

"Take Lafferty's place here." Norman makes a sweeping gesture with his hand. "Sure, it's a little better than average. It's a nine on good days, and an eight in the rain." He laughs and turns toward Bill to see if his assessment is meeting with approval.

Bill just shrugs.

"We're always under attack," says Norman. "I'm seventy years old, and we've been under pressure since I was fifteen. When you got places like ours and some gentleman farmer moves in next door, as soon as the wind starts blowing, he'll want you to move.

"Pig farms is just like landfills, like jails, hospitals. Everyone needs them, but they want them next to someone else's house.

"Hey, Vicki," says Norman, interrupting himself. "Give me some coffee to go with this doughnut."

"If we're going to recycle, we have to be near to where garbage comes from," Bill observes, cutting a piece of ham on his plate.

"All right. I'm going to give you a for instance," Norman adds. "We got thirty million people within fifteen minutes of here. Sure, I'd like to be way out on the middle of a desert someplace where no one would be bothered by what I'm doing. But there's no garbage on the desert!"

"Those hog farmers who feed grain and keep their animals in confinement barns think that we stink," Bill interjects, launching off onto a different track. "Well, did you ever go into one of those confinement barns where the pigs are crammed in so tight they can't hardly lie down? It smells so bad you can't breathe."

"They stink," exclaims Norman, holding his nose. "All that crowding, stress and disease. No wonder they have to give them all those antibiotics, otherwise they'd all drop dead!"

"Stay away from those pigs raised inside in confinement barns," Bill admonishes, wagging a warning index finger in my direction. "As soon as we get any of those pigs here, they always break down and become sick. They live on drugs and have no resistance to disease or weather. They're weak pigs. We don't use a lot of drugs. Maybe we spray a little sulfa on the garbage when the animals first get here, but then most of them develop their own natural resistance. I always tell my dealer, 'Get me a good barnyard pig that's been raised on dirt and I'll be happy.'"

"Some people even say that garbage-fed pigs taste sweeter than ones that are grain-fed," chimes in Vicki.

"Somewheres I read about how they put twenty judges up eating pork to see if they could tell the difference between grain-fed and garbage-fed pigs," Norman adds, jumping enthusiastically into the polemic. "They couldn't tell the difference! No difference! Norman thrusts out both upturned palms like a debater who believes he has just leveled an irrefutable argument.

Like performers of a musical work that gains in tempo as it progresses toward a crescendo, Norman and Bill have both begun to speak louder and more rapidly as our discussion has continued.

While outsiders may assume that all hog feeders feel a common fraternity, in fact deep schism between those farmers who feed their pigs grain and those who feed garbage divides the industry. It revolves around fears of the grain feeders that the garbage feeders have been responsible for the spread of hog cholera.

"We haven't had any hog cholera since 1975," proclaims Norman. "We've got a good program to cook the garbage, but still we get blamed."

"Hey, Norman," Vicki says. "What was that meeting you all went to when the grain feeders wouldn't even walk on the same side of the street with you?"

"Oh, yeah. I think that was down in Louisville. Some health meeting," Norman replies. "When us garbage feeders came into a room, the other farmers would say, 'Oh, God! Here comes the boys from Jersey!'"

"The thing of it was . . ." Bill begins.

"No. Wait. Let me really put my story across," Norman says, raising his hands like a conductor, signaling the others back into silence. "Everyone was blaming us. They were talking about eradicating hog cholera by eradicating us! We were the most hated people in the country!"

Having delivered this sweeping estimation of how garbage-feeding hog farmers are viewed by the outside world, Norman gets up and begins to prowl around the kitchen.

Spotting two cold uneaten slices of toast and a piece of ham on Bill's abandoned breakfast plate, he begins to make a ham sandwich.

"Oh, no, no, Norman! Take a fresh piece," Vicki protests, trying to wrest the hastily constructed sandwich from his grasp.

"Stop it! Leave me have it," Norman cries, wrenching it away from her. "Conservation! I believe in it! I believe in it every hour of the day!" He holds his recycled sandwich aloft as if it were the torch from the Statue of Liberty.

"The whole world except America is doing what us garbage feeders are doing, allowing pigs to eat what we've finished with." Norman smiles at the apparent simplicity of it all.

"In this business you get a little bit of everything," continues Norman, sitting down again. "You get spoiled melons and peaches, melted ice cream, Campbell's soup, candy. You name it, we get it. We even get stuff that has never been inside a garbage can. Right now, I know where you can get all these Navy survival rations. The thing of it is, they are all in small cans."

"When I was a kid, my father got a load of condensed milk one time," Bill says. "Us kids had to sit around all day with openers and open cans."

"We got the same item once," remembers Norman.

"I used to get wastes from a dog-food factory," Bill says.

"I used to get screenings from the Shake 'n Bake plant," parries Norman, as if he were in a game-show competition trying to top Bill's stories. "Or sometimes we'd get a whole batch of dough from a bakery that had screwed up. You might get two or three tons of dough that way."

"Yeah, but don't go trying to haul it on a warm day," Bill adds with a knowing chuckle. "If you put all that dough into a garbage truck when it's hot, the yeast will start rising, and you could blow your whole truck up."

"Then there was the time back in the fifties when I got a couple loads of fruitcake out of Baltimore because they had wrapped it in the wrong paper or something." Norman pauses for a moment, smiling as he remembers. "Oh, the pigs loved it. They go for anything sweet."

After these tales of porcine gastronomy, it is time actually to feed the pigs. Norman departs, and Bill Lafferty heads out to his pens. He backs one of his steam trucks, now full of cooled, cooked garbage, up to one of the concrete pallets where the pigs can get up out of the mud to eat.

His arrival induces a pandemonium of oinking and squealing among the pigs. Opening a small trap in the rear of the truck tank, Bill allows the swill to begin flowing out onto the slab as if he were pouring concrete. There is a brief and intense scramble as the hungry animals struggle to position themselves advantageously for their meal. Then suddenly, the cacophony diminuendoes. In a moment, except for the noises of hundreds of smacking lips, which sound like waves gently lapping against the underside of a pier, there is silence.

8

"All banner carriers should go to the south end of the field," booms a voice out of the loudspeaker system inside the University of Illinois football stadium in Urbana. The stadium's synthetic-grass playing field is awash with high school bands, majorettes twirling batons and pom-pom girls rehearsing for today's game between the Fighting Illini of Illinois and the Hoosiers of Indiana.

For many Illinois loyalists, today is just another football weekend, but for members of the Fighting Illini Pork Club, it is something more. It is Pork Day, an annual event for which hundreds of Illinois hog farmers take the day off and come to Urbana with their families to cook and distribute free "taste treats" or "finger sandwiches" (small patties of ground barbecued pork) to football fans as part of a promotional effort by the Illinois Pork Producers' Association.

From blocks away one can see a great cloud of gray smoke rising up over a group of tennis courts where volunteer hog farmers tend two long barbecue pits. As cars stream up onto the surrounding lawns that serve as parking lots for the game, people open up tailgates and trunks, haul out coolers of beer, and set up picnic tables until the whole area around the stadium looks like the encampment place of a massive army.

As game time approaches, a phalanx of twenty or so Pork Queens begins to assemble near the barbecue area. Each of these unpretentious and wholesome-looking young women is outfitted with a rhinestone tiara and a beauty-contest sash inscribed with the name of the county in which she reigns (Macoupin, Rock Island, Grundy, Wabash, Iroquois). Next year's Illinois State Pork Queen will be chosen from their ranks and will ultimately go on to compete for the title of National Pork Queen at the American Pork Congress. I have come here to Pork Day to find Pam Carney, this year's Illinois Queen.

"All right, Queens! Let's go!" yells Bonnie Bohlen, head of the Porkette Promotion and Project Committee of the Illinois Pork Producers' Association. A strong, cheerful woman with no-nonsense short hair and a ready smile, Bohlen runs a 120-sow operation with her daughter in Fithian, Illinois, while her husband farms their 1,200 acres of corn and soy.

"I want each queen to grab a plate of finger sandwiches, find a place at a table and stick with it!" Bohlen calls over the hubbub, as if she were a choreographer blocking out a dance piece involving a large corps de ballet.

Once the distribution system for the barbecued pork has been mastered by the queens, Bonnie Bohlen comes over to where her daughter Tammy and I are sitting next to a giant papier-mâché pig which has been towed here to Pork Day by the Heingold Hog Markets Co. on the back of a truck trailer. Sitting in the shadow of this pork-producer totem, I ask Tammy and Bonnie to tell me a little about the Porkettes.

"Mom here is a former president of the Illinois Porkettes," begins Tammy, putting a hand on her mother's shoulder with filial pride.

"We have about eight thousand pork producers and two thousand two hundred Porkettes here in Illinois alone," says Bonnie, getting right down to some statistics. "We're a completely volunteer organization, and I think all of us Porkettes do what we are doing as a kind of service, to help our own cause. Hogs are no laughing matter around here. Us Porkettes are all farm wives. We realize pork has had its image problems. But we also know how good it is, and we want it to be number one.

"We have Porkettes in every pork-producing state," continues Bonnie. "We have all sorts of activities. We go into
schools, shopping malls, dietetic associations, talk about pork
and give out taste treats, free recipes, answer questions and
deal with some of the many myths about pigs." An uncharacter-
istically dark look crosses Bonnie's face as she reflects for a
moment on some of these troubling myths.

"People still think they're going to get trichinosis if they eat
pork," interjects Tammy. "They think pigs are dirty and fat
and that pork is high in calories. Well, that's not true. Our new
breed of lean hog is just not that way."

"Today we're going to serve thirty-three hundred pounds of
complimentary pork. I believe that comes to about twenty
thousand taste treats," says Bonnie with renewed cheerfulness,
like a missionary suddenly recalling all the free bibles that
will be dispensed among the heathens. "I think we're raising
one of the best-tasting and most economical meat products
today, and that's something that makes us all real proud."

Bonnie Bohlen glances over to the phalanx of queens standing in front of their platters and smiles, seemingly reassured
by the hundreds of people still trying to elbow their way forward to the tables. While we have been talking, the dense
cloud of smoke billowing over the barbecue area has diminished to a mere wisp. The thousands of tailgate parties, which
only moments ago were in full swing, have almost all ended,
and their merrymakers have left to hurry toward the portals of
the stadium.

The throng that crowded in on the Pork Day serving tables
has dissipated, and the queens have broken ranks when suddenly a roar explodes from the stadium. The teams are on the
field. From here on, the only hog product worshiped will be
the pigskin.

After the game, the next event of the day does not begin
until evening, when the Fighting Illini Pork Club Banquet is
to be held at the Ramada Inn, where the antebellum white

columns of its front portico and brick exterior suggest the
cross-breeding of a Southern plantation mansion and the University's Meat Science Lab down the road. Inside, at a no-host
bar, I find several hundred farmers talking, laughing and milling around with drinks in hand.

"We all tend to get a little loony when we're let out after
being cooped up on the farm," says one hogman, throwing a
wadded cocktail napkin at a comrade and then laughing
gleefully.

As the farmers begin to drift into the banquet hall, I finally
spot Pam Carney attired in her tiara and a formal gown. When
I introduce myself and tell her that I would like to talk with
her, she says that after the banquet she will be returning to
school at Jacksonville, where she is an undergraduate at Illinois
College majoring in business administration and economics.
We arrange to meet there tomorrow, Sunday.

In the banquet hall, I find a seat between Tammy Bohlen
and her family, and a professor from the University of Illinois's
Department of Animal Sciences. While an electric chord organ
plays a medley of rumbas, I ask the professor his views on the
prevalent use of subtherapeutic antibiotics in swine feed. He
assures me with professorial authority that there is no cause
for alarm and then concludes our conversation peremptorily
by saying, "Actually, I get a little sick of being asked about
this sort of thing all the time." Thereafter, he busies himself
carving up one of the smoked pork chops that have just arrived on his plate, the way a seatmate on a crowded plane who
wishes to withdraw from conversation will concentrate intently
on the meal tray before him.

After dinner the speeches and awards begin. Standing under
a banner that says, "Welcome to the 1981 Pork Club Dinner,"
the chancellor of the University of Illinois gives an address
heavily larded with allusions to football and sex.

The football coach gives a speech and is awarded a pigskin
jacket. "Oh, this is fantastic," he exclaims from the podium,

caressing his new jacket. Then, looking deadpan out at the room filled with hog farmers, he asks, "Now what-in-the-hell did you say it was made out of?" Everyone howls with laughter.

We have already heard from the chancellor and the football coach, basketball coach, football captain, a high-scoring running back, a black basketball star, a U.S. senator, and numerous Illinois Pork Producers' Association officials, when suddenly a door bursts open into the banquet hall, and a truncated version of the university band enters, led by one Illini costumed like an Iroquois chief in a huge feathered headdress.

The hog farmers rise, clap their hands and whoop and yell as the band bleats and oom-pah-pahs in the background, and the make-believe Indian goes into a frenzied war dance.

Then, as suddenly as the hog farmers were stirred into action by the band's entry, they fall silent. The professor of Animal Sciences next to me claps his right hand over his heart, and the band breaks into a dirgelike tune. The entire room, sounding like a severely warped record, begins to sing "The Loyalty Song," evidently the anthem of the Fighting Illini.

"We've promoted animal science, we've promoted athletics and we've promoted pork! That's what it's all about!" bellows the president of the Pork Club as the anthem trails off.

This trilateral battle cry ushers in the auctioning of a grand-champion barrow (a castrated male), donated to Pork Day by Refco (a Peoria commodities company), with the proceeds going to the university's athletic-scholarship program and my dinnermate's Department of Animal Sciences for livestock-show judging. The pig has, of course, long since gone to its ultimate reward, since as a barrow it had no reproductive future. What will be auctioned off tonight are its remains, neatly cut, frozen and wrapped in orange paper.

The auctioneer summons Pam Carney up onto the dais. The various cuts of the grand-champion barrow are brought out in an ice chest. As the auctioneer prattles on, trying to goad the assemblage of hog farmers into making bids, Pam Carney, swathed in her own pigskin sash embossed with the words *Illinois State Pork Queen*, holds up first a ham, then a loin roast for the bidders to see.

Not ready to bid $600 for a ham or $285 for a side of bacon, I quietly bid Tammy and Bonnie Bohlen good-bye, and slip out the back door into the parking lot.

I arrive in Jacksonville, Illinois, about 12:30 P.M. on Sunday. I have an hour and a half before my rendezvous with Pam Carney. In anticipation of a leisurely Sunday repast in Jacksonville, I have purposely not stopped for breakfast along the way. By the time I reach the city's "miracle mile" on Route 36 and begin looking for a restaurant, I am famished. I pass up a Howard Johnson's and a pizza place. Nearing the far edge of town, I see a sign in the distance that appears to spell out the word *Waffles* in large neon letters. The idea of a few crisp golden waffles with butter, syrup, a few links of pan-browned sausage and a steaming cup of coffee occurrs to me as a perfect meal.

I turn my directional lights on, take my foot off the accelerator and am just about to begin making my turn when I see that the approaching sign does not say *Waffles*, but *Mufflers* instead.

Feeling betrayed, I wrench the car back into the flow of traffic. As I drive, my mind begins to conjure up images of cups of hot coffee, fried eggs, bacon and English muffins.

Steak 'n Shake, Hardees Charbroiled Burgers, Bonanza Sirloin Pit, Steak and Cakes, Sirloin Stockade. The entire highway seems consecrated to beef. I pull into one roadside franchise that advertises a "New Platter Breakfast," only to be told that they stopped serving it at 11:00 A.M.

Passing Howard Johnson's again, hungrier than ever and aware that time is running out, I grudgingly decide to stop. I take a seat at the counter. A waitress in a prim uniform immediately brings me some coffee in the kind of plastic urn one expects to find on a hospital bedside table.

I begin to order breakfast, which she tells me that they have also stopped serving. Handing me a menu, she points to the luncheon section.

Since it appears to be too late to get breakfast anywhere here in Jacksonville, I decide to make the best of the situation and order a real Sunday dinner. Violating my own guideline to eat only pork while on a hog leg of this journey, I order the turkey dinner, which is advertised as "white and dark meat with oven cornbread stuffing."

The idea of roast turkey, the symbol of Thanksgiving and Christmas feasting, has an aura about it that is satisfying at this moment. These lonely days on the road tend to make one crave a little ceremony, to yearn for the ritual of a formal meal as an antidote to the dizzying succession of fast food that otherwise punctuates the gastronomical day.

As I sip my cup of coffee and await the arrival of my meal, I relish the idea of a brown turkey with its knobby legs sticking up out of the roasting pan, a great white swath cut across one breast where the slices of meat have been carved for my Sunday dinner. These reveries (or perhaps it would be better to call them hallucinations) are quickly interrupted, however, when the young waitress who has taken my order reappears with a steaming plate and sets it on the doily in front of me.

Looking down, I see an ice-cream scoop of instant mashed potatoes convexed at the top like a volcano and filled with a starchy tan gravy, a heap of Army-surplus–colored peas and a stack of what I assume is turkey, although it is hard to tell, obscured as it is under a sludge of the same gravy that covers the potatoes. Probing it with a fork, I find that it is not a slab from the imaginary turkey breast in my mind's eye, but perfectly flat slices from a boneless restructured turkey breast.

Turning it over to its ungravied side, I can make out thin veins of gelatinous protein binder where one turkey breast has been fused together with another to construct this boneless, tasteless loaf. Excavating the slices of turkey further, I discover that they actually form a thatch over a soggy, mucusy bed of "oven corn bread stuffing," as if their function was to hide the stuffing from detection as long as possible.

For a moment I find myself gripped by indecisiveness, the same hesitancy one might feel before summoning the wine steward at a fancy restaurant to send back a questionable Bordeaux. Then, suddenly discovering that my turkey dinner contains no "dark meat" (as promised on the menu), I feel armed with at least a technical breach of contract and beckon for the waitress.

"Excuse me," I begin politely, but glacially, "there is no dark meat in this turkey dinner like the menu says."

"We don't have any dark meat. Turkey rolls don't come with dark meat," says the waitress, furrowing her brow with bewilderment.

"I'm sorry, this turkey dinner just isn't . . ." I don't quite know how to couch my complaint in understandable language. "This turkey just isn't acceptable. Bring me the ham. I'll have a ham dinner instead."

The gravy is already beginning to congeal and form a scum on top of the meat and potatoes as the waitress removes the plate. She carries it back to the cash register, where she presents it tentatively to her supervisor. They whisper to each other. The waitress holds the rejected turkey dinner out in one hand as if it were a collection plate and begins pointing in my direction, a gesture that she suddenly attenuates when she notices that I am watching her with a beetled brow.

The supervisor prods the turkey with the fork that lies fallen across the plate as if such an inquest might uncover a piece of broken glass or some other obvious contaminant that would make my refusal to accept the dinner more comprehensible. When she discovers nothing unusual, she gives her head a what-is-this-world-coming-to shake and slides the turkey back through the stainless-steel opening to the kitchen from whence it came.

When my ham dinner is ready, the waitress sets it down in front of me without making eye contact and walks back to the sanctuary of the cash-register area.

The pieces of rubbery pink ham taste good if not spectacular. I am reminded that it is hard to ruin ham, and hurry through my meal so as not to be late for my talk with the Illinois Pork Queen.

Pam Carney is a cheerful and eager-to-please young woman whose father is a partner in a six-hundred-sow operation in Milan, Illinois, near Moline. She is slender and has reddish-brown neatly permed hair. Today she wears a pair of slacks and a beige striped sweater adorned with a small gold pig pin just above her left breast. With the exception of a suggestion of mascara about her eyes, Pam wears no makeup. Her fingernails are neatly trimmed. As she begins speaking, her mouth emits a faint aroma of toothpaste.

Once we are settled on a couch in the common room of her dorm at Illinois College, I ask her if she has actually ever worked on a hog farm.

"Oh, for sure. The summer before I became queen I worked every day in the barns for my dad from six in the morning until seven at night. I think that experience was one of my strongest points in winning, because it made me knowledgeable about things like cost of production, prevention of disease, and why pork is really such a terrific meat and stuff like that."

The way Pam Carney describes her job, she sounds as much like a Socialist model youth as an American Pork Queen. And she wants it made perfectly clear that she did not win because of her pretty face.

"Oh, no!" says Pam, sitting bolt upright on the couch when I ask her if the Pork Queen contest has a bathing-suit-pageant component. "They say that your appearance is only supposed to count for ten percent. And personally, I wouldn't want to be in a beauty contest, because I wouldn't feel comfortable being viewed in my swimming suit. I suppose that's fine for some girls who are beautiful, and our society has always rewarded the beautiful girl. But I enjoyed the kind of contest that Pork Queens go through so much more than I would have a beauty-type contest, because the judges are looking for girls who have a few smarts upstairs, who can speak in public, although I am sure there are some beauty queens who are smart too."

"What did the judges ask you to do?"

"Well, besides questioning us about hog farming, how to cook pork and things like that, each county queen was given five minutes to give a kind of dramatic presentation or read an essay. I decided to portray an animal called Lean Jean, because "leanness" is the theme of this year's national pork promotion campaign."

"You mean you acted out the role of a pig?"

"Well, I kind of told about myself from the perspective of being a pig," replies Pam, giving a squeal of embarrassed laughter. "I told them all about my virtues, how I grew very quickly, produced lots of piglets, provided nutritious meat that was actually very lean in spite of what people thought.

"Then I made what I like to think was a smooth transition and began to talk about the whole question of animal welfare from the point of view of Lean Jean. You see, we're getting a lot of questions from people now who are for animal rights and who are worried about pigs being put into small pens and farrowing crates. So, I talked about how much we pigs liked the new confinement barns as opposed to living outside in the natural environment, because a herdsman can keep a close eye on us, watch for disease, give us warmth, good feed and clean water."

"Do you run into many people who make fun of your title because of the association with pigs?"

"Oh, yeah. I hear all kinds of things, especially when I have my Pork Queen banner on in parades and stuff. The title is kind of an open invitation for jokes and comments that thoughtless people might want to make."

"What kinds of things do people say?"

"Oh, I don't know," says Pam hesitantly, as if she were not sure she wanted to get into the negative aspects of being Pork Queen. "I mean, if a person is not familiar with agriculture, pig farming and all the purposes of our producers' organizations, he just won't . . . well, what's the first image that comes to mind when you hear the words 'pork queen'?"

Pam allows a rhetorical pause to elapse. I think better of responding.

"Like I've been called Pig Woman, Miss Piggy, Petunia Pig," continues Pam, a touch of defiance in her voice now. "This last summer, when I was taking a tour of the Chicago Mercantile Exchange, someone referred to me as Pork Belly Queen. I try to laugh with people about it to some extent, but I don't want to make fun of the job itself. For hog farmers it's an important thing to promote our product, and being Pork Queen is a respectable position that I take seriously."

"Do you think a homely woman could become a state or national queen?"

Pam squinches up her face and reflects for a moment. "I think so," she finally replies. "I mean, if you're really sharp, why should you be denied an honor that you deserve?"

Once again she falls silent. "But, of course, it would be bad to have a . . . well, let's just say a plump kind of girl, because . . ." A broad smile begins to form around Pam's eyes and mouth. Like a tickle in the nose that leads uncontrollably to a sneeze, the notion of a "plump" Pork Queen has begun to trigger in her an uncontrollable laugh in spite of the fact that the import of what she is saying suggests that she does not find such a stereotype humorous at all.

"Why?" I ask, just as she is overcome with laughter.

"Well, OK. I know it's not something to laugh about," replies Pam, flustered now. "This is something we queens have talked a lot about recently. We think maybe we should be called something like 'Pork Industry Queens,' rather than 'Pork Queens' so we don't encourage comments and open ourselves up to this thing about pigs and fatness, you know, the whole image thing."

Although much of Pam's work as Pork Queen involves getting people to buy more pork chops and bacon, she and other queens also have to wrestle with a far subtler task. Unfortunately, as she herself has suggested, pigs have historically carried with them many unflattering associations. They are viewed not only as fat, but as muddy, enamored of garbage and carriers of disease, all parts of an identity that pig farmers feel is grossly erroneous and would like to see queens like Pam Carney help to eradicate.

"Why do you think many people see pigs as such humorous animals?"

"Personally, I think pigs look great, particularly when they are small and all cute and cuddly," replies Pam, smiling. "When they get older, I'll admit that they get a little less attractive. But even then, their faces have real expression. The boars get all these worry lines across their brows and down onto their snouts, which make them look a little sad. But I also love the way the sows' mouths curve up at the ends so they look as if they are always smiling."

Not wishing to dwell too long on unserious aspects of her trade, Pam launches off into a discourse of pork Kultur of her own. "Through all this other stuff, my job is to help promote pork for all Illinois farmers," she continues, getting back to what she considers to be the business of being a queen. " 'Leanness' is going to be our new theme. We want to counteract how people used to think about pork.

"You see, pork has improved in quality immensely in the last twenty years. Now we're promoting ground pork, what we served at the football game. That's eighty-percent lean, more digestible and lower in calories than hamburger. When I speak to people, I always like to emphasize this calorie thing, because ..."

Pam is on familiar rehearsed Pork Queen territory now. She speaks with conviction, reciting facts and figures without getting flustered. I feel almost cruel interrupting her, but there are other matters about which I am curious to ask her. What, for instance, are her views on the way antibiotics are used in pork production?

"Well, you've really caught me off guard on this one," she replies after a long pause. "That's a subject I haven't really thought much about as queen. We've never been prepped in this area, and no one has asked this sort of thing before, although I have read that there is some consumer concern."

"Is it something that concerns you or hog producers whom you know here in Illinois?"

"Well, it's hard for me to say, since I am not really exposed to any of your true orthodox health food types or vegetarians," replies Pam as if she were referring to members of a strange ethnic group that lived outside of town.

"But if you want to talk about health questions, I'll just say that my family has always had a freezer full of beef and pork, and we eat meat at every meal," she replies cheerfully. "It's just a way of life with us, so I don't think much about it. I don't worry that I will be hurt by anything that I might buy at the grocery store like some of the environmental-type people, who I think are in a kind of alarmist situation. I believe our government has strict regulations and good control over things like drugs and chemicals. Personally, I don't have any worries about the sort of thing you're asking about."

9

Dr. Stuart Levy is professor of medicine and of molecular biology and microbiology at the Tufts University School of Medicine. Although the drab gray-brick building that houses his office and laboratory on downtown Boston's Harrison Street seems a far cry from Illinois, the research Levy has been conducting on antibiotic resistance may ultimately have a profound impact on the way meat animals are raised in the future.

I find Dr. Levy in a small but cheerful corner office affording an unspectacular view of the Massachusetts Transit Authority car yards. He is of medium height, with dark, curly hair and a well-trimmed mustache, and is wearing neatly creased slacks and a pullover sweater. His interest in antibiotic resistance, he tells me, was first aroused in 1962, while he was on a leave of absence from medical school and working at the Institut de Radium, in Paris, on radiation genetics. Learning of the work of Tsutomo Watanabe, the discoverer of R plasmids, he arranged to go to Tokyo in 1964 to work with him for several months at Keio University's School of Medicine. Through his work with Watanabe, it became evident to Levy that drug resistance was a highly transferable trait. He was aware that the overuse of antibiotics in human medicine was accountable for much of the rising tide of resistance that clinicians around the world were witnessing, but, like Richard Novick, Stanley Falkow and a growing number of other scientists, he was also concerned about the other half of all antibiotics manufactured in this country—those being fed subtherapeutically to livestock.

"We simply must think in terms of establishing appropriate uses for antibiotics, whether for human beings or farm animals," Levy says when I ask him about antibiotic feed additives. "To allow people who do not understand how these drugs work to use them by the ton without even a prescription is to my mind worse than just throwing the drugs to the wind. It is exactly this kind of indiscriminate use that is making them less and less effective. My intention is not to try and make the animal-health people seem to bear the responsibility for all our antibiotic-resistance problems. Even if farmers stopped using tetracycline and penicillin in animal feed, we would still have a problem. But the use of such drugs as growth promotants is one clear area where we can cut back on the total quantity of antibiotics being pumped into our environment."

With funds from the National Institute of Allergy and Infectious Disease and the Animal Health Institute (a drug-company lobbying group in Washington), Levy and several colleagues began in 1974 a study on R-factor transfer between animals and human beings. On a small Massachusetts family farm, they set up six cages of leghorn chicks, fifty to a cage. Testing the enteric, or gut, bacteria of the animals at the outset, they found that from 1 to 10 percent of the species of organisms found in the birds were already resistant to tetracycline. Levy and his colleagues then began to feed the chicks in one of the cages tetracycline-supplemented feed. Within thirty-six hours, fecal samples from 90 percent of the animals showed that virtually all the tetracycline-sensitive *Escherichia coli* from the intestinal tracts of these chicks had been replaced by resistant ones. As had been expected, resistance levels measured in the fecal samples from the other chicks, which, as a control group, were not receiving tetracycline-supplemented feed, remained unchanged. Then, toward the end of the third month, the researchers observed an unexpected phenomenon: The chicks in the control group began to show higher and higher levels of resistant organisms, even though they were in cages fifteen yards away from the birds that had been receiving tetracycline feed additives. By the fourth month, at least 30 percent of the control-group chicks were excreting enteric bacteria at least half of which were resistant. Was it possible that resistant organisms were somehow being passed from cage to cage? "We were not set up to ascertain what sort of transfer was actually going on," Levy says. "But it did seem quite logical that wind-blowing debris around the barnyard or insects such as flies could be responsible. Although we couldn't draw any scientifically based conclusions about such transport from our observations, we were reminded that there are a lot of natural vectors that move bacteria from place to place."

By January, four months after the tetracycline feed had been introduced, Levy and his colleagues found dramatic increases of resistant intestinal bacteria in those members of the farm family who were helping to care for the chicks. While only one of fifteen neighbors sampled was excreting high numbers of resistant bacteria, fecal samples of three of eight farm-family members contained levels of bacteria that were as much as 80 percent tetracycline-resistant. What was even more surprising (Levy described it as "alarming") was a finding that these three also showed rapidly rising levels of resistance to six other antibiotics, completely unrelated to tetracycline. This suggested that the antibiotic in the chicken feed was selecting for strains of bacteria that were resistant not only to tetracycline but also to several other antibiotics.

The increase of resistance levels in the farm family provided Levy with strong circumstantial evidence that they were being affected by the animals. That the acquisition of this resistance was not a regional phenomenon characteristic of everyone in the area was demonstrated by the lack of similar findings among families living within a two- or three-mile radius and among students attending the same school as the farm family's children. Nonetheless, Levy and his colleagues had not yet established a direct cause-and-effect relationship. It could still be argued—as representatives of drug companies had argued often in the past—that the resistance showing up in the human beings might be coming from some unidentifiable source, even though they were in contact with animals fed on antibiotics. Moreover, while Levy assumed that the resistance was coming from the chicks, he did not know whether it was because bacteria from the chicks were colonizing the guts of the family members (where their R plasmids could be easily transferred to indigenous microorganisms) or because the antibiotic feed additive itself was inadvertently being ingested by the family and then selecting for resistant strains of enteric bacteria already present in small numbers.

Returning to his lab in Boston with bacteria isolated from both the chicks and the farm-family members, Levy attempted to mate resistant strains of chicken *E. coli* with special sensitive animal strains of *E. coli* used for laboratory experiments to see if R-plasmid transfer would take place. Once again he made a curious discovery. He found that R plasmids that carried only genes for tetracycline resistance did not readily transfer *in vitro*, but that plasmids bearing multiple resistances (to streptomycin, ampicillin and carbenicillin as well as tetracycline) successfully transferred from every donor cell tested. This suggested to Levy that at least some organisms such as *E. coli* with multiple resistance are better equipped to transfer their R plasmids than those with only one.

In an effort to trace the pathways of the R plasmids that seemed to be spreading so widely, Levy and his colleagues returned to the farm, set up two cages (A and B) of fifty chicks each and inoculated two birds in each cage with a special brew of *E. coli* harboring R plasmids with four resis-

tance factors, one of which (the gene for resistance to chloramphenicol) had been modified genetically, so that its host
plasmids would be easy to distinguish from any other multiple
R plasmids already present. (The modification used caused
this particular resistance to be expressed at a temperature of
32 degrees Celsius, rather than at the normal temperature
of 42 degrees Celsius.) One cage of chicks was put on
tetracycline-laced feed, while the chicks in the second cage
were given feed without any additive. Within a few weeks,
the *E. coli* with the marked plasmids began showing up, as
expected, in large numbers in the fecal samples of all the
birds in the first cage—an indication that these bacteria had
successfully colonized the guts of the chicks on tetracycline.
They did not, however, spread throughout the second cage
of birds, which were not ingesting drugs, and, in fact, began
to disappear from the fecal samples of the two inoculated
birds in that cage. Levy concluded that the tetracycline feed
additive was the critical variable determining whether or not
these resistant organisms were able to establish themselves
and thrive in new hosts. To his surprise, Levy noted that after
a period of weeks the marked *E. coli* began to appear in a
third, completely separate cage of chicks some forty-five feet
away from the other two cages. The chicks in this cage were
uninoculated, but were also being given tetracycline-supplemented feed, which evidently had selected for resistant bacteria somehow transferred from the inoculated birds in cage A.
They also began appearing in bacterial isolates from the
feces of two of the farm-family members, which, as Levy wrote
in an article describing his experiment in the *Journal of Infectious Disease*, "clearly indicated a chicken-to-human transmission of resistant bacteria." Although in this particular case
the antibiotic resistance that was derived from the chicken
strains was not detected in any pathogenic bacteria, Levy
went on to warn in his article that "the transfer of these
plasmids from non-pathogenic to pathogenic bacterial strains,

and from animals to humans, is a potential consequence of the widespread use of antibiotics in the farm environment, as well as in other settings."

"What I would like to ask all of these drug companies who claim that antibiotic resistance isn't being spread around from animals to man is this: Where *do* you think it's coming from?" Levy says combatively during our conversation in his office.

"In a study we've been working on, seventy-five percent of the people we have observed are carrying *E. coli* at least ten percent of which are resistant to one antibiotic or another," Levy tells me. "We are finding that even people who are not taking antibiotics harbor strains with resistance to anywhere from four to seven drugs. Where are these people picking up the original R factors? Obviously, from the environment, but we're not sure where. That's the frightening part. But if we look at the total use of antibiotics, we do know that almost half of what is manufactured is going into animals, so I believe we have to look very carefully at this as a potential source. What happens, for instance, when these animals are finally killed? Their offal, which is full of microorganisms, has to be disposed of, and their carcasses, which also contain tremendous amounts of bacteria, have to be handled, cut, packaged, shipped and rehandled. The meat and by-products are moved all over the country, finally coming in contact with the consumer. So I don't see how anyone can say that there isn't much possibility of bacterial crossover."

Levy throws up his hands in exasperation. "We're talking about a reservoir of microorganisms shared by both animals and human beings. And what is the most important complement of that reservoir? The lowly *E. coli* from the gut—bugs that get around and share a common pool of genes, which they readily swap with other bacteria. What the people who sell animal-feed antibiotics want us to believe is that we are picking up the rising level of R factors almost exclusively from hospitals and from people under antibiotic medication. But I am not aware of one single study showing that gut bacteria transfer frequently between human beings. On the other hand, there are plenty of studies showing that human beings pick up bacteria from animals as well as from a great variety of other sources, such as fruits and vegetables, which may come in contact with animal wastes. Cows, chickens and pigs are not being kept on some outer planet. No! They're right here in our own environment!"

Levy stabs the air in front of his chest with an index finger. "The drug companies like to look at these animals as closed systems, as kind of dead ends. But I don't accept that. I recently heard that the staff at the New England Aquarium, which had been treating their marine mammals with chlor-amphenicol, suddenly began to encounter a lot of resistance to that drug. Where did the seals get the resistant bacteria? From the dolphins?" Levy raises his eyebrows to express his incredulity. "I would think it more likely that they picked it up from the general environment, or possibly from their han-dlers. If a marine mammal can acquire resistance from man, one must assume that the process also works in reverse. Just think about it! We have five hundred million chickens eating antibiotics every week, and that's just the chicken population. What about the pigs, cows, goats, sheep? How many billions of bacteria does that make resistant out there each day? It's beyond me why it is so hard to understand that eventually these bacteria and their R factors are going to migrate, so that finally it doesn't matter whether you're using antibiotics on animals or on people."

A growing number of studies that Levy has in his files lend plausibility to his presumption that antibiotic resistance gen-erated in animals is spreading to human beings. From 1963 until 1967, an epidemic of enteritis caused by the bacterium *Salmonella typhimurium* type 29 swept through herds of English cattle. Before it could be determined that the bacterium was resistant to eight commonly used antibiotics, it had infected and killed numerous animals and had been transmitted to people, seven of whom ultimately died of the infection. *Salmonella* is a genus of bacteria (of which there are ten species) that can colonize both animals and humans with little difficulty. The ability of the salmonella bacteria to survive on both sides of the animal-human divide renders people vulnerable not only to the diseases they induce but also to increased levels of antibiotic resistance from whatever transferable R plasmids these bacteria may have acquired while in their animal hosts.

Following the prolonged outbreak of salmonellosis in the sixties, the British secretary of state for social services and the minister of agriculture, fisheries and food convened a special Joint Committee on the Use of Antibiotics in Animal Husbandry and Veterinary Medicine, known as the Swann Committee, to determine whether or not antibiotics commonly used in human therapy, such as tetracycline and penicillin, should be regulated as animal-feed additives. In 1969, the Swann Committee released a provisional draft that recommended banning the use of these antibiotics in livestock feed and requiring veterinary prescriptions for *any* antibiotic used for cattle. Two years later, the committee expanded its recommendations, calling for all subtherapeutic antibiotics for swine and poultry to be sold only by veterinary prescription. These recommendations were adopted by the British government, and during the 1970s an increasing number of other European countries, including Norway, Sweden, Denmark, West Germany, the Netherlands and Czechoslovakia, imposed similar restrictions.

Repeated attempts to regulate the use of antibiotic feed additives in the United States have failed, however—in no small measure because of the enormous pressure that farm-lobbying groups and drug companies have succeeded in bringing on the FDA and on members of Congress. As the

largest producer of farm antibiotics used in Great Britain,
American Cyanamid is, of course, concerned lest the willingness of England and other countries to restrict the use of
subtherapeutic drugs encourage a similar move in this country. A pamphlet entitled "The Swann Report: An Appraisal,"
printed and distributed in America by the company, disputed
the conclusions of the Swann Committee, stating, "More than
one hundred billion head of livestock and poultry have been
given medicated feed and water [in the United States and
Canada] since 1950. Yet not a single medically annotated case
of disease outbreaks in humans caused by the use of antibiotics
in animals has been recorded." Invoking the name of their
former employee, Dr. Thomas Jukes, the discoverer of the
benefits of subtherapeutic doses of antibiotics in livestock
feed, the pamphlet went on to claim that the Swann Committee had provided no credible evidence that "the use of
antibiotics on the farm will develop resistant pathogens that
will make antibiotics useless in the treatment of human
disease."

Another pamphlet, which Cyanamid issued in the late seventies, when the FDA was considering the regulation, by veterinary prescription, of penicillin and tetracycline as feed additives, was called "Antibiotics Under Fire." It urged farmers to
begin a letter-writing campaign in defense of the unrestricted
use of these drugs. Under the headline "Make Your Voice
Heard—Your Support Is Needed," the pamphlet announced,

> The F.D.A. Commission's proposal to restrict the use of tetra-
> cycline feed additives can be reversed. . . . Tell the Commis-
> sioner and your Senators and Congressmen how necessary
> these antibiotics are to farmers. . . . Tell them you don't be-
> lieve American farmers should lose valuable, economic, disease-
> preventing antibiotics because of a speculative hazard—a
> "possibility" which has never actually occurred in more than a
> quarter of a century of widespread testing. . . . Don't put off
> writing until it is too late!

FDA attempts to regulate the subtherapeutic use of tetracycline and penicillin produced a 1980 report by the Committee to Study the Human Health Effects of Subtherapeutic
Antibiotic Use in Animal Feeds, of the National Academy of
Sciences. After an exhaustive review of the existing literature,
the writers of the report refused even to recommend any action, because of what they termed "a lack of data." They did,
however, make at least a theoretical admission of the problem,
noting that the salmonellosis epidemic in Britain presented
"a clear demonstration that the sequence of events involved
in the transmission of R-factor organisms to humans via food
is possible." And they acknowledged that in their survey of
completed research "the majority opinion . . . was that an
increased prevalence of antimicrobial resistant organisms presents a threat to human health and that the subtherapeutic use
of antimicrobials increases the prevalence of R-factor organisms in animals" and that "majorities of individuals in these
various studies recommended policies aimed at restricting the
subtherapeutic use of antimicrobials in animal feeds, particularly for those agents used in the therapy of diseases in
humans." But when it came to ascertaining the actual degree
of risk and recommending guidelines, the report backed off:

> The postulations concerning the hazards to human health that
> might result from the addition of subtherapeutic antimicrobials
> to feeds have been neither proven nor disproven. The lack of
> data linking human illness with subtherapeutic levels of anti-
> microbials must not be equated with proof that the proposed
> hazards do not exist. The research necessary to establish and
> measure a definite risk has not been conducted and, indeed,
> may not be possible.

"I just can't understand that report," Levy says, his voice
rising in a crescendo of frustration. "I try to stay unemotional
about this issue, and just stick to the scientific facts. But, as I

see it, there is simply no justification for refusing to deal with the problem."

In a recent book that Levy and two colleagues edited, entitled *The Molecular Biology, Pathogenicity, and Ecology of Bacterial Plasmids,* two British contributors—Bernard Rowe and E. J. Threlfall, of the division of enteric pathogens at Public Health Laboratory Service in the United Kingdom— present evidence that the epidemic that led to the Swann Committee's recommendations was far from unique in England. They note in their article that before 1963, when the use of additives in that country's livestock industry began to be widespread, only about 3 percent of *S. typhimurium* bacteria isolated from cattle were drug-resistant, whereas between 1963 and 1969 the level of drug resistance skyrocketed to 73 percent. They also note that even after the ban on subtherapeutic doses of antibiotics, strains of *S. typhimurium* carrying multiple R factors swept through cattle herds in various parts of England—once in 1974, twice in 1977 and again in 1979.

The epidemics took a particularly high death toll among newly weaned calves, deprived of the antibodies in their mothers' milk. These strains of *Salmonella* were not only multiply resistant but unusually virulent: They killed as many as half the animals in some herds. Furthermore, British medical authorities reported that at least 305 people became infected with resistant strains of *Salmonella* that were demonstrably of animal origin. Most of the infected patients survived after eventually receiving treatment with alternative drug therapies, but two adults and one child died.

A similarly well-documented case of animal-to-man transfer of resistant pathogens occurred in this country in 1976. On August 16 of that year, a shipment of calves arrived on a farm in northern Connecticut. When the farmer unloaded them, he found that several of the animals had severe cases of scours, or bloody diarrhea. Almost immediately, one of the calves died. Four days later, the farmer himself contracted a mild case of diarrhea. Then, on August 24, his pregnant daughter, who had been helping him feed the young animals by scooping milk up to their mouths with her hands, went into labor and was admitted to Hartford's Saint Francis Hospital, where she gave birth to a son. Immediately afterward, she, too, suffered from diarrhea. Three days later, her newborn son began running a fever, and he also contracted diarrhea. By August 30, three other infants who had shared a common nurse and nursery in the hospital with the infected child exhibited the same symptoms. What was unusual about this case was that the Saint Francis Hospital staff, having learned about the infected calves, was able to document the transfer of the resistant disease organisms.

In most cases, of course, even when human salmonellosis is suspected of being of animal origin, it is difficult or impossible to locate a specific animal so that a bacterial culture can be taken and compared to the human isolate. In this instance, however, the medical staff at the hospital was able to study stool cultures both from the afflicted animals and from the sick people. A *Salmonella* variant known as the Heidelberg strain, and resistant to tetracycline, chloramphenicol, sulfa-methoxole, neomycin and streptomycin, was found in isolates from the farmer and from his calves. Similar strains were isolated from the mother and the three infants. These, however, were resistant only to tetracycline, chloramphenicol and sulfamethoxole.

Dr. Robert W. Lyons, of the Department of Infectious Diseases of the University of Connecticut, was the attending physician in the case. When I asked him if he was convinced that the case provided evidence of a transfer from animals to people of bacteria carrying R factors, he replied, "Yes. My own feeling is that the case quite clearly suggests that connection." And how did Lyons account for the fact that the bacteria isolated from the mother and the babies were resistant to two fewer drugs than those isolated from the farmer and the calves? "We postulated that the missing resistances in the mother and the children were lost in transmission," Lyons told me. "What impressed us was not the missing R factors but the fact that our tests showed that all the strains, both from people and from animals, were resistant to chloramphenicol. Resistance to that drug is extremely rare in New England. This in itself suggested to me that the resistant disease organisms found in the humans had a common animal origin."

In an article in the *Journal of the American Medical Association*, Lyons concluded, "The spread of salmonella from animals to humans is not unusual, and hospital epidemics of salmonella are far from rare. The occurrence, however, of a hospital epidemic with a multiple drug-resistant salmonella strain that had its origin in a herd of infected animals is remarkable."

His findings were disputed in the *Reviews of Infectious Diseases* by Dr. Charles E. Cherubin, then with the Microbiology Laboratory of the Jewish Hospital and Medical Center of Brooklyn, who wrote that "the episode does not prove the argument," because the strains isolated from the children and the mother contained two fewer R factors than those from the farmer and the calves. Lyons replied wryly in a letter to the editor, "As Thoreau said about watered dairy products, 'Some circumstantial evidence is very strong, as when you find a trout in the milk.'"

In the Hartford case, all the patients ultimately recovered. However, multiresistant epidemic pathogens such as *Salmonella typhi* have been documented as being responsible for many thousands of deaths, particularly in the Third World.

"The Hartford case was an unusual one," Richard Novick says when I query him about its significance. "There are, in fact, very few cases where we have actually been able to trace resistant human diseases directly to animal origin. The drug companies and the agricultural lobby always raise this

lack of data by way of defense. The truth is that without marking plasmids or doing complicated genetic analysis, it is very
hard to determine where the resistance genes came from. So,
until recently we have been left with largely circumstantial evidence. In my view this evidence is nonetheless very strong.
We know that the stuff is moving around in an enormous
pool of bacteria that are always interacting, but it has rarely
been possible to trace the specific pathways on a case-by-case
basis."

It is not simply the transmission of resistant pathogenic
bacteria that concerns people like Novick and Levy, because
there are only a few dangerous microorganisms that readily
survive in both animals and man, salmonella being one. They
are infinitely more exercised over the transmission of relatively innocuous bacteria like *E. coli*, which, although they do
not readily spread disease, most emphatically can transfer R
plasmids. In their view, the showering of the bacterial pool
with plasmid-borne R factors is far more dangerous in the
long term than a few outbreaks of salmonellosis.

Dr. Dwight Hirsch, professor of microbiology and medicine
at the University of California's School of Veterinary Medicine
at Davis, has long been interested in animal-to-man R-plasmid
transfer. As the head of the school's pathology lab, where
susceptibility tests for resistances to antibiotics are done on
animal bacterial cultures from all over the western United
States, Hirsch is in a unique position to keep track of such
resistance levels in the field of veterinary medicine.

"I wish that those who are playing down the problem of
resistance were in our diagnostic lab every day and could see
the nature of the strains that come through here," Hirsch says,
in a tone of exasperation when I visit him in Davis. "There
are strains of bacteria of both human and animal origin around
today that were very sensitive to antibiotics up until five or
six years ago but are now resistant, because they have acquired genes that they never had before, from the resistance

pool in our environment. To my mind, the greatest contributor to that resistance pool has been the food-producing animal."

Hirsch's first work with antibiotic resistance began at the University of Missouri almost ten years ago. Taking resistant strains of *E. coli* from cows, Hirsch and his colleagues fed them to human volunteers like H. W. Smith, mentioned by Cyanamid's Richard Gustafson. "We wanted to find out two things," Hirsch recalls. "Could these bacteria of animal origin live in the human gastrointestinal tract? And if we fed antibiotics to the volunteers, how would these bugs respond?"

The results of Hirsch's first tests confirmed the conclusions of the drug companies, for they demonstrated that it was indeed very difficult for most animal strains of bacteria to thrive for any length of time in the human intestine. But when he administered antibiotics to his volunteers at the same time he fed them the bovine *E. coli*, the situation changed. "We found that antibiotics enabled the animal bacteria to survive a lot longer," says Hirsch. "This was quite logical, because there is an inborn resistance in every animal to being colonized with alien bacteria. It works quite simply. The bugs in the human colon live there, and not in a cow's colon, because they are optimally suited to that environment. Although it can be done, it would even be difficult to take an *E. coli* from me and give it to you, because of your own colonization resistance." One good way to overcome colonization resistance, Hirsch found, is to administer antibiotics. This seems to give the resistant alien bacteria the competitive advantage they need in order to survive. Hirsch concluded that antibiotics not only select for resistant organisms in their own host animal but allow resistant alien bacteria to flourish in a new environment, where they would not otherwise have the competitive edge.

"Antibiotics can make it easier rather than more difficult for transmitted disease organisms to establish themselves," Hirsch says. "Apparently, the drug companies and the government want to see dead bodies before they admit that there is an inherent danger here. But we're not talking simply about disease—we're talking about resistance to drugs. If you're going to get sick from a particular microorganism, you'll get sick whether or not it is resistant to antibiotics. The problem arises not in the numbers of people that contract the disease but in whether or not they can be successfully treated. Obviously, if you're dealing wtih resistant bacteria, the disease will be harder to treat. But that's not what the government and the drug industry seem to be concerned with. They're asking for some proof that there is an increase in infectious disease as a result of the overuse of antibiotics. That would be an irrelevant piece of evidence. It just sidesteps the real issue— resistance. There is no connection between the problem of widespread resistance, on the one hand, and the prevalence of disease-bearing organisms, on the other."

Another researcher who became interested in the role that *E. coli* play as vectors for drug resistance is the British bacteriologist A. H. Linton, of the University of Bristol. Like Hirsch, Linton was concerned with the higher and higher levels of drug resistance that common, nonpathogenic bacteria appeared to be spreading. "Since salmonella reach man via the food chain, no doubt animal *E. coli* also reach man by the same route," he surmised in a 1977 article in the *Royal Society of Health Journal*. "The question then arises as to their ability to colonize the human gut, or even if this does not happen, to transfer their R plasmids to resident flora during temporary passage through the human gut."

The year before, Linton had designed an experiment that would enable him to analyze this ability. Stopping at random in different grocery stores in the Bristol area at intervals throughout a three-month period, he bought fifteen frozen chickens. Taking them back to his lab, he cultured juices from each of the birds to determine the kinds of resistance factors their *E. coli* harbored. After he had catalogued these, he distributed the chickens to five volunteers, all of whom, not having recently taken antibiotics, had relatively low levels of resistant enteric bacteria. He told each volunteer to prepare and eat three chickens in any form he or she wished over a set period of days. Linton took fecal samples from his volunteers twice weekly for several weeks and cultured samples of the *E. coli* to see if any of the strains of resistant organisms he had previously identified in the chickens or any of the plasmids from those strains were appearing in the human beings. Even without the selective pressure of antibiotics, one of Linton's volunteers became colonized by the poultry *E. coli*, and Linton concluded, in his 1977 article, that "strains of animal origin can colonize the human gut at least from time to time . . . and can persist in the human gut for a significant time."

"What we do not know yet is how often this sort of event may occur," he wrote later in the *Journal of Applied Bacteriology*. "But upwards of three hundred million frozen or chilled chickens were consumed in the U.K. in 1975, and therefore [this] type of event . . . is likely to occur widely." Noting that calves and pigs as well as poultry appeared to provide major reservoirs for resistant bacteria, Linton reminded his readers that even animal bacteria that were nonpathogenic were capable of transferring R factors to pathogenic bacteria that could cause potentially virulent epidemics among human beings, and he warned that "every effort should be made to limit this flow as far as possible."

As Richard Novick pointed out, even when there has been overwhelmingly convincing circumstantial evidence (as in some cases of salmonellosis) of the connection between animal and human disease, it has been difficult to identify with absolute certainty the specific source of a piece of DNA. The problem confronting clinicians is that the presence of a given combination of resistances in, say, bacteria isolated from calves and bacteria isolated from human patients cannot be regarded as conclusive proof that the same plasmid or plasmids were involved, or that the resistances were transferred from animals to people. Since a particular combination of resistances could arise by a variety of evolutionary pathways, what is needed is a means of determining whether the genes themselves are the same, are carried by the same plasmid and are arranged in the same way on the plasmid. Only with such information, or in cases where scientists have laboriously marked plasmids, as Levy did, have their pathways been traced with certainty. But in the last few years, using recently developed techniques to analyze the sequential arrangement of the DNA nucleotides, or subunits, that make up a plasmid, molecular biologists have been able actually to "fingerprint" and compare R factors that they suspect to have been transferred from animals to humans.

A recent study documenting R-plasmid transfer from animal bacteria to human bacteria that was contracted by the FDA and undertaken by Dr. Thomas O'Brien, director of the Microbiology Laboratory at Brigham and Women's Hospital, in Boston, was published in the *New England Journal of Medicine* in July 1982. For two and a half years, O'Brien and his colleagues studied isolates of a subspecies of animal- and human-borne *Salmonella* that they had collected from a number of bacterial reference laboratories around the country. They tested each isolate to see which R factors it carried. Then they extracted the R plasmids and, by using a restriction enzyme, they fragmented them. Restriction enzymes are a kind of "chemical knife," and each type will cut a particular type of plasmid in a characteristic way, thus enabling researchers to compare the DNA sequences of one plasmid with those of another. This technique has enabled molecular biologists for the first time to take a plasmid from a human-borne bacterium and conclusively identify it as having a common origin with a plasmid from an animal-borne bacterium, or in other words, to "fingerprint" it genetically.

According to O'Brien's report in the *New England Journal of Medicine*, "identical or nearly identical antibiotic-resistance plasmids may be found in salmonella isolated from animals and persons in widely separated parts of the United States." Lamenting the fact that no other researchers have thus far systematically searched out such identical plasmids in other bacterial species common to humans and animals, the authors point out that "our findings . . . using a limited sample of human isolates, suggest that a comprehensive surveillance in the U.S. would uncover additional examples," and go on to note,

> Although suited as the tracers of the spread of resistance, iso-
> lates of salmonella may greatly under-represent its magnitude.
> Among human beings, each culture-documented case of infec-
> tion due to *Salmonella* has been estimated to represent as
> many as a hundred undocumented cases. Moreover, other far
> more prevalent Enterobacteriaceae such as *E. coli* may acquire
> resistance plasmids as readily, and spread in much larger num-
> bers through the same routes as the rare but traceable sal-
> monella.

Novick and Dunny's report on their FDA-funded study on streptococci and staphylococci came out a few months after the O'Brien paper. By using similar techniques for finger-printing the DNA sequence found on R plasmids in bacteria isolated from their test pigs, handlers and random samples from FDA reference laboratories across the country, Novick and Dunny reported that many of the R plasmids they iso-lated from their gram-positive bacteria were "similar and indistinguishable," and "freely transmissible between live-stock and humans." Not only was drug resistance transferred from the Tylosin-fed pigs to their handlers by the strepto-cocci and staphylococci, but the R plasmids they harbored were almost identical to those appearing in human bacterial isolates from places far away from this particular batch of test animals. They concluded that R-plasmid transfer was not only possible across the animal-human divide, but common, since there is "no obvious barrier to interfere with the transmission of resistance from animal to human bacterial flora."

"What impresses me about data of this sort is the fact that, molecularly speaking, the R plasmids found in animals do not differ much from those we are finding in human bacteria," Novick tells me later. "This overall similarity is, I think, strong proof of significant interaction. If the two pools were really separate, one would expect that evolution would have changed them in very different ways, because, after all, DNA is evolutionarily a very active substance. Instead, what we are finding is a striking molecular resemblance. After seeing the Cornell results and O'Brien's study, I am more firmly convinced than ever that livestock feed additives are contributing to the growing levels of antibiotic resistance we are finding in human beings."

In September 1984, a study conducted at the National Centers for Disease Control in Atlanta was published in the *New England Journal of Medicine*. Referred to by many researchers as the "smoking gun," it provided irrefutable evidence of the way in which harmful resistant bacteria can migrate from animals to humans. The study, directed by staff epidemiologist Dr. Scott D. Holmberg over a period of a year and a half, traced an outbreak of drug-resistant salmonella from eighteen people (one of whom died) in four Midwestern states back to a herd of beef cattle in South Dakota.

The offending bacteria originated in calves raised in a feed lot who had been fed chlortetracycline in feed-additive form. They were resistant not only to the tetracycline, but also to two kinds of penicillin, ampicillin and carbenicillin. The humans became infected with these resistant strains of salmonella by eating hamburger from the slaughtered animals. Twelve of the eighteen victims had themselves been taking penicillin for a variety of colds and infections which had depleted their own intestinal flora, allowing the salmonella to proliferate without competition and cause salmonellosis, just as Dwight Hirsh's earlier studies at the University of Missouri had demonstrated.

Holmberg, who had traced the beef from South Dakota to various supermarkets in Minnesota via newly available computer records, told the *New York Times*, "To my knowledge, this is the first time we've been able to actually demonstrate the complete sequence of events, starting with feeding animals additives and progressing through the distribution to people who become seriously ill."

"The study demonstrates that antimicrobial resistant organisms of animal origin cause serious human illness and emphasizes the need for more prudent use of antimicrobials in both human beings and animals," concluded the CDC study bluntly.

In an accompanying editorial in the *New England Journal of Medicine*, Stuart Levy noted, "This important missing link is now provided by the elegant detective work of Holmberg and colleagues. Although only one outbreak is described, the findings are compelling."

"The discussion about transmission of all this stuff from animals to man may sound a little esoteric to a layman," Stuart Levy had told me earlier after we had discussed his own studies. "But when you're involved in actually treating patients as well as doing labwork, as I am, you begin to see the problem of antibiotic resistance—wherever it's coming from—in terms of its impact on individuals. I encounter the problem as a practicing physician, particularly in the treatment of cancer. In this field of medicine, one of the severest problems we face is vulnerability to infection. A cancer patient may be given some kind of chemotherapy that, while treating the cancer, temporarily wipes out his bone marrow, so that he gets an infection because of his reduced white-blood-cell count. What do we do? We try treating him with one or two antibiotics.

What happens? The infection turns out to be resistant to those drugs, and by the time we get other antibiotics on board, their mixed toxicity and the bone-marrow suppression have ganged up on him, and he dies of the infection. And what kind of infection? Just a resistant strain of *E. coli* that any normal person could handle but the system of an older person or a cancer patient can't."

Levy pauses and then says, "This is where the question of antibiotic resistance really comes home to me. Just recently, I had a cancer patient—a man from Brazil. We treated him with chemotherapy, which wiped out the leukemia cells but also temporarily destroyed his bone marrow. Unfortunately, an *E. coli* from his gut had got into his bloodstream—where it can cause septicemia and become a serious problem—and proved to be resistant to everything we tested. We couldn't find *any* drug combination that would work, and eventually the man died. It's true that he arrived at the hospital with the resistant organism in his gut, and certainly his own indiscriminate use of antibiotics without prescription had helped to establish it. But where did this resistance originally come from—animals or human beings? We don't know. This is the critical question, and it's still unanswered."

Concerned by the government's failure to act and stem the use of penicillin and tetracycline as animal feed additives, the National Resources Defense Council began circulating a petition calling on President Reagan and Secretary of the Department of Health and Human Services, Margaret M. Heckler, to take "expeditious action to ban subtherapeutic uses" of these drugs. By October 1983 more than three hundred scientists, physicians and biologists, including some within such government entities as the Center for Disease Control and the National Institutes of Health, had signed the petition which warned against the "indiscriminate use" of antibiotics in animal feed, and called government refusals to act "unconscionable."

"I think, however, that any intelligent person who is familiar

with the data will come to the same conclusion; namely, we've
got a problem that is creeping up on the whole community of
modern man, and we can't just blame hospitals for it when
half the antibiotics in this country are going into animals,"
comments Levy. "One of the things I find unsettling is that
most countries don't have a ghost of an idea what their present inventory of R plasmids is. What's in India, Indonesia,
Africa? We just don't know. But whatever they have is slowly
being spread around the world."

With a fatalistic shrug, which does nothing to dispel my
impression of his obvious concern, Levy continues, "People
simply don't want to take notice! But when they have to pay
three hundred to five hundred dollars for some of the new
drugs instead of five dollars for the old first line of antibiotics
that no longer work, they're going to start asking, 'Hey, what's
wrong with penicillin and tetracycline? Why can't we use those
terrific cheap drugs anymore?' And if the cost of the new drugs
is going to hurt people in a rich country like ours, think of the
impact on a poor Third World country, where even now there
is barely enough money to keep epidemic diseases under
control.

"We're caught in a global web. Bacteria don't pay attention
to international borders and customs. Bacteria don't even
acknowledge the boundaries that we once thought were so
absolute between animals, humans and plants. They're moving
around! That's their evolutionary imperative. It's getting
harder and harder to stay ahead of resistance. The old drugs
are becoming less and less effective, and the new generation
of antimicrobials are not only more costly but more toxic.
Wouldn't simple prudence dictate that we should try to
salvage the ones we already have by cutting back on their
overuse? As soon as we cut back, sensitive strains of bacteria
will return. It will take time, but it will happen. And when it
does, we will have succeeded in extending the lives of some
drugs that in my estimation are irreplaceable."

II

FEED TECHNOLOGIES

The use of subtherapeutic antibiotics in animal feeds is only one of the better publicized technologies that have transformed the ways in which livestock have been fed over the past few decades. There are, in fact, a whole host of other innovative feed technologies that have gone largely unnoticed by the meat-eating public at large. While some of these innovations are irrefutably ingenious and productive, and bear out the old adage that when better mousetraps are made, Americans will be there making them, there is also an aspect to feeding cattle plastic hay, cardboard roughage, artificial flavors and aromas and oral insecticides that is disturbing, although it is sometimes difficult to say precisely how.

When I asked one FDA official how he personally felt about the trend toward feeding so many new and bizarre things to the animals we eat, he just laughed and said, "I don't think I could answer that question without going and getting all metaphysical, and that's not my job."

One does feel a little absurd getting "metaphysical" about something as mundane as livestock feed. But since the state of our knowledge does not always allow us to assign quotients of benefit and risk in a more practical way to the kinds of new technologies that we so often seem intent on embracing without first making a careful examination, we are sometimes forced "to get metaphysical" to make any sense at all out of what is happening. For ways of doing things that have been tested and proven safe over long periods of human history are now rapidly being abandoned and replaced by new ways that appear to be more efficient. But what their long-term consequences may be are as yet unknown, because we have no means of assaying their cumulative effect on us and our environment.

What we can say about the kinds of technological intervention into the stomachs of animals that I will describe here is that they are in their way marvels. The kind of restless energy that provokes people to invent substitutes for hay and pleasing artificial flavors for moldy grain is truly admirable, and in its way expresses the genius of America's quest for progress. But that such boundless forward motion often has unintended and untoward consequences is also a fact of life worth bearing in mind in spite of the "metaphysical" connotations of that notion.

1

I have come to Kansas State University in Manhattan, Kansas, to see Dr. Erle Bartley, professor of animal sciences and the inventor of plastic hay. I find Weber Hall, a low, nondescript structure that houses the Department of Animal Sciences. As I walk down the corridors past the offices of the faculty, it is evident that many professors not only have special agricultural fields of study, but also prefer animals about which they feel chauvinistic. Like diplomatic missions, which fly the flags of their respective countries prominently out front, many of these representatives of the animal sciences have office doors emblazoned with bumper stickers extolling the animal of their specialty.

"Eat More Pork, You Turkey!"

"Promote Beef! Run Over a Chicken!"

Although Erle Bartley's specialty is cows, his door is unadorned with any such pledge of allegiance. As I am glancing at the bulletin board outside his office, Bartley comes down the corridor, having just returned from KSU's Sixty-ninth Annual Cattlemen's Day, where he has given a speech entitled "The Effect of Bovatec and Rumensin on Grain and Legume Bloat."

Erle Bartley, a mild-mannered, friendly man with gray hair, has taught at KSU for thirty-four years. He greets me with disarming affability and suggests that we retire to his office to talk.

"I think artificial roughage is an idea whose time has come," begins Bartley after we have settled down around a table inside. "When you fatten feedlot cattle, you want to get as much energy into them as possible, which means you want to put them on a high-grain diet. That's what makes for good marbling and taste in a steak at the other end.

"The problem is that since cows are ruminants, they have to have some roughage as well. Unless they get about fifteen percent hay, they begin to develop real problems in the rumen [the first of a cow's four stomachs], where feed is initially digested before being regurgitated as cud and rechewed. Hays are not so nutritious as grains, but they are essential because of the way they form a floating mat and keep scouring the cow's rumen so that bacteria won't build up. The stomach lining is covered with thousands of little nodulelike papillae [which give tripe its familiar appearance]. Unless these papillae are constantly scrubbed, they act as breeding grounds for bacteria that can penetrate the bloodstream and finally cause liver abscesses."

As Bartley searches a drawer for an article he has written, I glance around his office. In one bookcase he has a complete bound set of the *Journal of Dairy Science* and volumes of the *Journal of Animal Sciences*. His shelves are filled with books and papers on feed and feedstuffs. His walls are adorned with pictures of cows, feed-mill calendars and award plaques from such organizations as the American Feed Manufacturers Association.

"These photos will give you a more graphic idea of what happens if a ruminant does not get adequate roughage," continues Bartley, opening up a copy of a scholarly article he has written and turning to a page that shows photos of two different cow's rumens.

Like the before-and-after depictions of bald men whose tonsorial splendor has allegedly been restored by some tonic

or other, these two photos show the state of the rumen with
and without roughage in its diet.

The first shows a bed of flattened papillae lying collapsed
and in disarray like a growth of seaweed on a rock that has
been exposed to the sun too long at low tide. The second
photo shows a healthy forest of papillae standing stalwartly
upright as if at attention, evidently eager to play their role as
absorbers of nutrients to make more tasty marbled steaks.

"Cattle enjoy chewing roughage," continues Bartley, smiling so that all the wrinkles around his eyes suddenly flex into
a deeper relief, making him look older than he first appeared.
"In fact the scratchiness of roughage is what makes a cow
regurgitate its cud. This is not only satisfying, but it also
causes a cow to salivate, which is beneficial because its saliva
contains bicarbonate of soda, which is vital to controlling the
pH in its stomach. You take an animal like a big Holstein, and
she'll secrete up to four hundred pounds of saliva a day, which
will give her about a pound or two of bicarb.

"No matter how you look at it, even when a cow is getting
plenty of food value from grain, it has to have roughage. So,
all I have tried to do is find a suitable roughage substitute to
provide what nature provides, only I've tried to provide it
more efficiently for a feedlot situation."

Just the way many people in the swine business tenaciously
refer to pig farmers as "pork producers," so Bartley seems to
prefer the terms *artificial roughage* or *roughage substitute* to
the more vernacular term *plastic hay*, which has caught my
fancy.

Bartley reaches back onto a windowsill that frames a vista
of the campus outside, produces a plastic bag and dumps the
contents out onto the table. "These are the pellets we are now
using," he announces.

On the tabletop is a small heap of plastic lumps (80 to 90
percent ethylene and 10 to 20 percent propylene), which at

first sight look very much like pale kernels of corn. A closer inspection, however, reveals that the pellets are actually shaped like miniature derbies.

"We've tried cylindrical pellets and disc-shaped pellets," Bartley explains, "but the cattle detected them in their feed and wouldn't eat them because they were too slippery. I guess they didn't like the feel of them. So then we went to the present shape, and that seems to satisfy things pretty well."

Bartley picks up a handful of his pellets and lets them fall through his fingers as if he were a prospector playing with his stash of gold nuggets. "This roughage requirement of cattle is a real pain in the neck for most feedlot operators," Bartley continues. "Hay is heavy, bulky, dusty, hard to grind up and mix with grain, and difficult to run through mechanical feed-delivery systems. So a lot of people have been scratching their heads for some time trying to come up with a substitute.

"The reason why these work," says Bartley, rolling a pellet between his thumb and forefinger, "is that when a cow chews them, they get shredded. Once they're swallowed, they float on top of the rumen in a kind of mat, just as hay does."

Bartley reaches behind himself once more and produces another plastic bag, this one filled with clumps of grated white material that looks as if it might be some kind of exotic sea-weed from an Oriental specialty store.

"This is what it looks like once the cow has chewed the pellets and swallowed them," says Bartley, proffering a pinch of the substance to me for examination. "The nice thing about this roughage substitute is that none of it is absorbed into the animal's bloodstream. We've traced it with carbon-fourteen and find no sign of its leaving the digestive tract."

The phone rings, and, reassured by what Bartley has just said, I quietly pop a pellet into my mouth and begin to chew as he answers. My first impression is that Bartley's artificial roughage is extremely unhaylike. The pellet is hard, and the sensation is not dissimilar to how I imagine it would feel to try to chew a fragment of hockey puck.

Gradually, however, as it warms up in my mouth, and as my bicuspids do their work, the pellet begins to yield and acquire the consistency of a Jujube candy. By the time Bartley has finished his phone call, the little derby-shaped piece of plastic hay has actually flattened out in my mouth and become a rather satisfying, if challenging, chew.

After his phone call, Bartley picks up where he left off. "Now, another thing about this product that I think makes it a winner is that when an animal is slaughtered, you can recover about twenty pounds of the stuff from each cow's rumen, melt it down and recycle it back into new pellets. That will make it a great boon to meat packers, because it will help cut down on the amount of offal that they have to dispose of at the packing plant." Bartley says that the 30 percent of the plastic roughage that is lost from the cow's stomach through elimination is biodegradable and will hardly be noticed in a feedlot environment, where thousands of tons of manure deposited annually often pose a massive disposal problem.

"We've done field tests, too," adds Bartley. "They show that cattle on this roughage substitute do as well or better than those on conventional hays. It's cheaper and more efficient. For instance, it takes only one-tenth of a pound of plastic roughage a day to accomplish the same end as four pounds of hay. That's a forty-to-one ratio, which could save cattle feeders about eleven cents a head a day." Bartley pats his bag full of plastic pellets with custodial affection.

When I first read about Erle Bartley's plastic hay, I must confess that I felt a sense of horror. In recent times it has become somewhat of a cliché of derogation to refer to this or that as being "plastic." But that this plastic world had actually extended right into the stomachs of the beef cattle that produce our burgers and steaks seemed to be going too far.

And yet here I am, sitting with the founding father of plastic hay, finding it not only fascinating, but possibly quite sensible. In fact, I find myself enthralled by Bartley's invention. Erle Bartley and his "artificial roughage" may be tolling the death knell of the American haystack, but it cannot be said that his invention doesn't have a certain logic on its side. For while plastic hay is made of petroleum itself, it can not only be recycled, but will save enormous amounts of petroleum necessary to produce and transport fodder.

Leaving Bartley's office, we head toward the Rumen Metabolism Laboratory in the back of Weber Hall, where some of the Department of Animal Sciences' experiments in bovine nutrition are done. On our way down the corridor, we make a brief detour into another lab to round up a graduate student clad in a white smock to accompany us on our tour. Bartley is still dressed from his Cattlemen's Day speech in what he calls "my best bib and tucker," and does not wish to get too close to any livestock.

We enter the Rumen Metabolism Laboratory through a large metal door marked with a sign that warns, Experiment in Progress. Do Not Enter!, and find ourselves in a dimly lit, windowless room where three cows stand docilely in head stanchions facing a wall. The scene in the room is unexceptional at first glance, but scanning it as though it were one of those children's puzzle pictures that require careful scrutiny to figure out which elements in them are awry, I soon notice that there is something unusual about the cows.

As the graduate student pulls on an elbow-length plastic veterinarian's glove and then walks over to the side of one of the animals, I notice a curious round black object about the size of a tuna fish can protruding from its side. As I draw closer to examine this possibly illusory protuberance, the graduate student reaches for it and suddenly plucks it right out like a stopper from a bottle, exposing the interior of the beast's stomach.

"This is a fistulated cow," says Bartley, noticing my astonishment. "We make openings surgically so that we can look in on the animal's digestive tract and see what is going on."

I draw closer, bend over and peer into the humid recesses of this living creature, feeling as if I were inside a submarine looking out through a tiny porthole into the dark underwater world of the deep. I can see the mat of half-digested hay floating on top of the reservoir of liquid in the cow's rumen, just as Bartley has described in his office.

Reaching into the gurgling stomach of the cow (who stares at the wall in front of us with a total lack of interest), the graduate student pulls out a handful of half-digested, khaki-colored hay. He holds it out for our inspection. It steams in the cool air and drips on the floor. Then, like a naturalist returning an unfledged baby bird to its nest, he reaches back into the stomach of the cow and delicately restores the soggy handful of roughage to its proper place.

"This animal has a healthy rumen," Bartley announces, as the graduate student neatly restores the rubber plug. "You can tell by that nice mat of hay, which provides the vital scratching action. And that is exactly what our roughage substitute does."

Walking over to a second cow, the graduate student unceremoniously pulls out the second plug. The animal lurches and gives a wheeze. No sooner is the plug out than a sickly-looking gray froth, like dirty shaving cream, begins billowing up out of the hole and splats in a bubbly cloud on the floor.

"Now, what we're seeing here is a very unhealthy cow," Bartley says. "It's being fed a high-starch diet with no hay, and the bacteria in the rumen are overproducing and creating all this froth. It's a bad situation that usually causes the animal to become weak and generally refuse to eat altogether. That is precisely the problem we are addressing with our product."

Indeed, this particular cow does look lethargic and depressed, standing listlessly in its stanchion, back slightly swayed and feet apart as if it had all it could do just to keep upright. As Bartley talks, foam keeps frothing out of the fistula in the cow's side, until finally the graduate student claps the plug back into the opening, causing a small jet of gastric juice to squirt out and land on one of Bartley's well-shined shoes. He smiles indifferently.

As we walk back to his office, I ask Bartley when he expects his plastic hay to be on the market. He doesn't immediately respond. His usually affable mood seems to darken.

"When I began to see if I couldn't develop a more efficient and compact roughage substitute in the 1960s, Exxon got interested, so we ended up doing our research under contract to them. It was a grant-in-aid sort of thing that gave them the license to whatever we came up with. At that time no one could foresee what we might develop—no one, I guess, but those smart Exxon lawyers." Bartley gives a wry laugh.

"Anyway, Exxon has gone and licensed everything to Ralston-Purina. They're not doing anything with it yet. They're just sitting on it. But even if they did do something with it, we wouldn't get any money from it, because they hold all the patents. We'd like to get the rights back and get it moving. Actually I even have a group together that has venture capital and three big feedlots with a hundred and fifty thousand head signed up ready to try the stuff, but right now there is nothing we can do."

Bartley sighs and for a moment falls silent as we walk. Then shaking his head dolefully from side to side, he adds, "Maybe I hadn't ought to be telling you all this, but sometimes I feel it's such a ridiculous situation. Sometimes I just feel so downright disgusted that I could . . ."

Bartley does not finish this sentence, as if he did not feel it becoming to dwell on such negative thoughts. Instead, he smiles broadly and adds with finality, "This product of ours has so few drawbacks and works so well that it's almost hard to believe it. I'm sure it will have a bright future."

Dr. Erle Bartley died in February of 1983, before seeing his artificial roughage, for which he had such high hope, developed as a commercial product.

2

Several minutes before Bruce Boyd turns his dusty and aging Mercedes sedan into the back parking lot of the Orlando, Florida, Frito-Lay, Inc., plant, I smell the aroma of frying corn chips drifting in the balmy tropical air.

We stop beside a red tanker truck backed up to a large industrial building. A pipe that extends out of a tall piece of machinery inside is emptying a pasty gray sludge into the truck's tank.

"That's our rig," says Bruce proudly, removing his own Frito-Lay cap and scratching his balding head. "What you see going inside there is corn and potato starch from all the snack foods they make here."

As Bruce speaks, his wife, Vi, gets out of the Mercedes and begins to climb gingerly up the utility ladder on the rear of the truck for a peek inside. Reaching the top, she peers down into the dark recesses of the tank, where the flowing starch makes echoing plopping noises. Then, looking up with a pleased smile, she yells over to Bruce, "It's getting up there!"

"Just the way I like it," Bruce calls back gruffly, thrusting one upturned thumb up into the air in satisfaction. "We pay Frito-Lay seven hundred dollars a month and earn back sixteen hundred dollars reselling that stuff as livestock feed," Bruce informs me. "We got a five-year contract. Before we came along, the Frito-Lay people were having a hell of a time getting rid of all this waste."

Bruce and Vi Boyd are the owners and operators of B/V By-Products, Inc., a company that specializes in reclaiming waste products and converting them into what Bruce refers to as "exotic feeds" for dairy and beef cattle. Their specialties right now are the waste matter from this Frito-Lay plant, waste scraps from a carton-box factory, and dust from a plant that manufactures cardboard frozen-orange-juice containers.

Actually, the Boyds are only two of a growing number of entrepreneurs who are trying to beat the high cost of livestock feed by finding ways to convert various kinds of industrial and agricultural wastes into rations for food-producing animals.

Bruce Boyd, who fought as a marine in the South Pacific during Word War II, is a tall burly man whose craggy, weathered face has a scar slashed across the nose. He is sixty-six years old, chain-smokes and wears dark glasses, a checkered short-sleeved shirt, a baggy pair of powder-blue slacks held up by a belt that strains against his ample girth, and an omnipresent Frito-Lay cap. He usually speaks with a forced brashness, which makes even his monologues sound as if he were in a heated argument.

His wife, Vi, on the other hand, is a rather quiet, sweet fifty-eight-year-old woman whose wistfully expressioned face is framed by red hair. Today her zaftig body is wedged into a pair of tight white toreador pants and a turquoise blouse. Although she frequently has interesting observations of her own to make, more often than not she defers to her husband, offering only such conversational embellishments as "Oh, Bruce is just talking," or "Bruce is just a man of strong convictions," after he has come out with a particulary extreme comment. Only when Bruce is not around does Vi become voluble.

"Vi and I have been in the business of exotic feeds for more than eight years," says Bruce as we stand in the parking lot waiting for Vi to climb back down the starch truck ladder. "When we first started, we sold peanut skins shipped down here from Georgia. Those skins were the best, eighteen percent protein, thirty percent fat. People just couldn't afford to feed their animals expensive hay and grain. Before we knew it, the demand was so great that we were bringing down three box-car loads a week, about three hundred and thirty tons every month. We got so famous selling them that people started calling us the 'King and Queen of Exotic Feeds.'" Bruce announces these pretensions to royalty with boastful pride.

As we talk, Vi regains terra firma and walks across the parking lot to join us.

"What finally killed the whole deal was when the cost of freight started skyrocketing," continues Bruce, a sourness creeping into his voice.

"Well, I'm going to tell you something. Those goddamn unions just strangled our transportation system, and now they want to strangle everything else too. Where the hell is it going to end?" asks Bruce belligerently, as if he expected me or Vi to answer for the unions. But I am beginning to guess that Bruce is not the sort of man who really wants to hear an answer. I don't believe in unionism, communism, or any other ism except Americanism," he says. Having made his point, Bruce strides off into the Frito-Lay warehouse to talk with an employee.

"Bruce gets carried away sometimes," says Vi with an apologetic smile. "But, you know, without all those strikes I really do believe Bruce and I would have been wealthy by now. I remember one time there was a glass strike up there around Georgia. The glass strike made the peanut butter factories close down because they didn't have any jars. That meant we couldn't get any peanut skins, and so we lost all our customers.

"When we started on this starch-and-cardboard route, all the livestock people thought we were crazy. Bruce couldn't get anyone to listen to him for a long time." Vi shakes her head with a faraway look in her eyes. Then, in a soft but proud voice she adds, "Bruce is always ten years ahead of his time."

When Bruce is through talking inside, the three of us pile back into the Mercedes. No sooner have we regained the road than Bruce turns off again, this time gliding into the Frito-Lay front parking lot. He pulls the Mercedes up beside a large truck and several dumpsters that stand next to the plant's main building.

"Just have a look in the back of that truck," says Bruce with a cocky smile.

Getting out of the car, I climb up on the back of the dump truck and peer over the sides into its bed. It is filled almost to the top with mounds of corn chips.

"Rejects," yells Bruce. "They screw up on them or something and have to get rid of them."

Before me is the biggest aggregation of junk food I have ever seen, even imagined, in my life! I am reminded of perennial collegiate legends about pranksters pouring massive amounts of Jello-O into swimming pools to create the largest gelatin desserts in history, and of Scrooge McDuck, whose comic-book fortunes had grown to such a level that he needed bulldozers to move his money around. This mammoth dune of chips made the small Mylar bags in which Frito-Lay finally markets its product seem like subatomic particles by comparison.

"This stuff is excellent, just excellent," exclaims Bruce as if he were a wine enthusiast appraising a choice vintage. "These chips are seventy percent protein and fifty percent fat." (I do not ask him how a corn chip can be composed of 120 percent of anything.) "We get fifteen tons a week from this plant. It makes great cattle feed." For a moment Bruce's rapture over these chips causes him to lose his usual gruffness, and he becomes almost childlike in his enthusiasm.

"We've had a lot of trouble with people here at the plant

just throwing any old kind of junk into the bins along with the
rejected chips," offers Vi as I climb down from the truck and
Bruce steps up to check the load. "We had to put a sign up so
that they wouldn't ruin the feed." She points to a placard that
reads, "Please no salt, paper, cardboard, rags, metal, wood."

While Vi speaks, Bruce is squinting up into the glare of the
sky with an intense look on his face. Following his gaze upward, I notice a flock of birds circling over the plant. When
they swoop down toward us, Bruce, his face showing great
agitation, suddenly starts waving his arms in the air like a
human scarecrow. Just before landing, the birds evidently
notice him because they suddenly break formation and fly cha-
otically back to the safety of a higher altitude.

"Damn those birds," says Vi with exasperation. "They're a
big pain in the neck! Some people get angry: they claim the
birds come here to eat chips and then fly over that stadium
there and shit on the people watching sports events." She
points out past the parking lot to where one can just make out
the top of a stadium in the distance.

"Well, let me just tell you something, mister," says Bruce
cholerically, turning back to where Vi and I stand. "If the
government hadn't gone and made all them endangered species, I'd sure as shit have taken care of a few of these birds a
long time ago." Bruce's eyes are narrowed behind his sunglasses
to mere slits.

"We believe in eating anything we feed to our animals," says
Vi, reaching into one of the dumpsters and extracting a handful of corn chips, which she begins to munch. "Sometimes if
we're in the neighborhood we'll just drop by here for lunch."

"The big problem with this country is the ecologists and
legislators, who all work for the government," says Bruce, who
has also started to munch on some corn chips. "These com-
munists are on their way to taking over. Anyone who is a tri-
lateralist and for one world is a communist in my book."

Bruce pauses, but only long enough to light a cigarette and exhale a first lungful of smoke. Then he's off again on a new theme, the NAACP.

Bruce is still holding forth when we get back into the Mercedes, this time on Hitler. He doesn't stop until we hit the highway and are well on our way to the Cloyd Dairy, where he is going to show me B/V's other line of waste-made-into-feed, shredded cardboard.

In order to receive the requisite amino acids to build muscle tissue and grow, pigs (like humans and other omnivores with one stomach, or monogastric digestive systems) must be fed relatively high-protein diets composed of such feed ingredients as meat, eggs, dairy products, soybean meal, cottonseed meal or peanut meal.

By contrast, ruminant animals (with more than one stomach), such as cows and sheep, are able to produce their own amino acids from cellulose through the action of certain microorganisms that dwell in their rumen, or first stomach. Thus, cows and other ruminants are able to utilize grasses, hays and legumes, which are high in cellulose, as complete feeds, while a pig or a human cannot. Although not usually thought of as an animal food, wood is, of course, largely cellulose. And since cardboard is nothing more than crushed or "pulped" wood, it has as much potential nutritional value for a cow as other conventional cellulose feeds.

"We've marketed cardboard as a cattle feed for eight years," says Bruce as we drive along. "There's not a damn thing wrong with it. We've even tried marketing sawdust and bark, but the only problem is that we can't get a steady cheap supply. There are too many other uses for chipped woods now—Presto logs, Masonite, fiberboard, even animal bedding. So we went to cardboard."

As Bruce drives, he has a habit of jackknifing his beefy left arm out over the window ledge so that his elbow protrudes outside the car; at the same time he slings his right hand over the top of the steering wheel so that he is in effect navigating the car with nothing more than the underside of one wrist.

And as we speed along, Bruce makes frequent gestures with his right hand, so that no part of his body, not even his wrist, is touching the helm. Moreover, to emphasize certain points, Bruce may turn his head—and occasionally even his whole body—around in the front seat to face me while he speaks. My most fervent wish at moments like this is that the oncoming traffic will be merciful and that Bruce will conclude his thought quickly and get his eye back on the road.

"Fiber or cellulose is what's short in the diet of a cow that is not grazing," says Bruce, looking right at me and allowing the Mercedes to sail down the road unguided. "In order for a cow to survive, it's got to have fiber. Without fiber a cow will get sick and die. Now, beef cattle don't need as much fiber as a dairy cow, because they're going to die soon anyway," says Bruce, making a slicing motion in the air with his driving hand. "You're just trying to get all the high-energy grains into them you can before that happens so they'll fatten up faster. But you could feed the animal hay or you could feed it cardboard boxes. Same thing. It would just take him a little longer to get to market size on hay or boxes, that's all." As Bruce talks, I am wondering to myself how Erle Bartley, inventor of plastic hay, would take to the idea of cardboard roughage.

"Hell," continues Bruce after a moment's pause, "there are people feeding cows on newspaper. Cows would even eat phone books. Nothing wrong with phone books if you can get a steady supply. Another thing you got to consider with your cardboards is that the price per ton remains pretty constant, while the price of newsprint is all over the lot. Sometimes it's free, then at other times it's one hundred and twenty-five dollars a ton. Now, how are you going to run a business with prices going up and down like that?"

Bruce lights up a cigarette and then adds, "You want to know something? Me and Vi did an experiment once. We fed out three head of cattle to slaughter-size on ground cardboard and grapefruit peel, and I want to tell you they dressed out real good. The taste on those guys was terrific. They were lean, but they made the best burgers I ever ate."

According to A. H. Peavey III et al., writing in the *Journal of Dairy Science,*

> Feeding waste papers to ruminants has created interest, because it utilizes a waste product which has the potential to become an economically feasible roughage substitute in complete feeds. The nutritional value of waste paper such as newsprint, computer paper, brown shopping bags and corrugated boxes varies with source . . . caused by type of pulping treatment, source of wood, and additives such as ink, glue, clay and plastic.

Peavey et al. noted simply that, "Further work indicated that animals preferred newsprint without ink."

I ask Bruce if the ink on newsprint isn't something that might be harmful to animals or the people who will ultimately eat their meat. He dismisses the idea with a wave of his driving hand. "Newspaper ink is all safe," he says. "The goddamn government with all its regulations isn't going to let you feed anything injurious to anyone, although, if you ask me, they don't know what the hell they're doing."

Later, I check with Paul Volpe at the National Association of Printing Manufacturers. At first he seems a little incredulous when I tell him that people are actually feeding cardboard boxes and newsprint to animals. "Letterpress inks, which are what most newspapers use, are composed mainly of carbon black, mineral oil and certain hydrocarbon resins," he finally offers with a bemused congeniality.

I ask him if there is anything he knows about these inks that would make them unsuitable for consumption by meat-producing animals. "Well, there's been a lot of panic in the streets about inks," he says, a tentative note creeping into his voice. "But I don't think any tests have been done on the long-term effect of eating this sort of thing. I mean . . . well, they're not designed to be eaten.

"The thing that you have to remember in all this is that we're using petroleum derivatives," he adds, when I probe some more. "What's in the ink depends on what's in the crude oil that is used. You might get certain fractions of polycyclic aromatic hydrocarbons in the mineral oils, or benza-alpha pyrenes, some of which have been found to be carcinogenic to lab animals. But it's not a cut-and-dried thing in inks because the rate at which these compounds appears varies from one kind of crude oil to another. Anyway, it all depends on what studies you read. There are so many published, you don't know what to believe."

"Are these inks an environmentally controversial subject?" I ask.

"Well, you might say that it's a delicate subject," Volpe replies. "I'm cautious because there are certain lawsuits out now in which people claim that they were harmed by newsprint ink. So, even though my personal opinion is that ink isn't highly toxic, I can't guarantee that. If an animal was fed his whole life on nothing but newspapers, I guess I'd take a jaundiced look at it before I'd eat it."

Back in the Mercedes, Bruce has just said something I did not hear, which has caused him to turn toward me with a smile of satisfaction on his craggy face, when . . .

Zooooooooooooooooom! A truck and trailer followed by a whole string of cars sheers past us in the oncoming lane so close that they seem almost to graze Bruce's protruding elbow.

"Do you know what our B/V By-Products' letterhead motto is?" asks Bruce. He hands me an envelope off the top of the dashboard. In the upper left-hand corner just under a drawing of a cow I find the motto, "What We Have, We Owe to Udders." Bruce gives a wink. Vi smiles.

A hand-painted sign that says "Dairy Calves 4 Sale" flashes by, and Bruce peels off the main highway and bounces down a dirt road. We pass a shantytown of collapsing calf sheds with rusting corrugated iron roofs and come to stop in a sandy parking area. Around us is a veritable sculpture garden of broken-down equipment: rusted tanks and drums, worn-out tractor tires and gutted car bodies. Several men in *Deliverance*-type bib overalls silently watch our arrival from a distance. This is the Cloyd Dairy

While Bruce goes over to one of the silently watching figures to explain our presence, Vi and I walk over to a row of large bins made out of railroad ties and sheets of plywood, which are filled with fermenting peels from one of central Florida's orange-juice plants.

Florida is the home of some 864,000 acres of citrus trees. Besides producing a bountiful harvest of fruit and juices, the citrus crop also creates more than three-quarters of a million tons of citrus peel and pulp waste each year. High in carbohydrates (a rich energy source for bovines), citrus pulp makes a palatable and nutritious feed when mixed up to 40 percent with other ingredients. In the case of the Cloyd Dairy, the other ingredient consists of Bruce and Vi's line of shredded cardboard.

Vi is just beginning to explain to me how the citrus pulp (which is a brown, fermenting mush under a thick cloud of flies) is mixed with the shredded cardboard to form a complete cattle ration for the Cloyd herd, when Bruce beckons us over to several large bales wrapped in sheets of polyethylene.

"What we got here is dust from the cardboard-container plant," he announces like a tour operator. He reaches through a rip in the plastic skin of one of the bales and pulls out a handful of the substance for my inspection. The idea of a living creature actually eating this dirt-colored dust is not an appealing one. But Bruce hardly seems to share my view.

"You mix this with a little citrus peel, potato starch or cottonseed meal, and it makes a beautiful feed," says Bruce, allowing a little of the fine powder to sift almost lovingly through his fingers to the ground.

Eager to see where this unusual feed comes from, I tell Bruce that I would enjoy visiting one of the cardboard plants itself. Bruce seems dubious. Vi says she wants to go back to the motel where she and Bruce frequently stay for the night in Orlando. When I offer to drive my rented car, Bruce finally consents to take me down to Auburndale to the International Paper plant, where he contracts for the factory's wastes. Arriving at the motel, Bruce heads back to their room to call the plant while Vi lingers out in the parking lot with me.

We are chatting with each other, when suddenly her voice lowers to a confidential whisper and she says, "When you're finished with this story on exotic feeds, I've got a *really* sensational one for you." I look at her animated face and begin to feel intuitively wary.

"Do you want to know what it is?" she asks enthusiastically. I nod circumspectly.

"Bruce and I are nudists, and we'd like to take you to our camp. It is beautiful. It has a natural spring-fed lake and fifty-three acres to roam in. We feel it's a sensational story. And . . ."

My mind, programmed as it is for waste cardboard boxes and their conversion from cellulose to protein, finds it hard to shift mental gears to nudism. But Vi is speaking without the faintest suggestion of salaciousness and with such unalloyed enthusiasm that I find myself not wanting to puncture her evident pleasure at having extended this special invitation.

As I am fumbling for a polite demurral, I see Bruce emerge

from the motel and head toward us. For the most fleeting moment I try to imagine this large, bulky, opinionated man naked at his nudist colony, but I cannot quite make the leap. My mind's eye is successful in removing most of his clothes, but like an indelible stain on an otherwise blank sheet of paper, no matter how I conjure the image, Bruce continues to wear his Frito-Lay cap.

Just before Bruce arrives within earshot I manage to say, "Thanks, Vi. That sounds like an interesting story. I'm sorry I don't have more time." She gives my shoulder a confidential squeeze.

Bidding Vi good-bye, Bruce and I head off to Auburndale with me at the wheel. We drive on the back roads of central Florida through seemingly endless groves of orange trees. Their blossoms fill the warm air with a heavenly scent. But Bruce appears unaffected by the pleasant smell, and soon slides back into one of his vituperations.

"There's too much ass kissing among government bureaucrats," he begins out of the blue. I am beginning to view Bruce like a twenty-four-hour evangelical station that's never off the air. Anytime you want a little political hellfire and damnation, all you have to do is turn on your mental radio, and Bruce will be there broadcasting his own unique commentary.

For the moment, I tune out Bruce's programming. The beauty of the countryside, the warmth of the sun and the aroma of the orange blossoms all put me into another state of mind. The car gently swings down the curving road past more groves and crudely lettered signs advertising everything from Hot Boiled Peanuts and Wigglers to Goat Milk Citrus Fudge.

When I reconnect with Bruce's monologue, he is advocating some new forms of cruel and unusual punishments for prisoners as a deterrent to crime. However, as we approach Auburndale, Bruce's bravado seems to moderate. In fact, by the time we bounce across the railroad tracks that run parallel to the International Paper plant, he has become almost completely silent.

"You know, International Paper is one of the biggest. It's real big," says Bruce, after we have parked and are walking toward the massive complex of steel buildings, his ardor for bombast evidently chilled by the scale of the plant.

When we reach the front steps, Bruce almost meekly doffs his Frito-Lay cap before going inside. "I know this fellow Johansen, the manager, pretty good," he tentatively offers.

Inside the lobby Bruce lights up a cigarette and then picks up the house phone to announce our arrival. After five minutes the locked door that separates the small lobby from the workshop area opens, and Plant Manager John Johansen emerges. Bruce shakes his hand and mumbles a few words to him about me. Johansen nods politely, if not enthusiastically, and then leads the way back into the roar of the plant, where the air is filled with the uniquely dry and dusty smell of cardboard.

As is so often the case in Bruce's work, his vested interest in a production line does not begin until everyone else's leaves off, namely at the end, where the effluvia of the manufacturing process comes out for disposal. Like the Frito-Lay plant where Bruce and Vi's trucks and dumpsters wait out back to capture waste starch and rejected chips, their province of concern here at International Paper does not begin until one reaches the very rear of this industrial complex.

To reach this area we walk through the main workshop, a huge indoor space filled with machinery connected with conveyors. As we pass a machine that staples cartons together, Johansen stops for a moment to chat with a worker on the line.

"We have a helluva time when these metal staples end up in our feed," says Bruce gravely as we pause. "It's not so bad for the big milk cows. You can drop a cow magnet into their stomachs and pick up all the bits of bailing wire, staples and other hardware they might have eaten. But the young cows can't take it. Cuts them all up. I've been talking to the plant about the problem." The manner in which Bruce describes his negotiations does not make them sound fruitful.

Moving on, we pass an area where collapsed folded cartons have their labels printed on them. The finished products, with names like Minute Maid, Budweiser, Leaf Lettuce and Smoked Pork Loin, lie stacked in orderly piles all around us waiting to be banded and shipped.

As we continue toward the back, I notice that many of the cartons are coated with wax. I ask Johansen over the roar of machinery what they do with the scraps of wax-coated cardboard, assuming that animals would find it unpalatable and that Bruce probably wouldn't want them.

"Actually, that's all Boyd gets," replies Johansen. "He has contracted for the waxed cardboard, which we can't recycle ourselves." Bruce looks uneasy. Johansen makes a white scratch across the surface of one of the boxes with a fingernail.

"What kind of wax is it?" I ask.

"It's a petroleum-based paraffin," responds Johansen.

"Is it good for animals to eat this wax?" I ask, turning to Bruce, who has been listening to our conversation.

"No problem," he replies. "The animals metabolize the wax just as if it were fat. We've been doing this cardboard for eight years and haven't had any trouble."

(I later had occasion to ask Dr. Barney Harris, a professor from the Dairy Science Department, University of Florida, Gainesville, his views on feeding wax-coated cardboard to cattle. He tells me that ruminants cannot in fact metabolize wax like fats. He goes on to note that while he knows of no ill effects from feeding cardboard coated with wax, one could expect it to be from 25 to 30 percent less digestible than regular cardboard, and thus significantly less valuable per ton as a feed.)

After walking through the plant, we finally arrive in the cavernous rear warehouse, where whole railroad freight cars are parked and are being loaded with pallets of cartons by fork-lifts. Bruce and Johansen walk over toward one side, where ten or so automobile-size bricks of fuzzy brown matter (which looks as if it might be some kind of wall insulation) are stacked one on top of another.

"This is it," says Bruce, smiling rakishly and placing a hand proudly on one of the bales, which towers over his head.

Just then the warehouse is filled with a deafening noise, which comes from directly overhead and sounds like a four-engine propeller aircraft flying at full speed through the tops of a grove of large trees. "That's the grinder," yells Bruce, gesturing upward to a large device that is fastened overhead on the girders of the warehouse. "It's some baby. It's got a hundred-horse motor hooked up to it. First, it really tears hell out of those boxes, then it dumps them down here into this compactor." Bruce points to a square green device on the floor that compresses the ground cardboard into the huge fuzzy bricks that lie piled behind us like a pulp Stonehenge on the set of a low-budget film.

"I buy this stuff for sixty-five dollars a ton," Bruce yells into my ear, having to get so close to make himself heard over the high-pitched whine of the grinder, that I can feel the warmth of his breath. "It can handle ten tons of waste a day."

Leaving Bruce and Johansen to talk cardboard boxes, I climb the narrow steel ladder that leads up to the shredding machine overhead. I am just surveying the warehouse and thinking how even carton boxes ultimately raise the metaphysical question of what is waste and what is not when the whole catwalk starts vibrating as if it were being shaken by a powerful earthquake. A cyclone of cardboard scraps comes blasting through a pneumatic tube from the workshops and hits the blades of the oversized Waring blender behind me with a roar. In an instant it is transformed from waste boxes into cattle feed, soon to become milk and meat.

Gripping the rail around my precarious perch, I glance down to the floor. Johansen has gone off to talk with a forklift operator. Bruce stands alone below me, dwarfed by the immensity of the warehouse. A flurry of shredded cardboard is sifting down from where I stand and settling slowly on his Frito-Lay cap like a thin dusting of snow.

3

When I pull into the Fred Diehl Dairy on the outskirts of Dodge City, it is a hot Kansas summer day. I find Fred Diehl himself sitting alone in the processing room watching his wife and several employees pasteurize and bottle the day's milk. Even though he has not been working today, Fred looks tired. The fact is that over the last several years, he has been feeling so weak that he has hardly been able to work at all.

When I ask him what went wrong, he just rubs his brow as if to soothe a headache and replies, "Well, it was a couple of years ago. The flies were so thick on the cows that summer that a person pretty near had to do something. A salesman showed up and sold me this sprayer that had a trigger on it so that it went off automatically and sprayed my cows with Vapona each time they left the milking parlor. I'm not denying it helped keep the flies down pretty good, but the wind used to blow right back through the door off the prairie, and after breathing that mixture of Vapona and diesel for a while I got a cough. When I went to see a doctor he looked down my throat and told me that I had a cold."

Diehl talks in a thin voice, which is barely audible over the noises in the dairy. While he speaks he keeps running his hand across his pale brow and through his graying hair as if he were trying to massage away a deep inner pain.

"Those pesticides ruined my husband's lungs," interjects Diehl's wife bluntly from behind him where she is ringing up sales from the day's milk on an old cash register to the steady stream of local customers. "Now he coughs all the time, has no energy and feels awful. That's what that spray did to him." She looks down at her husband on the chair before her with an expression of pain and frustration. Then, as if she did not wish to appear too abject over her husband's condition, she turns and busily begins to carry just-sealed cases of chocolate milk into a walk-in cooler.

"We're the only small dairy open around here now. But I'm not really up to it. My wife does pretty much everything these days," says Diehl softly, staring out the window where an old delivery truck with flat tires and side panels that read, "Diehl Dairy. Farm Fresh," is parked under a cottonwood tree—a reminder of better times.

"It got to the point where that spray was just driving me crazy," continues Diehl. "Of course I was suspicious, so finally I went on over to the University of Oklahoma Hospital and told the doctors something real bad was wrong with me. They put a thing down my lungs and took a tissue sample. When I asked them what was wrong, they just said it was 'farmer's lung' and wouldn't go any further except to tell me that they had seen quite a few guys like me."

Diehl gives a muffled cough. "Now, I can't prove that it was that pesticide that done this thing to me," he finally continues dispiritedly, "but I'll tell you something, I never smoked in my life, and now I can't hardly breathe without my medication."

"That sprayer should never have been in the doorway. It should have been far away from this building," says Diehl's wife, returning to her post at the cash register. "But that salesman said, 'No! Go right ahead and put it on the milking-parlor door.' So we did." She gives an exasperated smile.

"When I finally figured out what the hell was going on, I took the whole damn sprayer right to the dump," says Diehl, the memory of this final decisive act making him smile wanly.

"Now besides my medication I got this breathing machine. When that doesn't work, I go to the hospital, and they give me something in my veins."

Fred Diehl's cows are not the only ones bothered by flies. Flies cause animals to interrupt their grazing and feeding as well as causing the spread of serious diseases such as pinkeye and IBR (infectious bovine rhinotraceitis).

An "Executive Summary" of the *Proceedings of the National Workshop on Livestock Insect Pest Management*, held at Kansas State University in 1979, estimated that the annual loss to the livestock and poultry industries from flies was around $4 billion. In 1979, some $60 million was spent on insecticides and associated costs for animals alone. The "Executive Summary" went on to note,

> Potential problems resulting from frequent applications of insecticides are contamination of meat, milk, eggs and the environment and the development of insecticide resistance by the insects. Current methods of livestock insect control are often inefficient and certainly expensive because of poor application methodology, improper timing and lack of understanding of pest biology.

Curiously, no mention was made of the hazards posed to the livestockmen, like Fred Diehl, who in 1983 was still not fully recovered.

There are two general kinds of flies that bother livestock—those that bite and those that suck. Sucking flies, such as the face fly and housefly, feed with their spongelike mouths on liquid material found around the eyes, mouth and nose or wounds of animals.

Biting flies, such as horn flies, stable flies, horseflies and deerflies, have mouths that are actually capable of piercing the flesh of animals and sucking out blood. Tests have shown that severe infestations of such flies can irritate cattle to the point where they can lose as much as half a pound a day.

There are numerous chemical sprays on the market for the control of flies around livestock. Vapona, which Fred Diehl used, is one of the most popular.

The active ingredient in Vapona is DDVP, or dichlorvos (2-2 dichloroethynyl phosphoric acid dimethyl ester), which is also known by a host of other trade names that sound like those of the dramatis personae in a *Star Trek* series. Besides Vapona, they include Benfos, Cekusan, Dedevap, Kerkol, Mafu, Nogos, Nuvan, Oko and several more explicit but prosaic names, such as Fly-Die, Duo-Kill, Fly Bait. The most common nonagricultural uses of dichlorvos are for fumigating aircraft and household No-Pest strips.

Much controversy has surrounded the use of Vapona around humans. Even the very low but prolonged levels of Vapona that humans might inhale as a result of having No-Pest strips inside their house has caused debate in the scientific community.

The World Health Organization has set its Acceptable Daily Intake of Vapona at 0.004 mg/kg, an amount that is exceeded by a person who stays indoors with one small No-Pest strip for nine hours, not to mention the daily blasting that a man like Fred Diehl (and presumably other feedlot workers) get through even the most careful livestock spraying program.

The active ingredient in Vapona, dichlorvos, is a clear organophosphorus liquid manufactured by the Diamond Shamrock Corp. It is listed on the National Institute for Occupational Safety and Health's "Emergency Medical Treatment for Acute Poisoning" chart in bold red letters as "Highly Toxic."

For labeling purposes, the Environmental Protection Agency divides up the more than four hundred registered insecticides (comprising some thirty thousand formulations) into three major groupings: "Danger Poison" (highly toxic), "Warning" (moderately toxic) and "Caution" (slightly toxic).

Vapona, or dichlorvos, falls in the first category, which means that "Danger Poison" must be clearly written on all insecticide containers and that the labels must advise users that Vapona is "Poisonous if swallowed, inhaled or absorbed through skin. Do not contaminate foodstuffs."

Like all organophosphates, dichlorvos is an anticholinesterase nerve poison. Although much less toxic, it is in the same family of compounds as Sarin and other nerve gases manufactured and stockpiled by various governments for chemical-warfare purposes.

Acetylcholinesterase (true cholinesterase) is an enzyme that plays a critical role in the functioning of the nervous system. When a nerve impulse jumps across a synapse, causing a muscle to articulate, it is transmitted by a substance called acetylcholine. But in order for that impulse to terminate properly so that the muscle can again relax, the acetylcholine must be destroyed and removed from the synapse. This is the role of acetylcholinesterase. Without it, a nerve will go into over-stimulation, causing severe muscular spasms, convulsions and ultimately paralysis and death. Organophosphates have a strong anticholinesterase effect, causing an overabundance of acetylcholine at the synapses and thus a breakdown of control in the nervous system.

Common symptoms of organophosphate nerve poisoning are involuntary defecation and urination, contraction of the pupils, blockage of the respiratory system (which tends to fill with liquids that cannot be expelled) by the contraction of bronchial muscles, as well as brain dysfunctions symptomatized by irritability, disorientation and lethargy, conditions with which Fred Diehl was all too familiar.

A leaflet put out by the University of California Division of Agricultural Sciences entitled "Fly Control on the Dairy" lists Vapona as having a "high toxicity to man" and warns in bold-face, "Do not use in milk rooms. Do not spray feed or contaminate water. Do not spray animals. Thoroughly flush mangers and watering troughs after application."

In the case of the Diehl Dairy, which has a reputation around

Dodge City for providing wholesome milk—"People come here and buy because they say the milk just tastes better than at a big store," Fred Diehl had told me—the sprayer, which blew a mist of Vapona back into the milking parlor onto Fred and the room where the dairy products were processed, could have been contaminating the milk as well as Fred Diehl's lungs.

Of course, milk cows are not the only animals to be sprayed with such insecticides as dichlorvos. In feedlots raising beef cattle, it is not uncommon to see large tractor-driven sprayers equipped with banks of high-pressure nozzles being driven down access roads, fogging the pens and sometimes the animals inside with a cloud of poison.

In larger feedlots, where such application by tractor is time-consuming and often ineffective, managers sometimes turn to aerial spraying. Crop-dusting aircraft are employed to fly back and forth over the cattle pens and spray the feedlot with insecticide from above. Generally this sort of application is done in the early morning, when it is more or less wind-still. The slightest breeze, of course, is capable of blowing the spray off target, so that people, animals and property downwind may end up being at least partial recipients of any insecticide applied in this fashion.

Another way in which people and animals may become exposed to toxic farm chemicals is through improper disposal of residues. This is a major problem for residues of compounds that are used for "dipping," where the complete body of an animal is immersed in an insecticide bath to kill scabies-producing lice. Farmers are legally required to take residues of insecticides (which can amount to hundreds or even thousands of gallons) to specially licensed toxic-waste-disposal sites. But since the transport of such materials is extremely inconvenient and costly, farmers will often seek alternative methods of disposal. For instance, one Illinois livestock operation I visited had a swim-through dip tank for pigs that was full of lindane, a highly toxic organophosphate used to control hog lice. When the farmer was finished running his pigs through the dip, he was left with several hundred gallons of muddy but highly toxic waste. His solution was to suck it up with his honey wagon (manure-disposal truck) and spray it out onto the surrounding cornfields.

Although the spraying of insecticide is still the most common means of getting rid of flies around livestock, the industry has recently developed a whole host of intriguing new technologies. For instance, Universal Cooperatives, Inc., in Alliance, Ohio, has come up with a curious alternative to spraying. They have developed something they call Insectaway, a paint that contains the insecticide chlorpyriphos. When this EPA-approved anti-insect paint is applied to buildings, crystals of chlorpyriphos bond to the surface, so that when insects land, the sticky secretions from their legs dissolve some of these crystals, making them absorbable and deadly.

"Most insecticide sprays used in farm buildings and in the home are effective for only a short time . . . whereas Insectaway . . . keeps killing insects month after month for up to three years," proclaims a flyer from Universal Cooperatives, Inc. This "war paint" comes in semigloss and can be used on "exterior and interior walls and ceilings of farm buildings, barns, confinement buildings, schools, warehouses, and every room in the house."

The promotional flyer does not explain what happens when it rains on an exterior surface or when a child with sticky hands leans against an interior wall of a freshly painted family rumpus room.

At the Colorado Cattlemen's Association Convention in Greeley, Colorado, I meet John Evans, a tall blond man in his late twenties who majored in entomology at Gustavus Adolphus College in Minnesota and who is executive director of the

Colorado Insectory, in Durango. While Evans mans the insectory's trade booth at the convention, he explains to me another, quite different concept of fly control called IPM, or integrated pest management.

"We don't believe that sprays or chemicals alone are an effective or safe way to control flies," he begins. "We've been working with a completely different idea. We're selling predator wasps to ranchers and feedlot operators who have fly problems. In fact, if you look carefully here, you'll be able to see some of our wasps right inside."

Evans lifts a glass chemist's jar stoppered with a large cork off the folding table in front of him and proffers it to me for inspection. Peering inside, I see hundreds of small brown fly pupae about the size of rice grains lying on the bottom. Flying above them are a number of miniature delicate wasps no larger than gnats, which make lazy loops around the inside of the jar.

"The idea of using one insect to control another is quite a basic one," says Evans. "And we think that we are selling a good way to control flies around livestock with these wasps. What they do is stop the reproductive cycle of the fly by burrowing down into the manure and either eating the fly's pupae or laying their eggs in them."

Just behind Evans is a promotional display that shows a blowup photo of two of his wasps perched on the opposite ends of a football-shaped object. Evans tells me that one of the wasps in the photo is just laying its eggs in the fly pupa, while the other, looking weak and wobbly like a chick just emerging from an egg, has just hatched out of the destroyed fly pupa.

What Evans's Colorado Insectory does is to market fly pupae that have been parasitized with eggs by these predator wasps, either the species *Spalangia endius* or the species *Pachycrepoideus vindemaie*, two species that not only are tiny but also neither buzz nor sting. Not only that, but once a colony is started, they reproduce themselves. When the first generation of parasitized wasps hatch out, they will in turn search out new prey and deposit their eggs in freshly pupated maggots.

"Effective control of flies has long been an elusive goal of man," says a promotional brochure from the Colorado Insectory entitled "Biological Fly Control." "Since World War II chemical agents have been the primary weapon. Now increased resistance of fly populations, widespread ecological damage and prohibitive costs necessitate other methods. Biological fly control is a process of combating flies by importing their natural enemies."

"Sure, there are a lot of feedlots where they still just go out there and spray the whole place with chemical insecticide," says Evans. "And it's true, in one day they can kill almost every fly. But chemicals are expensive—and guess what? The next morning it's just the same again because a whole new generation of flies has hatched out. The chemicals just knock the flies out of the air, but because they don't stop the reproductive cycle, they have no long-lasting effect. I've seen feedlots where they spray regularly, and still the hired hands have to turn on their windshield wipers in order to see through the windows of their pickups as they drive around inspecting pens."

Evans pauses to hand out a brochure and a name card, inscribed with the Colorado Insectory's motto, "Rearing beneficial insects for pest control," to a curious cattleman.

It is late Friday afternoon when Evans turns into the Tom Cooper Feedlots in Fort Morgan, Colorado, to deliver start-up colonies of wasps to a new client. He parks in a dusty lot next to a patch of green new sod that has been rolled out in front of a small office building in an apparent attempt to gussy up the entrance.

"Arch. The people are here with that wasp deal," announces Peggy, the feedlot office manager, over her CB radio once we have entered the air-conditioned coolness of the room in which she works. "We didn't do anything for the flies here last year," she says dispiritedly, looking out a picture window to the truck scales just outside. "Oh my God, it was something! You'd look out the window, and the glass would be black. I had to spray my way out of here at night. So this year we figured we'd better do something. Maybe get a crop duster to come in here and spray the whole place." She gestures out the window to where twenty thousand head of cattle mill about in the heat.

Evans has just unloaded a cardboard box filled with bags of parasitized fly pupae outside, when the feedlot foreman, Arch Tadolini, pulls up in a bright-red four-wheel-drive pickup, along with another cowboy.

Tadolini, a middle-aged man, and his younger comrade appear to have already begun weekend festivities. Beside them on the front seat of their truck is a cool, sweating six-pack of beer with several cans missing.

"Even though it's late in the afternoon, I'd like to show you how these wasps work," Evans tells Tadolini after introductions have been made. Tadolini does not look thrilled at this prospect. But Evans presses on. He takes several of the tiny parasitized fly pupae out of a brown-paper bag, and like a jeweler raising a precious stone to the light, holds one between thumb and forefinger and inspects it. Then, very painstakingly, he breaks it open to reveal the small, fragile wasps curled up inside.

"Hey. Watch out there, Arch! One of them little buggers might eat you up!" says the cowboy, rearing back in mock fear from Evans and slapping Tadolini on the back.

"Are you telling me that those little guys will actually eat up flies?" says Tadolini, shaking his head in disbelief, apparently unable to imagine how these minuscule wasps could ever be expected to devour a large fly.

"Well, you have to remember that it will take a few weeks before these wasps start showing any effect," explains Evans patiently. "First we have to build up the population so that they can compete with the flies. Each adult female fly can lay up to eight hundred eggs at one time, and under the right moisture conditions these eggs will grow into maggots in about seven to eight days. A few days later the maggots will start seeking drier ground where their outer surface will be able to harden into a dry brown shell. This is their pupal stage, when our wasps are able to attack them by parasitizing their pupae with their own eggs. The young wasps are then able to feed off the contents of the fly pupae inside as they develop.

"Actually, it would be helpful if your people could walk around with us as we distribute the parasites in the pens," says Evans, turning to Tadolini and picking up several bags full of pupae.

Tadolini, who has been listening without much interest, immediately deputizes the young cowboy to make the rounds with Evans. Then, bidding us good-bye, he gets back in the truck and starts the engine. Just before he drives away, we hear the hissing sound of a can of beer being opened.

Out on the feedlot it is searingly hot and dry. Other than the cattle, the fences, the feed bunkers and the huge bulldozed piles of manure that rise up in the center of each pen like mountains on the moon, the landscape is utterly barren. Clouds of dust, which form into miniature tornado-like swirls, sweep back and forth across the pens, so that in a matter of minutes the inside of my nostrils are coated with a powdery film.

"Okay. Let's stop here for a moment," says Evans, pausing before a muddy puddle left over from the last rain that is already beginning to crust over under the hot sun. "This is the kind of place we want to hit with the wasps, because this moisture is exactly what the fly eggs need to hatch out."

Like a prospector searching an outcropping of rock for a vein of gold, Evans falls to one knee in the next pen and begins to inspect a clod of manure. "All right. If you look here, you can see some fly eggs, just beginning to develop into maggots," he says, pointing with a pencil tip toward an encrustation of tiny white particles that, to the naked eye, appear like grains of sand. "It won't be long before these are into the pupal stage and spewing out flies like ash from Mount Saint Helens."

Evans stands up and casts several handfuls of parasitized fly pupae around like a farmer broadcast-seeding a freshly tilled field.

Moving over toward a line of feed bunkers, Evans stops to inspect another clod of manure. Scraping away a whole cache of dehydrated maggots that never made it to the pupal stage because they did not have a sufficiently moist environment, Evans explains, "The wasps are capable of burrowing into the manure, but they can still be killed by sprayed insecticides. When someone uses these chemicals, it disrupts a whole eco-system out here. The result is that the sensitive insects, like our wasps, get killed, and the hardier ones, like the flies, are left to multiply."

As we pass a dead calf, born to an accidentally bred heifer, whose body is crawling with maggots, Evans scatters another handful of parasitized pupae on the ground. By now the sun has worked its way down near the horizon. The first cool of evening is just beginning to settle over Tom Cooper Feedlots. Evans scoops the last few handfuls of fly pupae out of the last brown-paper bag and sprinkles them under a feed bunker that is wet from cattle urine. It is time to head back.

For five minutes or so we walk silently down one of the long dusty access roads that divide the pens of this vast bovine factory. As we near the office, Evans finally says, "We're not entirely against sprays, but we have to advise our clients to be careful so that they don't kill our wasps along with the flies. All I think we're trying to do is to get people to under-stand that chemicals are not the only answer."

In spite of the biological methods of control that have re-cently been developed and marketed by businesses like the Colorado Insectory, for most cattlemen "the answer" to fly problems is still chemicals. Wary of anything as new as "integrated pest management," but also increasingly concerned about the high costs, inefficiency and dangers of chemical sprays, many cattlemen are turning to another recently approved group of products called oral larvicides, which are insecticides that are mixed into animal feed and actually fed to livestock. Instead of using sprayers which make air the vector for an insecticide, these feed additives, or "pass-through" insecticides, simply avail themselves of an animal's gastrointestinal tract as a delivery system. The insecticides go into the mouth, through the stomach and intestines, and are then eliminated in manure, which they have rendered chemically toxic to the egg stage of the fly's life cycle.

To date the Environmental Protection Agency, which handles government approval for all insecticides (even when they are designed to be ingested), has approved several compounds for oral use. The most widely marketed is Rabon (trichlorvonphos [2-chloro-1 a,4,5, trichlorphenyl]vinyl dimethyl phosphate), which, like Vapona (dichlorvos), is an organophosphate. Originally patented by the Shell Chemical Co., Rabon is now manufactured by the Animal Health Division of Diamond Shamrock. Ciba-Geigy makes a similar product for chickens called Larvadex.

And what does this curious comestible for livestock look and taste like? It is a musty-odored substance, which comes in forty-pound bags of off-white granules that cost about one dollar a pound. For those cattlemen whose animals are out to pasture (and thus not consuming a feed into which an additive can be mixed), Rabon also comes incorporated into salt- or molasses-lick blocks.

The initial technical bulletin compiled by Shell Chemical Co. notes that "Rabon larvicidal rations may be fed to breeding cattle, lactating dairy cattle, or growing-finishing cattle in either dry lot or on pasture," and that it can be fed continuously to an animal while it is being milked as well as right up to the time it is slaughtered.

"We recommend about fifty to seventy milligrams per hundred pounds of body weight be fed to every animal each day," says M. G. Scroggs, a veterinarian who is manager of development and technical services at Diamond Shamrock, when I speak to him on the phone.

"Rabon is an organophosphate that reacts with the cholinesterase of maggots living in manure [just like Vapona] by overstimulating their nervous system so that they go into convulsions and die," continues Scroggs cheerfully. "One of its strongest features is that it remains active in manure for about three weeks after the cow eliminates it."

"Are any harmful residues absorbed through an animal's digestive system that might end up in meat or milk?" I ask Scroggs.

"There may be very small amounts absorbed," he replies. "But these are quickly metabolized and leave no residues above the allowable tolerance levels."

What if people ate Rabon?

"Oh, I don't know," says Scroggs, laughing. "The chances are it wouldn't bother them. It has a very low mammalian toxicity."

"Have there been any other problems with Rabon?" I ask, wary by nature of any poison that might be fed to a meat animal.

"If someone dumped a whole bunch of it into a stream or if a whole lot of it ran off from a feedlot into a lake, it could be toxic to fish," replies Scroggs. "But actually, we really haven't had any big problems with it, other than getting the compound approved by the EPA."

4

As soon as I step through the doorway from the cool fresh air outside, I am overcome by a powerful aroma, which smells like a mixture between a confectioner's shop and a public restroom in which the air-freshening machine has gone awry.

Once inside, I am greeted cheerfully by a receptionist who asks my name, squires me to a lobby couch and then disappears down a carpeted hallway.

"Mr. Schell is here to see you, Mr. Tribble," I hear her say.

"Well, fine. Tell Mr. Schell I'll be with him in a moment," I hear a male voice, with a suggestion of a Southern drawl, reply.

I have come here to Northbrook, Illinois, an industrial suburb of Chicago, to visit Dr. Talmadge B. Tribble, founder of the Flavor Corporation of America (a division of Agrimerica, Inc.), which develops, manufactures and markets synthetic feed-additive flavors and aromas to improve the appeal of feeds for animals.

I first became aware of "the exciting new science of animal-feed-flavor chemistry" (as Tribble puts it in one of his company's brochures) in a livestock-journal advertisement for one of Agrimerica's products called Ultra Sweet Pignectar. The ad described it as having that "original sweet sow milk flavor . . . [which] satisfies the 'sweet tooth' of baby pigs. . . . Just one pound provides the sweetening power of 100 pounds of sugar!"

A phone call to Northbrook revealed that not only did the

Flavor Corporation of America make a product that simulated the taste of a sow's milk, but it also made Ultra Sweet Calfnectar, which reproduced the taste of cow's milk, as well as a whole host of other flavors to stimulate the appetites of pigs, cows, horses, sheep, rabbits, cats, dogs and chickens. Moreover, I discovered that besides these flavors, Tribble's labs had created a whole line of synthetic aromas as well. "Aromabuds," which purportedly combined flavors and aromas, came (I was told) in twenty-four varieties (reminiscently similar to Howard Johnson's legendary twenty-eight flavors) and included such unlikely animal taste sensations as "Chocolate Milk," "Delicious Apple," "Jamaica Rum," "Licorice Stick," and "Roasted Almond."

Waiting now for my audience with Dr. Talmadge B. Tribble, I feel a little like Charlie in Roald Dahl's story just before he finally gains entrance to Willie Wonka's fabled chocolate factory.

As I wait in the lobby breathing the heavily scented air, I wonder why it is that animals that presumably have been contented to eat grasses, grains and other feeds for millennia now need to be coaxed to eat with such an elaborate battery of artificial inducements.

A brochure on the coffee table in front of me explains:

> As animal feed progresses toward perfect nutrition and promoted growth, and as the industry adopts least cost formulations, palatability problems occur. Antibiotics, wormers, growth stimulants, vitamins, mineral supplements and waste products often taste bad. But flavor and aromas can attract animals to feed and keep them on feed.

I think immediately of oral larvicides like Rabon, which was described as "musty" in a company brochure.

A blurb on "Aromabuds" goes on to note that "good flavor and nutrition in livestock feeds are equally important. A well-liked feed is more readily digested than one that is not palatable, and improved feed conversion [pounds of meat gained per pounds of feed consumed] is a natural consequence."

A copy of Agrimerica's newsletter, *Feed Sense*, explains how, "based on the pioneering research of Dr. Talmadge B. Tribble, a pharmaceutical chemist and founder of Agrimerica, we've learned animals' specific taste preferences by species and age, and have developed products for them."

I am just scanning a brochure on dog food (Tribble's canine flavors include "Bacon-juice," "Beef Hash," "Cheese Rind" and "Chicken-Gravy Liver Sausage"), when I look up to see a man walking down the hallway toward me. He introduces himself not as Talmadge B. Tribble but as Don Reisenberg, executive vice-president of Agrimerica.

Reisenberg, a mild-mannered, balding, thoughtful-looking man in a three-piece suit greets me and in hushed tones tells me, "Dr. Tribble is so glad you are here. He will receive you shortly."

Reisenberg and I retire to a meeting room, which, unlike the modern corporate style of the lobby area, is furnished in a curious mixture of decors that like an older woman who dresses up in the latest youth fashions, seems to be stylistically at war with itself. Like the lobby, the floor is covered with wall-to-wall carpeting, the chairs are fashionably contemporary and the walls are constructed out of minimalist-painted cement block. But mingled in with this corporate modernity is a mélange of other decorative items that are clearly from an earlier era.

An old-fashioned table with a slightly tilting marble top stands in the middle of the room. On one side there is an antique chemist's scale and a model of an old sailing vessel. The walls on the other side are adorned with a curious assortment of artwork, a yellowing photograph of a cow in an aging frame and three oil portraits with small hooded lights affixed to the tops of their frames so that they dominate the room like

ikons. The two side portraits, Reisenberg tells me, are like-
nesses of Tribble's sons. The center one, which is somewhat
larger and more imposing, is of Tribble himself.

I am just contemplating his imposing visage as portrayed
in the painting, when suddenly someone steps through the
doorway. The figure pauses just long enough for Reisenberg
to rise before regally continuing his entrance. Without speaking, he approaches the marble-topped table, puts down a
carved wooden cane and takes a seat. He scrutinizes me for a
moment, then nods his head and smiles as if granting approval.

This is Dr. Talmadge B. Tribble, seventy-nine years old. He
has a Kriss Kringle twinkle in his eyes, which are bespectacled
with horn-rimmed glasses. He has longish white hair, but is
slightly balder and has a few more lines on his thickset face
than in his portrait. But he still wears the same look of un-
shakable confidence. As I gaze back at him, I am struck immediately by his uncanny resemblance to Colonel Sanders of
Kentucky Fried Chicken fame.

"You might say that I am the grand progenitor of the
animal-feed-flavor industry," begins Tribble with patriarchal
immodesty. "I founded the Flavor Corporation of America in
1945. At the time I was also on the board of directors of
United Stockyards, which was a family-controlled company,"
he continues. "I was medically trained and could see that the
animals coming into our nine stockyards around the country
were under stress and not eating very well. These feed slumps
were taking a toll. So, I said to myself, 'Tribble, you've got
to find a way to get these animals on their feet!'

"Well, as a good Alabama boy who grew up on a small
farm, I knew a few old-time things. So I set out to see what
kinds of flavorings would make various animals want to eat
more."

As Tribble speaks, I begin to comprehend the unity of the
seemingly disjointed furnishings in the meeting room. Although Tribble is clearly a man who has been successful in

the modern corporate world, there is also an old-fashioned quality about him that is more suggestive of old oak furniture and clerks sitting around in green eyeshades and sleeve garters rather than of desktop computers. While the founder recounts his history of animal-feed flavors and aromas, I glance over at Don Reisenberg, clearly an embodiment of Tribble's more contemporary half. He is sitting quietly to the side, head respectfully lowered and hands clasped in his lap as Tribble speaks. If he has heard this historical narrative of the master before, he shows no sign of it now.

"I happen to have been blessed with a remarkable sense of smell," says Tribble, pausing, smiling and tapping the side of his nose with satisfaction. "I could and still can take a compound, smell it or taste it, and tell you what's in it. Taste and smell play an extraordinary part in the sensory apparatus of animals. A man has about nine thousand taste buds, whereas a cow has around thirty thousand. What I did was to just go out into the country and eat some green grass or a legume, take flavors like alfalfa, corn or other feedstuffs I knew animals liked and break them down chemically in my lab to analyze their structures into esters, ethers and so forth. That was long before we had gas chromatographers. When I identified a good flavor, I'd synthetically make some up myself and then run tests with it to see if animals would eat more when it was added to their feed.

"Here at Agrimerica we have a board of directors, and Don here is on it along with some of the other employees who I like to call 'Agrimericans,'" continues Tribble, as if he felt a brief précis of the command structure was required, although since I first laid eyes on Tribble there has not been the slightest doubt in my mind about who is in charge.

"Now, when I call a board meeting, we all sit down, and then I say, 'OK. Here's what we're going to do.' Then we do it!" Tribble gives a little explosion of laughter. "You see, I'm the president *and* the chairman of the board," adds Tribble.

"I've got all the stock right in my own pocket! I don't owe anybody or any bank anything, so I can afford to be auto-cratic."

As Tribble speaks, he fairly sparkles with smiling defiance. He evinces not the slightest apology for the way in which he dominates his company or the slightest contrition for the vast wealth he has evidently accumulated making artificial flavors and aromas for animals.

"What you see is mine!" he replies, making a sweeping gesture around the room as if he were a cattle baron surveying a twenty-thousand-acre ranch. "I have ten million dollars, and I intend to convert that to one hundred million before I am ninety-nine. I figure I've got twenty more years to enjoy mak-ing money." An elfin grin animates Tribble's face.

"I have two sons of my own, but they don't give a damn about chemistry," continues Tribble less enthusiastically and pointing to the dual portraits that flank his own on the wall. "So what I'm going to do is devote myself to pure research and appoint Don here as president." He looks at the future president of Agrimerica and gives an avuncular smile.

Reisenberg, who has been sitting in probationary silence as Tribble speaks, brightens considerably at the mention of his future investiture as president.

"But Don here will still have a boss. Don will be president, but I'll still be the chief executive officer," Tribble hastens to add, lest in acknowledging that he will soon renounce the office of president, I (and perhaps Reisenberg) get the mis-apprehension that the sun is about to set on the Tribble dynasty at Agrimerica.

"Now, where were we," says Tribble, leaning back sover-eignly in his chair, trying to find the thread of the conversa-tion that he has lost in this detour through the corporate chain of command.

"Feed flavors," reminds Reisenberg helpfully.

"Yes. Well, as I was saying, back in the forties, even though farmers were pouring huge quantities of molasses over feed to get animals to eat poor-tasting hay and grain, no one was very interested in feed flavors yet. Fifteen years of R and D went by before even I could develop a line of flavors that worked for each species of animal and their young. Over the years I developed some twelve hundred flavors, although we now actually only market about a hundred of them."

"Why not just give the animals corn, alfalfa and molasses like the old days and forget all the flavors?" I query when Tribble comes to a hiatus in his monologue.

"What is the object of feed?" asks Tribble rhetorically, rapping an outstretched forefinger on the conference table like a schoolteacher. "Feed is what makes animals grow. The idea is to stuff the animal with all the feed you can so that he will grow quickly and get off to market. Now, if an artificial flavor makes a feed, perhaps a poor-tasting feed, more palatable, the animals will naturally eat more."

I ask Tribble if he sees his flavors as competing with the various kinds of antibiotics and hormonal compounds that are also used as growth promotants in livestock.

"Absolutely not," exclaims Tribble, his brow furrowing in consternation. "Our products *help* animals utilize these sometimes off-tasting feed additives."

"And what about your work with aromas?" I ask.

(Tribble has written, à la Proust, in an article entitled "The Psychophysical Responses to Animal Feed and Smells," "The nose holds the key to the world of lively description that no other sense can unlock. Neither seeing, hearing, touching, or even tasting—so akin to smelling—can call up memories with such verity. . . . Odors can bring back unlimited memories to man, unimpaired by the lapse of time.")

"With the exception of chickens, which have no sense of smell at all, aroma is extremely important to animals," replies Tribble to my question. "Most animals will only eat what they can first smell. So here at Agrimerica we have a fine line of 'aroma boosters' as well as our flavors for sale."

"What's the aroma we are smelling right now?" I ask, referring to the fierce pungence pervading the conference room.

"It's just a conglomerate of all the aromas that we make out back. In spite of an elaborate ventilation system, they just continue to leak out," answers Tribble, the twinkle in his eye suggesting that perhaps he actually enjoys this constant olfactory reminder of his life's work.

"Oh, Lord, back when I was getting started, flavor was a dirty word," laments Tribble reflectively, with a distant look in his eye. "People thought this sort of thing for animals was just a big con game. Some called me Dr. Sharpie, as if I was trying to put something over on the public. It took fifteen years before I could get them to accept how important flavors and aromas are for animals.

"There's one thing I have been working on for years," says Tribble, suddenly leaning forward toward me across the conference table, his voice modulated to a low secretive whisper. "I've been in the lab trying to come up with one single flavor that can satisfy all species at once."

As he makes this confidential announcement, my mind is filled with images of a mad octogenarian scientist from some old movie, a demonic gleam in his eye, racks of test tubes bubbling and steaming, a white smock aflutter as he works feverishly in a drafty castle on the definitive synthetic flavor that will be so powerful that it will drive all species of livestock into frenzies of feeding.

"And now, at last, I have completed my work," announces Tribble triumphantly, picking a small brown glass bottle from off the tabletop and handing it to me.

"Go ahead," he urges, as if he were offering me a sample of his homemade jelly. "Take the top off and try some! I call it 'Omniflavor'!"

As soon as I have removed the top, a new aroma wells invisibly up out of the bottle, obliterating the already powerful background smell of all of Tribble's other products, the way a heavy mist will sometimes rise up off the ground, suddenly obscuring all the previously visible landmarks before one's eyes.

"Just touch a little to your tongue. There's not another product on the market anywhere in the world like it," says Tribble, goading me on with his own enthusiasm so that it is unthinkable that I demur.

The brown bottle is filled with tiny particles that look like dry coffee grounds. I reach my little finger into the bottle and dab one grain onto my tongue. Tribble and Reisenberg sit watching for my reaction as if they were waiting for a stick of dynamite with a lit fuse to explode.

As I smack my palate I am suddenly jolted with what is in fact an explosion of taste. It is an eerie feeling, for while the sensation is a massive one, which completely fills my mouth so that it seems to ring, there is actually nothing of substance in it but one tiny dissolved grain of Omniflavor.

"It's three separate things at once," says Tribble proudly. "It's an artificial sweetener, flavor and aroma all in one. One pound of Omniflavor is equivalent to a hundred pounds of sugar."

"Dr. Tribble has been working on this for twenty years," chimes in Reisenberg proudly. "Until now, however, the time has not been ripe to disclose it."

This last comment makes me feel somewhat ill at ease. I am wondering if they are using my presence as a journalist here at Agrimerica to announce their new product to the world. At the pace I write, Omniflavor will still be unknown in two years' time. I am just about to say something when Tribble gives his best Kentucky Fried Colonel smile and announces that if we wish to see the lab and mixing room, we'd better start now because it's almost closing time.

With Tribble, supported by his cane (he has recently broken a hip), in the lead, we file out of Agrimerica's executive offices. Stepping through a steel door, we are greeted by a new blast of concentrated sweetness even more intense than that in the conference room and find ourselves in the laboratory in which research is conducted.

As Tribble enters, a woman technician who is working over a piece of scientific equipment snaps to attention. He greets her warmly and, with a paternal hand on her shoulder, says, "All of our products are checked here with a gas chromatographer before they are shipped to our customers."

Walking slowly over to a long table, he picks up a plastic bag full of a gray powdery substance and hands it to me. "Smell it," he says with a sly smile. "Go ahead. See if you can smell it right through the bag." I raise the bag toward my nose and inhale. Even without opening the seemingly impermeable plastic, a sour, nauseating odor turns my stomach.

"That's guar meal," says Tribble, pleased that the smell has been so self-evident. "It has a very acrid smell and bitter taste, but it has about a forty-percent protein content [higher in crude protein than even soybean meal]. I've had it around here for six months trying to figure out how to mask its bad odor and taste so that we could use it for livestock feed. Now I've discovered the way to remove bitterness from saccharine and at the same time make it one thousand times sweeter, so I believe that in time I'll be able to get this meal to cooperate with me too." Tribble gives me a self-assured wink and then pats the bag of guar meal as if it were a small pet.

"Actually, these kinds of matters are really Don's specialty," says Tribble, turning toward Reisenberg, who has been standing quietly behind him.

"Well, you might say that these are our problem children," says Reisenberg, coming to life. "These bags here on the table are filled with various products and wastes that people send to us to see if we can invent ways to convert them into usable feeds." Reisenberg picks up a second plastic bag off the table-top and hands it to me. I give it a tentative squeeze. It contains a heavy, mushy substance the texture of tapioca. As Reisenberg explains, he is trying to figure out a way to suspend these fat particles in a liquid feed supplement so that they won't all sink to the bottom of a lickwheel tank.

"We are heavily involved here at Agrimerica with what we call recoverable resources," continues Reisenberg. "For instance, we've been doing some work for Weyerhauser, part of the large paper and forest product's company down in Oklahoma. They have a throwaway product of lignant sulfates high in ammonia that is left over after a paper-pulping process. Now, ammonia makes an excellent animal-feed ingredient. [Ammonia is a central compound that helps certain bacteria in a cow's stomach synthesize protein. These bacteria don't care whether the ammonia comes from the natural proteins in feed or from nonprotein sources, such as urea, as long as ammonia is present.] The problem with the Weyerhauser waste was that it had an aroma that would absolutely knock your hat off, and it looked exactly like a viscous black ink. I tasted some of that stuff once, and it seared the membranes in my throat." Reisenberg makes a face and grabs at his throat with both hands.

"What we had to do was to analyze the components in this waste and mesh them with products we developed here at Agrimerica so that this pulping waste could finally be consumed by cattle. And I'm proud to be able to tell you today that we have developed a flavor and aroma that now make this waste a recoverable feed resource." Reisenberg smiles with evident satisfaction.

"Quite frankly, Mr. Schell, it is my belief that recoverable resources are an area of animal-feed technology that no one has adequately looked into," continues Reisenberg. "The possibilities are almost limitless."

A brochure that Reisenberg later gives me describes Agrimerica's efforts to utilize nutritious wastes as "a solution to the problem of the constantly rising cost of conventional feed." It goes on to discuss what Tribble and Reisenberg call Newtrition, namely, their theory that "the same nutrients found in feed grains are available from a variety of other sources— both natural and man-made, sources that cost much less than feed grains."

One such source is waste cellulose—as Bruce and Vi Boyd down in Florida can attest—which is found in such varied end products as waste cardboard, paper, ground-up corncobs, straw, beet pulp, sugarcane fiber, wood chips and sawdust. Given the fact that agricultural cellulosic residues comprise over 50 percent of the solar energy utilized in cultivated plant life, one can understand Tribble and Reisenberg's fixation on them as a potential food source.

"There is an awful lot of this waste cellulose around," interjects Tribble. "If we could just convert six hundred million tons of it a year [a relatively small percentage of the whole] into usable animal feed, we would be able to nearly double the nation's agricultural capacity."

In his search for some kind of alchemy to enrich these sources of waste cellulose, Tribble has come up with an enzymatic substance called Agrimate, which he claims is capable of enhancing the food value of cellulose by predigesting it through fermentation into a more readily metabolizable form.

Cattle and other ruminants, unlike pigs, are capable of utilizing a raw cellulose (they are about 35 to 50 percent efficient, excreting the rest) by breaking it down into usable carbohydrates. By predigesting cellulose, Agrimate increases the nutrients that can be readily absorbed by ruminants, while at the same time making it a viable feed for nonruminant animals with monogastric stomachs, such as pigs.

Agrimerica is of course not alone in its quest to discover new and cheaper sources of animal feed. Numerous other companies and government agencies have been experimenting with a wide variety of truly "exotic" feeds in a search to cut costs and solve problems of waste disposal. For instance, researchers at the Finnish Agricultural Center report that they have come up with a new protein substance called Pekilo that can serve as a replacement for expensive fish and soybean meal. It is made from fungi that grow on the waste liquid from paper mills.

The U.S. Department of Agriculture's Research Service recently did a series of trials at their Beltsville, Maryland, research center in which they fed cement dust (high in calcium) to cattle as a supplement. They were surprised to find in their 112-day study that the test cows gained weight 30 percent faster than animals fed a normal diet of hay and grain. Two department scientists, William E. Wheeler and Robert Oltjen, claimed to find no abnormalities in the livers and other internal organs of the cattle when they were slaughtered. In fact, they reported that the beef from the cement-dust-fed cattle was more tender and juicy than that from cattle fed conventional rations.

"Tremendous amounts of cement-kiln dust are produced not only in this country but in many developing countries as well," reported Mr. Wheeler. "This opens up new avenues of research that could lead to low-cost production of quality beef."

Researchers at the University of Florida, Gainesville, have conducted feed tests with what they refer to as "manure roughage." "One of the most promising methods of cattle-manure disposal is recycling as livestock-feed ingredients," writes M. F. Richter in a recent issue of the *Journal of Animal Sciences.*

At first blush, the idea of feeding waste that has come out of one end of an animal back into the other is not a tremendously appealing one. But if one is aware, as Tribble and Reisenberg are, that of the roughly 30 billion tons of formulated feed fed to livestock and poultry in the United States, almost two-thirds will be deposited as partially digested animal waste (creating the country's single largest source of polluting organic waste), then the notion of finding ways to feed animal waste back to livestock becomes one of common sense if not cosmetic appeal.

And what effect does a diet supplemented with "manure roughage" have on the meat? After feeding diets of up to 60 percent recycled manure back to steers being fattened for slaughter, Richter reported that, "marbling, flavor juiciness, tenderness, and overall acceptance of the steaks was not affected."

In Alabama, cattlemen are turning to another inexpensive recycled feed, what is called poultry litter, which is composed of manure, feathers and old bedding from henhouses, combined with molasses and grain to make it palatable. "It's hard to mix, it's dirty and it's smelly," Bill Beasley, an Ariton, Alabama, commerical "poultry litter" retailer told a *Beef Magazine* interviewer. "But there's one thing about it . . . cows love it. We sell about all we can put together."

Beasley did admit to at least two problems with "poultry litter," namely its tendency to catch on fire through spontaneous combustion when it is stored and what he calls the people-acceptance factor of feeding chicken shit to cows. As Beasley jokingly noted, some people are hesitant to eat a "litter"-fed cow because they wonder "if they'll find a feather in their T-bones."

How good is the meat?

"It's as good as any I've ever eaten," proclaimed Beasley.

In the hog industry, it has been a common practice for some time to separate the undigested solids out of the manure that flows out of confinement barn gutters and feed it back to animals being fattened for slaughter.

But some of the most unusual experiments with what Reisenberg refers to as recoverable resources involve feeding hogs dried sludge from sewage plants used to treat human waste.

Although sludge from municipal sewage has proved to have adequate nutritional content to make it a "feasible" animal feed (crude protein level of about 25 percent), and although test animals eating up to 20 percent sewage sludge showed no immediately debilitating effects, one problem with it has so far proved insurmountable. Since it is impossible to control what people dump into their sinks and toilets, or what industries dispose of into public sewers, there is no way to prevent highly toxic substances from building up in the sewage sludge. When livestock consume such sludge, they in turn may become contaminated.

In fact, research recently done at the University of Florida in Gainesville showed a tenfold increase in lead and mercury, a twofold increase in cadmium and copper and elevated levels of PCBs (polychlorinated biphenyls) in the kidneys and livers of cattle fed a 15 percent diet of sewage sludge over a period of ninety-four days. The researchers also noted a decrease in body-weight gain of the animals.

As we leave the lab, once again Tribble is in the lead. Just as the intensity of heat increases as one draws closer to an open fire, so the intensity of smell has been growing as we have moved ever closer to its source, the Liquid Mixing Room. It is here, at one side of the warehouse, where the ingredients for Tribble's arsenal of flavors and aromas are electronically weighed and mechanically mixed in giant stainless-steel vats, that the smell is strongest.

Bacon Juice dog-food seasoning, Ultra Sweet Pignectar, Omniflavor, Wild Strawberry, Sweet Cream—the Liquid Mixing Room is the ecumenical meeting place for Tribble's whole pantheon of scents. In fact, all the aromas in the room wage such an intense combat for supremacy that I soon have a headache and yearn more than anything for the brisk, clear air of the outside.

Fifty-five-gallon drums of oils, alcohols and solvents, bottles and containers of Furfural, Flacoa, Invertase and other substances that sound as if they might be named after characters from a Tolkien novel are stored on shelves everywhere around the room.

"This is where we put it all together. That tank can hold a hundred gallons of liquid flavoring worth thousands of dollars," proclaims Tribble with proprietary affection as he taps one large mixing vat with the end of his cane.

By now it is well after five. Most Agrimericans have left for home. Except for some Muzak, which continues to play with an irritating softness, the Liquid Mixing Room is quiet and devoid of people.

As we stroll down corridor after corridor in the warehouse where silent forklifts stand beside tall racks stocked like a well-provisioned larder with Tribble's creations, Tribble and Reisenberg continue to regale me with their schemes and dreams of new mold inhibitors, all-purpose animal-feed flavors and aromas, wonder germ destroyers and miraculous new enzyme products capable of transforming the Sunday paper into steak, milk and pork chops. My mind begins to wobble. I am sated not only by the density of the odor, but also by the inventive energy and the seemingly endless succession of plans and ideas that gushes out of Tribble.

Just as my note taking begins to founder, Tribble leads us at last out through a door from the warehouse and back into the office section of the building. Reisenberg disappears while Tribble and I exchange small talk. When Reisenberg reappears several moments later, he is carrying a cap with a black-and-yellow Agrimerica chevron embossed on its crown. He presents it to me as if it were an award.

I put it on, although actually I feel a little foolish standing here in the lobby before Tribble and Reisenberg wearing this cranial advertisement as if I had just been inducted as an Agrimerican myself.

As I bid Tribble good-bye, Reisenberg unlocks the front door for me. With a grip every bit as firm as his remaining hold on Agrimerica, Inc., and the Flavor Corporation of America, Tribble shakes my hand and wishes me "all the luck in the world."

Still wearing my cap, I step into the crisp autumn air outside. Several hours later, as I drive through the darkness of central Illinois, my clothes still exude the curious sweet smell of Dr. Talmadge B. Tribble's emporium of artificial animal-feed aromas and flavors.

III

HORMONES

1

The human body is composed of a vast and complex conglomeration of cells that are coordinated by two pathways of communication: the nervous system and the endocrine system. The nervous system is essentially controlled by one organ, the brain, while the endocrine system is far more decentralized. Like a large territory that has no one single capital but is instead ruled by a number of far-flung regional power centers, the endocrine system is governed by means of a plethora of separate glands, tissues and organs, such as the hypothalamus, pituitary, thyroid, adrenal cortex, pancreas, ovary and testes. Spread throughout the body, these glands secrete various compounds into the bloodstream to form a network of chemical communication.

Since these hormonal messengers must travel through veins and arteries like maritime emissaries, endocrine communications move much more slowly than those of the nervous system, where a combination of electrical and chemical impulses move across synapses and nerves to the brain and back in a matter of milliseconds.

But for all its apparent sluggishness, the endocrine system nonetheless forms a masterfully effective network of communication. By means of minuscule amounts of highly active chemicals, it regulates a host of bodily functions including growth, metabolism, the reproductive cycle and the development of secondary sexual characteristics such as breasts, body hair and shape, voice changes and the onset of puberty and maturity.

This system of exquisitely well-integrated and interconnected biological controls can only function correctly, however, when it is in equilibrium; when the correct amount of each of the hundreds of different hormones ebbing and flowing through the bloodstream at any given moment are produced at the right time. An extremely small amount of one introduced exogenously (from the outside) or the failure of a gland to secrete quite enough of another endogenously (from within) can be enough to affect an important biological function. As one endocrinologist put it, if our taste buds were as sensitively attuned to flavors as target cells are to the appropriate hormones, our tongues would be able to detect several grains of sugar dissolved in a swimming pool full of water.

Hormonal imbalances can lead to a wide variety of disorders, such as obesity, infertility, diabetes, dwarfism, gigantism, kidney disease, hypertension, precocious puberty, hypoglycemia, masculinization of females, feminization of males and even cancer.

Sex hormones, one of the most important groups of hormones in the body, are generally divided into three types: androgens, progestogens and estrogens.

Androgens, such as testosterone, are male hormones produced in the testes that stimulate the activity of the male sex organs as well as the development of secondary male sexual characteristics, such as body shape, beard growth, pubic hair and voice change.

Progesterone—one of the progestogens—is a female hormone produced in the corpus luteum (a body of cells that forms over the ruptured egg follicle after ovulation in the female species) and helps prepare the uterus for implantation of the egg should fertilization take place.

Estrogens are hormones produced by the ovary and placenta

in females and in the testes, albeit in small quantities, in males. They stimulate the development of internal female sex organs and external secondary sexual characteristics, as well as regulating the menstrual cycles of women and the estrus, or heat, cycles of lower mammals.

Over the past three decades an increasing variety of natural and synthetic sex hormones have been used in raising livestock and poultry.

For reasons that are still incompletely understood, some sex hormones have an anabolic effect on the cells that are sensitive to them, namely, they cause those cells to synthesize protein and convert nutritive matter into living substance (such as muscle tissue) more rapidly than normal. This particular attribute has interested not only body builders intent on accumulating ever-greater muscle mass, but also animal scientists eager to find new ways to promote faster growth and greater feed efficiency in meat animals.

Since most of the hormonal growth promotants used on meat animals today contain estradiol (the most potent naturally occurring estrogen in mammals), it may be instructive by way of example to examine how this one sex hormone is produced, distributed and utilized by the mammalian body under natural conditions.

Like a Rube Goldberg machine where a ball falling off a tower into a pot causes water to overflow down a pipe and turn a dynamo that rings a bell, the production of estradiol begins when the hypothalamus secretes gonadotropin-releasing hormones (GnRH) into the bloodstream. The pituitary is stimulated by the GnRH to secrete gonadotropins—luteinizing hormones (LH) and follicle-stimulating hormones (FSH).

Traveling in the blood to the ovaries, the LH and FSH are picked up by cells around the egg follicle that have special LH- and FSH-sensitive receptors on their cell membranes. These receptors transmit a signal through the membrane (without the follicle-stimulating and luteinizing hormones ever actually entering the cell) by means of an enzyme called adenyl cyclase.

The adenyl cyclase stimulates the cell to produce a compound called cyclic AMP. It is this final burst of chemistry that triggers a cell to begin steroidogenesis, or the production of steroidal hormones such as estradiol. Suddenly now, surges of estradiol are released into the bloodstream in extremely low but active concentrations. And just as those ovarian and placental cells that produce estradiol have receptors that are sensitive to LH and FSH from the pituitary, so cells in certain other "target organs" (like the uterus, breasts and hypothalamus) have receptors that are sensitive to estrogens and are capable of taking up estradiol out of the vascular system as the blood is pumped past them by the heart.

Once an estrogen-sensitive receptor has absorbed a molecule of estradiol, it is channeled by the cell toward its nucleus. Upon reaching its target, the estradiol acts on the genetic material of the cell by stimulating the production of messenger RNA (ribonucleic acid), which in turn induces the cell, among other things, to synthesize protein more rapidly.

Sex hormones are, of course, only one constellation within a whole galaxy of hormones that interact to form the endocrine system. While each one is a separate chemical compound in its own right, they form a web of interaction that is so involved that authors of endocrinology texts often resort, by way of explanation, to visual aids which are such a muddle of arrows that they often resemble plans for razzle-dazzle football plays as much as they do medical diagrams.

But perhaps a more apt metaphor for the complexity of the mammalian endocrine system is that of an orchestra. Hormones, like individual instruments, may occasionally play brief solos, but they also play important passages together, cueing one another in—sometimes even resting—to create a rhythmically and harmonically intricate chemical score. As researchers have learned more and more about how the endocrine system functions, they have also learned how to manipulate it, not only to correct hormonal imbalances but to make it perform in new and unique ways.

Hormonal birth control pills are now widely used to suppress ovulation. Estrogens are given to women to counteract the effects of menopause. Transsexuals are administered massive doses of androgens and estrogens to reverse secondary sexual characteristics. Women with premenstrual syndrome (PMS) are now being given hormones to relieve severe cramps, tension and depression.

These advances in endocrine research have not gone unnoticed in the field of animal science. In fact, it would not be inaccurate to say that man's new ability to manipulate the mammalian endocrine system with both natural and synthetic hormones has revolutionized the process of raising livestock. It is a revolution in which one can not only discern an enormous scientific and technical ingenuity but also a certain blindness and hubris. For what is often forgotten is that hormones, substances that are active even in the minutest amounts, are now mass-produced and used with an unnerving indiscrimination. Not only are these compounds capable of bringing about the kind of imbalance of the endocrine system that I have described, but by exciting tissue cells that are sensitive to them, hormones are also able to promote carcinogenesis.

The recognition that sex hormones can be dangerous as well as beneficial to humans, and that they are now widely used in the production of livestock as well as in human therapy, has caused many people to become fearful of eating meat and in some cases to become vegetarians. Although the nature and potential danger of these drugs is often misunderstood, this wariness about their increasingly widespread use and presence in our environment is prudently cautious. For the truth is, we still do not know very much about the nature and long-term effects of increased burdens of sex hormones.

Who makes these animal drugs? How do scientists view their advent as commercial agricultural tools? How does the government endeavor to regulate their use and inspect meat to assure that harmful residues do not occur?

An incident that I became aware of one day while visiting the FDA's Washington headquarters in 1980 set me off on a three-year inquiry to find answers to some of these questions.

2

"We are going to take immediate action, including criminal sanctions against the violators. This drug has been used in plain violation of the law. We've got fifty thousand head of cattle out there illegally implanted with DES, and we're going to have to do something about it."

The speaker is Wayne Pines, associate commissioner of the Food and Drug Administration (FDA) for public affairs. Pines is an intense man in his thirties, with a beard and a head of curly black hair, and he wears wire-rimmed glasses. He has been talking on the phone in his Washington, D.C., office almost all morning. The desk at which he sits is overflowing with papers; even his briefcase, open beside him on the floor, is engorged with unattended business.

"I feel like I have been in the middle of a hurricane," he says with a weary smile when he finally hangs up. The "hurricane" Pines is referring to has been caused by the revelation that DES (diethylstilbestrol)—a synthetic estrogen commonly used as a growth promotant in meat animals since the 1950s and finally banned in 1979 after years of legal wrangling—has actually continued to be used illegally on a widespread basis. As the parent agency for both the Bureau of Foods (which sets acceptable residue levels of drugs and chemicals in food), and the Bureau of Veterinary Medicine (which approves animal drugs and sets guidelines for their use), the FDA is deeply involved in this affair.

DES, which was discovered in the 1930s, and became the

first inexpensive synthetic estrogen used in human therapy, was an ideal livestock-feed additive, since unlike other natural estrogens, it was capable of being absorbed through the gastro-intestinal tract after oral administration. Cattlemen were extremely pleased with DES. After all, according to the government's Office of Technology Assessment, DES increased weight gain from 15 to 19 percent and feed efficiency from 7 to 10 percent in steers.

DES would doubtless have continued to be used without challenge as a livestock-growth promotant were it not for the fact that in 1966 Dr. Arthur L. Herbst, a young gynecologist working at Massachusetts General Hospital in Boston, became aware of a fifteen-year-old girl with clear-cell adenocarcinoma of the vagina. It was the first time that anyone at the hospital had seen this rare kind of cancer in any female under the age of twenty-five.

In the next three years, six more cases of young women with clear-cell adenocarcinoma turned up at the hospital. Perplexed, Herbst and several colleagues began to make a study. They finally published their findings in the *New England Journal of Medicine* in 1971. What they had found was that the mothers of all the girls, save one, had received DES therapy (consist-ing of doses from 2.5 to 150 mg daily for as long as 212 days) while pregnant to prevent miscarriage. Not only was DES linked to the cancers, but for the first time doctors had grounds to suspect that other estrogenic compounds might be carcino-genic as well.

According to Herbst's last tally in 1980, 429 women between the ages of seven and thirty-one had developed clear-cell adenocarcinoma of the vagina. The mothers of 243 of these women were known to have been treated with DES during pregnancy. (Another 57 mothers had been treated for high-risk pregnancies with other types of hormonal therapies.) The mortality rate of this type of cancer has been approximately

50 percent. It is estimated that between 3 and 6 million women received estrogen therapy between 1941 and 1971.

Some of the male offspring of mothers who underwent these DES treatments were also affected, suffering congenital malformations of their reproductive organs, such as abnormally undersize penises, undescended and atrophied testicles, and abnormalities in sperm production.

When animals were exposed to DES in laboratory tests, they became sterile and frequently showed other malfunctions of the reproductive system as well as increased rates of uterine, vaginal, ovarian and mammarian cancer.

Researchers are still not quite sure what it is about DES that makes it carcinogenic, although in view of the fact that all natural estrogens are known to be cancer causing, they suspect that it may have something to do with its estrogenic activity. However, since DES is different from natural estrogens in chemical structure (it belongs to the stilbene rather than the steroid family of compounds), it is possible that its carcinogenic potential comes from another of its properties, or even from one of its metabolites (those numerous compounds into which it is broken down by an animal's metabolism), which are very different from the metabolites of natural estrogens.

In reviewing all the extant literature on the subject, the International Agency for Research on Cancer noted simply in its monograph "Sex Hormones" (part of its series *The Evaluation of Carcinogenic Risks of Chemicals to Humans*) that "diethylstilbestrol is causally associated with the occurrence of cancer in humans."

Administrative Law Judge Daniel J. Davidson, who ultimately recommended that the drug be banned in 1978, put it this way: "The agent(s) which cause the ill effects of DES are unknown. It could be its conjugate form or any one of several DES metabolites, some of which remain uncharacterized. The present detection methods cannot reveal the presence of most of these chemicals. When DES and its conjugates have been detected [in meat], they have occurred at levels very close to those that have produced cancer in animals . . . Therefore, DES lacks the necessary prerequisites to support a finding of safety . . ."

Both protagonists and antagonists of the continued use of the drug in livestock more or less agree that DES *does* cause cancer. But what they disagree about, sometimes vociferously, is the amount of DES required to make it cancer causing. Although protagonists acknowledge that the administration of massive doses of DES to pregnant mothers was ill advised, (and, as it turned out, useless as well), they are quick to point out that while the mothers were getting up to 150 mg each day for prolonged periods of time, a cow ingesting DES feed additives or implanted subcutaneously in the ear with a 36-mg pellet (which slowly releases its ingredients into the bloodstream over approximately 120 days) was only receiving about 0.025 mg a day, 600 times less than the daily dose given to DES mothers.

The Council on Agricultural Sciences and Technology (CAST), a research organization funded by the agricultural industry as well as various drug and chemical companies, took such a position in their report, "Hormonally Active Substances in Food: A Safety Evaluation," issued in 1977. They claimed that "from 1973 through the second quarter of 1976, no residues could be detected at the five parts per billion level in 99.4 percent of the 9,426 beef livers analyzed" by the FDA under the U.S. Department of Agriculture's residue-monitoring program and that "except under conditions of gross illegal overdosages, DES cannot be detected in muscle meat."

They calculated that the exposure that humans might get from DES residues in meat were 600,000 times less than the amount of estrogen in oral contraceptives. In their view, the benefits of using DES as a livestock-growth promotant far outweighed the risks, particularly since (according to CAST's calculations) DES saved farmers 7.7 billion pounds of feed a year, by enabling animals to gain slaughter weights more quickly.

However, the Delaney Clause, passed as an amendment in 1958 to the Federal Food, Drug and Cosmetic Act of 1938, states that "no food additive shall be deemed safe if it is found to induce cancer when ingested by man or animal . . ." Since DES was an undisputed carcinogen, this amendment should have effectively ended its use as a growth promotant in meat animals. But the Congress passed another amendment in 1962, the Kefauver-Harris Drug Amendment, or "DES Proviso," which made an exception for the drug's continued use. The proviso exempted DES from the Delaney Clause if the drug's manufacturers provided users with a set of directions that were "reasonably certain to be followed in practice," provided the FDA with a "prescribed and approved" technique for assaying residues and as long as no residues showed up in meat.

What conspired against the continued use of DES in the 1970s, the DES Proviso notwithstanding, was not only the bad publicity the drug had begun to get because of Herbst's revelations about the problems with the so-called DES daughters, but also the fact that techniques for detecting residues of drugs and chemicals in food had in general become more advanced.

Whereas in the early years of DES use it had been difficult to detect residual compounds in a tissue at less than parts per million, new technology and more sophisticated instruments now made it possible to detect them in parts per billion and trillion. This meant that while residues may not actually have grown in quantity or frequency, some meat that earlier had been tested and passed under the provisions of the DES Proviso was now showing up with "violative" residues. "Radioisotope studies combined with gas-liquid chromatography have shown that under the conditions of use upon which the application was approved [under the DES Proviso stipulations], DES and/or its conjugate finds its way into the heart, liver, muscle and kidneys of beef cattle," noted Daniel J. Davidson in his 1978 administrative law court opinion calling for the ban of DES. "The limited recovery of these chemicals has been up to 0.1 part per billion."

In at least one other case, a USDA/FDA-tested cow liver was found to contain 0.37 parts per billion. While these residues were minuscule, they did clearly violate the letter of the law, which did not allow for DES residues of any level.

By way of rebuttal, drug and livestock industry advocates of continued DES use argued that the residues were nonetheless infrequent and inconsequential. Moreover, they argued, that in tests with laboratory mice, there had been no evidence that DES induced tumors until it had been absorbed at levels of at least 6.5 parts per billion. And they even disputed the test that showed these results, claiming that it had been an isolated and probably defective study, since no other tests were found to induce tumors in mice until residue levels reached 50 parts per billion. (Tests at 12.5 parts per billion and 25 parts per billion had all come out negative.)

They also protested that whereas in the sixties and early seventies most cattlemen were using DES as a feed additive, now they were using implants, which were much tidier, since they contained smaller and more controlled amounts of the drug. But given the fact that DES was a compound that had proven to be carcinogenic, and that there was no way to establish safe residue levels because so little was known about its long-term effects, most researchers counseled in favor of an extremely cautious approach, in spite of the admittedly low levels being found in the edible tissue of meat animals.

They were mindful not only of the residues that were known to occur when the drug was used correctly, but of those that could be created as a result of misuse by farmers who might, for instance, implant their animals with more than one pellet or take them to slaughter before the 120-day FDA-required withdrawal time had elapsed after implantation. Some researchers were even concerned about that portion of DES used as a feed additive that had been simply excreted out onto the ground in urine and manure, where studies had suggested that it might be taken up by certain plants and small animals and possibly reingested by livestock before it was finally chemically degraded. One such study pointed to the fact that as late as 1978 over thirty tons of DES had been used annually as a feed additive and had presumably ended up somewhere in the environment.

Carcinogenicity was not the only toxic effect to be considered. After all, DES was also a very powerful estrogenic substance capable of causing profound physiological changes in humans. For instance, farmers who had inhaled or ingested DES in powdered form—from feed mills that used to grind grain and mix it with additives—sometimes exhibited symptoms of impotence, infertility, gynecomastia (elevated and tender breasts) or changes in voice register. Less acute symptoms, such as changes in menstrual cycles, may also have occurred among some farm wives but gone unnoticed or undiagnosed because DES was a synthetic female hormone and in small doses would have caused problems that could have easily been explained as nothing more than normal irregularity.

But one situation where DES contamination did not go unnoticed occurred in the South during the 1950s after DES implants had been cleared by the FDA for use in caponizing male chickens. When dogs who had been eating food containing chicken processing wastes, and even some males from low-income families who had eaten inexpensive chicken necks began to show signs of feminization, the FDA banned the use of implants for caponization in 1959, and the USDA ended up having to purchase some $10 million worth of contaminated chicken to get it off the market.

The scientific literature cites other, often bizarre, instances in which humans have inadvertently been exposed to DES. In one case two five-year-old children with breast enlargement were diagnosed as having taken daily vitamin pills that had been tableted in a machine contaminated with DES. In another case, two young boys who had developed breast enlargement were found to have been using hair tonic that had been accidentally contaminated with DES.

As Dr. Frank J. Lauscher, director of the National Cancer Institute, cautioned in 1972 as the issue was joined against the use of DES as a feed additive, "The whole nation is a research lab when it comes to this kind of thing."

In 1970 a report prepared by the National Cancer Institute, the National Institute of Environment Health Sciences and the Surgeon General of the United States summed up this conservative position on the drug's use when its authors stated that "no level of exposure to a chemical carcinogen should be considered toxicologically insignificant. A safe level for man cannot be established from our present knowledge." Judge Davidson, in his final argument in favor of banning DES, concurred in this judgment, noting that "no safe level has yet been established for DES ingestion."

With the pressure building, largely due to the enormous amount of publicity the DES mothers and their offspring received in the early 1970s and the revelation that in the same year the USDA had found violative residues in 2 percent of the beef livers it had sampled (up from 1 percent during the previous years), the FDA moved first against DES feed additives in 1972 and then against DES implants in 1973.

The livestock industry challenged the ban in the district court of appeals for the District of Columbia, claiming that the FDA had failed to hold a certain legally required hearing prior to taking action against the drug. On this technicality, they succeeded in overturning the ban without the court ever having to consider the merits of the case from the point of view of public health.

It was not until 1976 that the FDA began new legal proceedings. These culminated in 1979, when FDA Commissioner Donald Kennedy (presently president of Stanford University) ended almost a decade of legal wrangling by upholding the decision made by Judge Davidson to ban DES.

Ironically, the final ban was not based on the Delaney Clause prohibition against adding carcinogens to the food supply, but was rather based on the general-safety clause of the Federal Food, Drug and Cosmetic Act, which allows the FDA to withdraw approval of a drug or food additive if tests raise reasonable doubts about the conclusion of safety that was the basis on which it was originally approved.

As of July 13, 1979, further sale and shipment of DES finally became illegal. On November 1, after existing stocks of the drugs already in the hands of users were presumably to have been exhausted, further use became illegal.

Livestock producers were every bit as displeased with the ruling as the actual producers of DES. In their view, they had been denied an inexpensive and useful technology that helped them raise more beef for less money, simply because of emotional hysteria caused by the unfortunate use of DES as a human therapy. What particulary angered them was that in banning DES, the court had not attempted to weigh risks against benefits. This was one extra-legal consideration to which the court had, perforce of the law, been blind.

Wrote Administrative Law Judge Davidson in his Initial Decision banning the drug, "The Statute does not require that a generic risk benefit analysis, one which includes societal along with therapeutic benefits, be employed in the evaluation of the safety of DES. The balancing of socio-economic benefits against health risks is therefore inappropriate to the safety evaluation of DES."

With the case finally resolved in court against the drug companies and cattlemen, the whole issue of DES seemed to disappear from public consciousness. But its disappearance was short-lived. In March 1980, shortly before my visit to Wayne Pines's office in Washington, D.C., the FDA was suddenly informed of a shocking occurrence: Fifty thousand head of cattle had continued to be implanted with DES in Texas in spite of the ban.

Assuming that USDA or FDA inspectors had unearthed the violations in the normal course of vigilant duty, I ask Pines, back in his FDA office, to explain how the government had first discovered that their ban was being broken. I am unprepared for his answer.

"It began back on March 14, when after requesting a kind of rush meeting with the Bureau of Veterinary Medicine, representatives from Allied Mills Incorporated in Chicago [a division of Continental Grain] rushed here to Washington with their legal counsel," begins Pines, like a storyteller. "When they arrived, they announced that two of their feedlots—real big ones down in the Texas Panhandle—had been illegally using DES all along. They said they wanted to know what they should do to salvage the animals."

Before Pines can continue his story, the phone rings. While he talks, I am left alone to ponder what he has just said. It is an anomalous situation. A corporate wrongdoer that has effectively evaded the clutches of two large governmental organizations dedicated to regulating just the kinds of crimes it has committed suddenly turns itself in and asks the surprised constabulary to assist it in its own rehabilitation.

"The story is that some cowboy who didn't get promoted in one of their feedlots down there in Texas wrote to Allied in Chicago protesting, and also mentioning that all their cattle were illegally implanted with DES," I hear Pines say on the phone.

"No. We don't know what we're going to do with the cows

yet," he continues after a pause. "We're discovering new lots every day. The options range from destroying the animals to reconditioning them. But I think what they'll probably do is make the feedlots surgically remove the implants and wait for sixty days or so before allowing the animals to be slaughtered.

"Everyone in the farm press wants to know what's going to happen to the animals," says Pines, shaking his head as he hangs up. "We don't regulate cows here at the FDA. That's the USDA's job. We are supposed to regulate drugs."

I ask Pines if he feels that the FDA has done an effective job of regulation of drugs such as DES. In very measured tones, as if he were addressing someone who spoke English only as a second language, Pines replies, "We operate on the presumption that people are basically law-abiding. If we assumed that there would always be these kinds of repeated and flagrant violations, well, hell, then we'd need a huge staff of inspectors just like a police force." He shrugs.

Again the phone rings. "All I can tell you about the possibility of legal action is that some violations of the Food, Drug and Cosmetic Act have occurred, and that the act establishes three-year prison terms and ten-thousand-dollar fines for each count," replies Pines after he picks up the receiver. "If you call me back tomorrow, maybe I'll have something more for you."

"Do you think that the FDA or the USDA would have found out about these violations on their own?" I ask Pines as he hangs up once again.

He looks at his overloaded desk, then at his watch. "I would certainly hope that we would have found out about them ourselves," he replies. "Sure, a lot of us are surprised and outraged to find such a flagrant violation of the law. This is the first time we have confronted such a widespread use of a banned drug."

3

The next day, on Wednesday, April 2, I walk over to the Washington office of the National Cattlemen's Association to see Burton Eller, the NCA's director for Washington affairs.

Entering the lobby, I find a young woman with a name block on her desk that identifies her as Karen Darling, speaking on the phone. "Well, sir. All that I can tell you at this point is that the newly revised list says that seventy thousand head of cattle in thirty feedlots have been identified as being illegally implanted with DES, but that the FDA says that there is no appreciable health risk for consumers."

"Good grief, but hasn't this been a hot one!" exclaims Darling, shaking her head as she hangs up.

Smiling in agreement, I ask Darling if Burton Eller is in the office.

"He is here, but he's not seeing anybody until he finishes the statement he has been working on," she replies apologetically.

During a temporary lull in her switchboard and receptionist duties, I ask Darling whether the revelations of the last few days have alarmed her.

"Frankly, DES doesn't bother me a bit," she replies, her otherwise cheerful manner now tinged with testiness. "DES is just like those antibiotics and everything else that is getting banned without any scientific basis. I just think what has happened is a damn shame because of how it might affect the industry." She pauses a moment and then adds more tentatively,

"Of course, the problem with this incident is going to be the illegality of it. That's going to be a hard fire to put out."

As Darling and I chat, the lobby slowly fills with a group of men wearing cowboy hats, Western-style suits and boots and carrying briefcases and clothesbag-type suitcases. One after another they arrive, stow their gear in a corner, then, still standing, confer with each other in grave voices. They are members of the NCA's Executive Committee which, like a high command of wartime generals, has been hastily convened to plan strategy against a sudden enemy breakthrough.

"We are just as concerned with the wholesomeness of meat as the next guy," says C. W. "Bill" McMillan, vice-president of the NCA's Government Affairs Office (later to become assistant secretary of agriculture under Ronald Reagan in charge of the USDA's Marketing and Inspection Services), when I ask him what position the association intends to take. "We don't condone the use of DES in the illegal sense, but we've never been in support of the ban. We feel that if it is properly used, DES present no dangers to the consumer and will provide great economic benefit. Our concern right now is to minimize the bad impact all this could have on our industry."

"How did all this happen?" I ask McMillan.

"Well, I'm not sure I can tell you, but you have to realize that there was a great deal of confusion in the minds of cattlemen about when all the different stages of this ban actually went into effect."

"In our view, there is no problem with DES as far as being a cancer-producing compound," adds David Bechtol, a veterinarian from Palo Duro Vet Services in Canyon, Texas, who has just flown in for the Executive Committee meeting. "They talk about residues, but they have only appeared in the liver and kidneys of a few cattle, never in the muscle tissue. A person would have to eat a hundred and ten pounds of liver a day to get a dose equal to what they gave those pregnant women to prevent miscarriage."

Bechtol is a cool, unsmiling man in a green Western-style leisure suit, white shirt and striped tie. It is more than evident that he places little trust in the reportage of prying journalists. I ask him if it is not true that the FDA has in fact isolated residues in the muscle tissue from some DES-implanted cattle.

"They claim to have done some testing out in Maryland that has isolated residues in muscle tissue through radioactive isotopes, but we've never seen any evidence of tissue residue. Maybe you get some occasionally in the livers, but we'd be willing to throw those out if that's what the government wants."

I am wondering how it would ever be possible to know which livers contain residues and which do not unless each one was tested—a monumental task. But Bechtol's expression does not invite further questioning about this matter. He has another point on his mind.

"When the FDA banned DES, they didn't go out and recall the stuff themselves. Why not? It was their ban. Did they expect that we would do it for them like a government messenger boy?" Bechtol gives a sardonic laugh. "Hell! We've been fighting this damn ban a long time. Still, we informed our people about it, but it's not our job to go out and play inspector for the FDA!"

Although reluctant at first to become deeply engaged in conversation, Bechtol has now gathered a certain momentum, impelled onward by a deep sense of frustration with what he repeatedly refers to as the "regulatory process." "Now, we've got tens of thousands of animals out there ready to go to slaughter," he continues. "I mean, these animals are still wholesome food, and we have to figure out some way with the USDA and FDA to move them to market. We're heading over to talk with Lester Crawford, the director of the Bureau of Veterinary Medicine, in just a moment."

"If you ask me, there's too much coming out of the press

that's making the consumer upset," offers McMillan, looking right at me.

"That is what hurts," adds Bechtol severely and extracts a consumer publication from his briefcase that bears the head-line "Consumers May Get DES Tainted Beef." Slapping it with the back of his hand contemptuously, he says, "This isn't facts. This is just a story that's gotten all blown up in the press. Hell, this so-called 'DES Tainted Beef' is what people have been eating for years, and I haven't seen any big problem, have you?"

When Burton Eller finally emerges from a back office, he is holding a much-corrected draft of a proposed NCA official statement. He passes it around the room. Members of his Executive Committee read it quickly and nod with approval.

"The National Cattlemen's Association does not condone in any way the use of any product that has been ruled illegal," the statement begins. "The NCA reminds the public that there never have been any DES residues in edible tissue as a result of commercial use of DES" (a statement that is not strictly true). It goes on to say, "There is no cause for concern about the safety and wholesomeness of beef. As noted by an FDA spokesman, the current situation 'is more a legal situation than a health situation.'"

The FDA has in fact made statements to this effect. For this whole affair has indeed been difficult for them in the sense that for more than twenty years, as Bechtol has just pointed out, the FDA has allowed DES to be used in meat animals. Now that it is illegal, the FDA people find themselves in the awkward position of suddenly having to claim that its con-tinued use constitutes a health hazard. If they expect anyone to obey their regulations in the future, they must give this situation some appearance of gravity, if not as a health hazard, then at least as a serious legal infraction.

When Eller has finished his consultation with the NCA's

Executive Committee members, I manage to ask him one question before he leaves for the meeting at the FDA's Bureau of Veterinary Medicine.

"How could such a widespread violation involving so many different operations have taken place for so long without the government knowing about it?"

"I guess you'd just have to say that it was one hell of a well-kept secret," replies Eller, his voice tinged with an air of challenge, suggesting that he might be indirectly applauding the cattlemen for their successful conspiracy. But before I can query him any further, he and his committee members sweep out the door, leaving me alone with Karen Darling. She gives a shrug and says, "Right now, those guys are some busy men!"

4

It is April 3. Almost as if they were casualty figures during wartime, the FDA has just issued another revised account and now reports that 105,000 head of cattle have been illegally implanted with DES in forty-six separate feedlots throughout the West and Midwest.

Two days have passed since I first spoke with Wayne Pines, and already I find unanswered questions about this whole affair piling up in my mind. Does the regulatory system often overlook such gross violations until corporations like Allied Mills turn themselves in? Why did Allied Mills turn itself in? What other hormonal agents are now being used to replace DES in the feedlots of America? How do they work? Are they potentially hazardous? How are they being regulated?

Like an avid mystery reader who, having once casually glanced at the first few pages of a good thriller, becomes irretrievably drawn into the plot, I find myself involuntarily wanting to get to the bottom of this affair. I head back over to the FDA building hoping to talk with Lester Crawford at the Bureau of Veterinary Medicine.

For several hours I try to reach him on the telephone. But like everyone else within this expanding ring of fire, Crawford is either in a meeting or on the phone. When I finally get through to him, it quickly becomes evident that he feels involved in this affair in a very personal way.

"Quite frankly, I'm disappointed, shocked and angered by this whole thing," he tells me when I ask how he is feeling about the ballooning statistics.

"What particular aspect of the affair makes you so shocked and disappointed?" I ask.

There is a pause at the other end of the line, then the sound of either a long sigh or a lungful of smoke being exhaled. "Well, perhaps you are not aware of it, but before that discontented cowboy wrote his letter, I made a trip down there to the Texas Panhandle to visit the Allied Mills feedlot outside of Dalhart that was responsible for starting this whole thing," recounts Crawford. "It was a fact-finding/goodwill sort of a trip. I went out to the feedlot and met the manager, some guy with a Norwegian name. He was kind of the host. I remember him telling me how he didn't think the implants he had had to switch to after DES was banned were as good or as economical. He said that they were feminizing his steers and causing them to bull [mount] each other. He had all this computer printout that showed that they were using another hormonal implant called Ralgro. But actually he was just standing in front of me and lying. The whole feedlot was actually implanted with DES."

Like a husband who has just found out that he has been cuckolded and is still unable to comprehend the full magnitude of the deception perpetrated on him, Crawford stops speaking. "We not only gave the cattlemen a lot of advance notice before this ban went into effect, but also a whole interim period of time after it was illegal to buy DES—from July thirteenth to November first—to use up their already existing stocks," continues Crawford. "We wanted to avoid inconveniencing them as much as possible. But now we discover that many of them not only stockpiled DES, but went right on buying it illegally from drug distributors after the ban. And to my way of thinking, that sort of behavior flies right in the face of the kind of cooperative spirit that the industry people are always claiming they want to establish with government.

"Perhaps they thought they wouldn't get caught, or that no one would take any legal action against them because of all the rapport we've built with industry, and all the recent stress on the need for self-regulation. Well, if that's their presumption, they've got another thing coming."

For several minutes more Crawford continues to talk with a candor and passion that is quite surprising. It is only when I ask him for the actual name of the feedlot and its manager in Dalhart that he begins to cool down and regain a certain bureaucratic aloofness. And when I ask Crawford if he knows the name of the cowboy who wrote the letter to Allied he suddenly rejoins, his curtness contrasting markedly to his earlier garrulousness, "I'd rather not say anything more on this matter. This is really a legal matter, and it's just going to have to take its own legal course."

Three months later Crawford tells an Animal Health Institute meeting, "To say that the DES problem has been personally painful is to understate the case. To say that I am worried about more of the same is the reason I stand before you today."

Trying to analyze how such a widespread flaunting of the law could happen, Crawford went on to say that in his view there were three myths of the "pioneering spirit," which, unless tempered, would presage even more lawless use of dangerous drugs and chemicals. "Original pioneers sometimes defiled the land, wildlife, the natives and anything else in their path because they were mindful of the horizon," said Crawford. "Some suggest we are still at it, but with different horizons in mind.

"How many times have we heard the refrain, 'You'd have to eat a carload of this or that to get cancer,' as if there were a known level below which any carcinogen can be surely shown not to cause cancer. Anyone who spreads the half-truth about having to eat a carload of this or that in order to get cancer is guilty of contributing to the national confusion that is crippling us . . .

"We still live in a nation where people have difficulty accepting the world as a grand, yet delicate ecosystem. . . . What we do to our livestock is our business alone only if we expect to eat every one of them ourselves. But it is not rational and is abjectly unconscionable for us to exercise anything less than the utmost care, concern and vigilance over the human food supply."

5

It is Monday April 7. Each day the magnitude of the DES affair continues to grow. This afternoon when I once again stop by the press office in the FDA building on C Street, in downtown Washington, I find that the number of illegally implanted cattle of which the FDA is aware has risen to two hundred thousand from fifty different feedlots across the country.

The USDA has just announced that their Food Safety and Quality Service (which oversees the inspection of meat and which is now known as the Food Safety and Inspection Service) will permit feedlots that are known to have used DES to slaughter cattle only after an accredited vet has certified that implants have been surgically removed, and after the animal has been "reconditioned," by allowing it to remain alive and unimplanted for thirty-five days before slaughter. (If cattlemen wish to market the livers and kidneys of illegally implanted animals, they will be required to wait an additional twenty-six days.)

Wanting to know more about how a drug like DES is approved by the FDA for use in livestock in the first place, I leave the press office to find Robert C. Livingston, who is chief of the Food Additive and Animal Drug Chemistry Evaluation Branch of the FDA's Bureau of Foods. Livingston's office is reputedly in the same building as the press office, but since I have failed to ask his floor number, I soon find myself roaming mazes of corridors seeking directions like a wayfaring stranger lost in a confusing network of backcountry roads.

I ask two women in white lab smocks if they know where the Food Additive and Animal Drug Chemistry Evaluation Branch office is located. They give each other blank but searching stares.

"Does that have anything to do with the Bureau of Veterinary Medicine?" one asks the other.

"I dunno," is the reply. "I think you'd better check the directory."

Curiously, when I first arrived here at the FDA just a week ago and asked the Public Information Office for a directory of the agency (which I hoped would help unravel the tangle of interlocking offices, staffs and jurisdictions), I was given a sheet that had been compiled not by the U.S. government, but by *Food Chemical News*, a private chemical-industry publication.

Nonetheless, after having studied the *Food Chemical News* offering conscientiously, I am still only able to visualize the roughest approximation of the organizational scheme on which this agency is built. In fact, as I pass scores of offices and labs, each filled with employees and emblazoned with bureaucratic names (Division of Chemical Technology, Genetics Toxicology Branch, Division of Food Technology, Food and Cosmetics Microbiology Branch, and so on), it seems miraculous that this whole ungainly aggregation of bureaucracy can ever coordinate itself and act in concert at all.

When I finally arrive at Livingston's office, I find him to be a congenial man in his mid-thirties wearing a conservative gray suit, black wing-tip shoes, a white shirt and tie, with neatly combed hair. "People here in Washington claim that the FDA is one of the better-run agencies in the government," begins Livingston cheerfully. "Even though there is waste and red tape here that sometimes terrifies me, there is no doubt in my mind that the FDA is a necessary organization when it comes to regulating drugs and chemicals in livestock production."

I ask him what the FDA's most critical role is in this regard. "The pharmaceutical industry will usually weed out drugs that are obviously hazardous before they are submitted to us for approval," he replies. "Obviously they do not want to be caught marketing something that is clearly dangerous. But where we run into problems is with drugs whose effects are rather subtle, ones where it is often difficult to determine whether or not they may have some kind of long-term deleterious impact on human health. Our particular concern here is drug residues in meat."

I ask Livingston how his branch goes about determining what residue levels of a drug are unacceptable?

"Well, let's start from the beginning," he says. "When a company is applying for approval of a new animal drug, they are required to do extensive studies with lab animals to see if it will show up as a meat residue and what the effects of it will be. Then the company sends its data and conclusions to us, along with an acceptable method for detecting such residues, and we make a final appraisal about their toxicological effects on humans.

"The question of residues, however, is not as simple as one might suppose," continues Livingston. "If all we had to do was to test a piece of meat for one drug, well, that would be relatively straightforward. But what you have to remember is that whenever any chemical compound goes into an animal, it doesn't just vanish. It is transformed, or broken down, into a whole new set of compounds, or metabolites, by organs such as the liver."

When metabolized, some drugs like DES break down into ten, twenty or even thirty derivative compounds, creating a bewildering new array of chemicals that may, in their own right, be toxic or carcinogenic to humans. To identify each one, much less test for the myriad number of their possibly toxic effects, is a Hydra-headed proposition that makes it virtually impossible for men like Livingston ever to feel that their job is completely done.

"We require companies applying for approval to market a new drug to tag their drug radioactively in their tests so that when it is metabolized we can see what it turns into and where the metabolites go. But there are still drugs on the market for which we have not identified all the metabolites." Livingston gives a fatalistic shrug.

(Just such a problem prevails in the case of DES. Although methods for detecting residues have been developed so that one or two parts per billion can be identified, scientists have not yet even catalogued all its metabolites, much less determined whether or not they are carcinogenic.)

"Suffice it to say," adds Livingston, "these metabolites have complicated our testing procedures beyond belief. Be that as it may, the main way that we have of controlling residues of the original drug or its metabolites is to require a withdrawal time, that is, to make it mandatory that farmers stop using the drug on an animal a certain number of days or weeks before slaughter time so that residues will have a chance to be naturally cleared out of its system."

I ask Livingston how the FDA decides on a withdrawal time for a given drug.

"Well, each drug application has to be gone over," he replies. "Residue levels are measured, and our chemists and toxicologists will consult together. They might agree that a two-week withdrawal time would be advisable. But then the Bureau of Veterinary Medicine, which decides whether the drug is effective and what the proper dose should be for a given disease in an animal, will come in and say, 'Hey! We can't let that go through! An animal can't get correct treatment that way!' You see, their whole concern is very different from ours. They're worried about treating sick animals, while we're worried about protecting humans.

"Then what happens is that while we are battling it out with them, the National Cattlemen's Association, the National Turkey Federation or the National Pork Producers' Council will troop in here to lobby for the drug, saying they can't possibly make out with such a long withdrawal time. Then we have to work out some sort of compromise."

I ask Livingston whether or not he is alarmed by the growing reliance of the livestock industry on ever more sophisticated drug and chemical technologies.

"Well, no, not really," he says after staring pensively at the ceiling for a few moments. "We try to be really conservative here at the FDA. For instance, in considering a drug, we say that it should be safe for someone to consume it over a thirty-year period if it appeared constantly in a food that comprised a third of his diet. So, theoretically all these drugs can be used safely *if* people will follow the labels on dosage and withdrawal time. But that's a big *if*," continues Livingston. "Compliance is the crux of the matter, and that really isn't in our hands."

Finally, I cannot resist asking Livingston how he himself feels about eating meat that has been raised with so many drugs and chemicals. He smiles and then laughs nervously, unaccustomed as he apparently is to responding about professional matters in a personal way.

"Well, if you want to have enough inexpensive meat for everyone, you're going to have to use some of these drugs," he replies. Then he pauses, shakes his head and laughs before adding, "But personally, I'd rather eat meat that was raised without them."

6

The weather gets warmer and warmer as I make my way from the Northeast down to Texas.

A dispatch from Washington in a local paper along the way reports that the FDA now claims to have identified 344,000 head of cattle from 115 feedlots in sixteen states that have been illegally implanted with DES.

They also report that Patricia Harris, secretary of HEW (the FDA's parent department), has just spoken to a conference of federal attorneys about the DES violations and has said, "If the FDA investigations warrant, we will seek your help in prosecuting these cases. If such prosecution results in convictions, we will ask your help in persuading the judges that prison sentences are both appropriate and imperative."

I read, moreover, that the FDA, having made a mistake in its initial calculations of a no-risk residue level, is lengthening the "reconditioning" time DES-implanted cattle must be held back after explanation before they can be slaughtered, from thirty-five to forty-one days. (If cattlemen wish to market organ meats from implanted cattle, they must now wait sixty-one days.)

Considering that the average slaughter steer sells for around seven hundred dollars on the current market and that only about twenty to twenty-five dollars of that is profit, these added costs will be a significant burden for violators. As I mull over

this new regulation, I find it hard to imagine Lonestar cattlemen, who have already ignored the DES ban with such defiance, surrendering to this new government intrusion without
resistance.

I cross the Mississippi at Hannibal, Missouri (next stop
Carthage), my mind filled with images of weary elephants
trudging over snowbound passes in the Pyrenees. But the
legendary Carthaginian general is not the patron saint of these
parts, if the neon signs that flash outside my car window are
any indication. It is Mark Twain, born here in 1835 as Samuel
Clemens, who appears to be best loved. Everywhere the
names Huck Finn, Jim, Tom Sawyer and sundry other Twain
characters blink on and off in front of motels, restaurants and
stores in the rainy darkness.

Spotting a cheerful yellow sign on the edge of the Huck
Finn Shopping Plaza that announces the Ponderosa Steak
House, I decide to stop and consecrate the evening to a piece
of beef, possible DES contamination notwithstanding. Stepping inside the front door, I quickly discern that rather than
being a sitdown restaurant, this steak house is a fast-food,
cafeteria-style eatery. But before I actually make up my mind
to stay, I find myself swept inside by a family of six to the head
of a line of people waiting beside a stack of trays.

Les jeux sont faits! Like a bare car chassis moving irrevocably
down an auto assembly line, the six family members and I
quickly acquire trays, napkins and silverware and are soon
passing down a gauntlet between a chrome railing and a food
counter where people are ordering various kinds of steaks,
potatoes, biscuits, soft drinks and desserts. By the time I
reach the cash register in front of a case of blindingly colorful
dishes of Jell-O (each tarped over with Saran Wrap lest the
gaudy cubes of gelatine become dehydrated like the bodies
of so many Portuguese men-of-war washed up on a hot, dry
beach), my own tray has acquired a medium-size cup of Mr.

Pibbs, a baked potato, some biscuits and a rib-eye steak. Opposite the Jell-O, the line of Ponderosa customers flows in swift single file, like a river being squeezed through a narrow flume. But once it passes the cash register and approaches the salad bar, it fans out into a broad delta of people.

Spotting Roy Watson, a young man who is identified as "manager" by a small plastic badge affixed to his shirt just to the left of his Ponderosa Steak House string tie, I ask if he has time to answer a few questions.

"Who owns this steak house?" I ask, after I have introduced myself and explained my interest in meat.

"No one in particular," he replies solicitously. "I mean, not just one person. We're part of a large chain owned by ESI [Elkhart Steak Inc.] meats out of Bristol, Indiana. There are a whole lot more of these steak houses around the Midwest."

"Do they send sides of beef down periodically to keep each franchise supplied?" I ask, my mind imagining butchers in stained white aprons at work in the back room slicing up steaks from hanging carcasses.

"Oh my goodness, no!" he exclaims, an indulgent smile creeping across his otherwise serious face, as if I had just asked whether or not his steak house raised its own cattle by grazing them out on the highway dividers in front of the Huck Finn Shopping Plaza. "No. No. In this business we're all boxed. Our meats are all prepackaged. They come forty-five to ninety-six steaks in a box, depending on their size. They are all frozen and shipped out to the individual franchises in refrigerated trucks. Each portion is cut and scientifically weighed. All we do at this end is to take the boxes out of the freezer, unwrap the meat and thaw it out."

"How many portions do you go through in a day?"

"Hooo! Jeez!" says Watson, drawing his right hand across his brow like a silent-film star getting the vapors. "On a good Saturday or Sunday we'll go through six hundred pieces of meat. But then on a normal weekday we'll drop down to two to three hundred."

"Is a steak house like this a profitable business with beef prices so high?"

"Oh yeah," he answers confidently. "We're profitable. Of course it helps being owned by a big meat company. That cuts your costs right there because of your volume. But you still need good promotion. Like, when we run a coupon sale in the papers, oh my God! Our business just shoots up! People who are counting their pennies recognize good value, you know, like people on Social Security. They watch for those discount coupons like hawks, because they know we're giving them one helluva deal."

Thanking Roy Watson for his time, I move on to the salad bar. When I can fit no more into my small bowl, I move slowly toward an empty table like a tightrope walker so that my unstable tower of roughage will not topple to the floor.

Sitting down, with no thoughts of drug residues or other chemical contaminants in my mind, I cut off a piece of my rib-eye steak and pop it in my mouth. It is very tasty, and I note with satisfaction that my entire meal has cost only $3.26.

When I later check with ESI headquarters in Bristol, Indiana, Dave Rawson, head of planning and development, tells me that the Hannibal Ponderosa Steak House is just one of about 550 ESI outlets located in twenty midwestern states and that they sell up to one and one-half million pounds of meat each year. When I ask Rawson what is unique about ESI meats, he tells me that they are all what he calls "portion controlled," meaning that each piece weighs, looks and tastes the same. He also tells me that ESI menu items are as inexpensive as they are because many of them come from "subprimal cuts" that are tenderized mechanically and with special enzymes at their Bristol plant.

"We're the largest outlet in the budget steak house segment

of the restaurant industry," he adds. "And from a profitability sense, you'd have to say that we are doing quite well."

When I ask Rawson if he has been aware of any DES problems in cattle slaughtered for ESI, he responds, "DE what?"

After I have explained what DES is, he replies, "To tell you the truth, we don't hear much about that sort of thing."

7

On April 14, I arrive in Amarillo where between four and five million head of beef cattle are raised each year in the surrounding high plains of the Texas Panhandle. My first stop is at the 1980 Texas Beef Conference, being held this year in the Hilton Inn on I-40 just east of Amarillo International Airport.

Sponsored by the Texas Cattle Feeders' Association and Texas A & M University, the Texas Beef Conference is an annual event. This year's program, "Efficiency and Economics in the Eighties," features a series of lectures, a social hour and steak dinner sponsored by the Texas T-Bone Club, where a Texas Beef Cook-Off Award, an event run by the Texas Cowbelles, the Cattle Feeders' Association's Women's Auxiliary (analogous to the Porkettes in the National Pork Producers' Council), will be presented.

Arriving at the Hilton Inn, I find myself inside a huge, glassed-in atrium filled with little paths that wind through an undergrowth of lush foliage. This elaborate landscaped interior has so little to do with the dry plains outside that it is not difficult to forget completely where one is.

Just as I arrive, the last symposium of the afternoon, "Where Is the Beef Industry Headed?," concludes. Chatting in groups of twos and threes, the conference goers drift out of the lecture room back into the atrium, where they congregate around a bar for a drink or two before their Texas Steak Dinner.

As I wait at the bar, I find myself standing next to a tall, heavyset man wearing hand-tooled cowboy boots, a brick-red western-style suit, a checked shirt with mother-of-pearl snap buttons and a massive silver belt buckle, the size of a small shield, embedded in his expansive girth. His conference badge identifies him as hailing from Deaf Smith County, Texas

After eyeing my notepad and pen, he inquires with a drawl about what brings me here to the beef conference. With an instinctual foreboding, I reply that I am a journalist covering the "so-called" DES affair. I use the term *so-called* reflexively, the way one might refer to a counterpart government when one is visiting a divided country, so as to please one's host with at least the suggestion of nonrecognition of the other side.

Such politesse does not seem to soothe my conversant. At the mention of the words "DES" and "journalist," his eyes narrow. Very slowly he exhales a plume of cigarette smoke over the top of my head, much as a warship might fire a warning salvo across the bow of an intruder into its territorial waters.

For a full minute he does not speak. Then, in very measured but hushed tones, he says, "If I was you, I'd be pretty careful around here," then turns to face the other direction until the line advances him to the bar and liberation from my presence.

I find myself not only standing alone now, but suddenly feeling extremely alien. Walking over to a thicket of shrubs to study the program, I hear two voices speaking on the other side.

"Well, as far as I know, we're in complete compliance," says the first voice.

"Never mind about that," says the second voice. "All I know is if one of those sons-of-bitches from the FDA comes snooping around our lot, he's going to get his teeth knocked so far down his throat, he's going to have to stick a toothbrush up his asshole to clean them."

"That cowboy up at Coronado in Dalhart who squealed is one fellow who is going to be unemployed around here for about three thousand years," replies the first voice menacingly.

I make a mental note that evidently Coronado is the name of the feedlot at which this epic began.

Although I have only been at the Texas Beef Conference for twenty minutes, it is evident that there is little contrition here among these men for the violations of law that many of them have committed. When Lester Crawford referred to the "myths of the pioneering spirit" that he felt were still extant among cattlemen, he was doubtless referring to men like these who are accustomed to doing what they want, when they want, and without government interference, much less threats of legal action and jail by a woman, even if she is the Cabinet secretary for the U.S. Department of Health, Education and Welfare.

In front of one of the guest rooms that open off the atrium, I notice a small sign that says "Syntex Agribusiness, Inc." Walking over, I find that it designates a "hospitality room" where conference goers can stop for a free drink and literature about Syntex's animal-health products. Syntex Agribusiness, Inc., of Palo Alto, California, manufactures growth-promoting hormonal implants for cattle called Synovex-H (which contains estradiol benzoate [estrogen] and progesterone for heifers), and Synovex-S (which contains estradiol benzoate and testosterone for steers). Since the banning of DES, large numbers of cattlemen have switched over to Synovex, now making it the largest-selling hormonal implant in the United States.

Inside the hospitality room, I find several cattlemen drinking Scotch and water around a table heaped with brochures and ads. I pick up a brochure which shows two grinning trainers in a boxing ring with a steer that has a gym towel draped around its neck. One of the trainers wears a T-shirt with the words *Synovex Implants* printed boldly on the front in red letters. A headline beneath the photo says, "Synovex Implants Can Make Heavyweight Champions Out of Lightweight Contenders for Pennies a Day."

"You Can Bank the Difference Synovex Makes," proclaims another ad. "Implanting with Synovex means better feed con-

version, faster daily gains and less time in the lot; an investment that puts you days and dollars ahead."

"I just don't know how to put it into words, but even though
we never made DES implants at Syntex, we still hated to see
them go and get banned," says Syntex's Animal Health Division's area sales representative for the Southwest, Carl Cooper.
Cooper is a tall, orderly young man who wears a tie and white
shirt.

"Sure we were competitors," he continues, stirring ice cubes
around in a plastic cup with his index finger. "But let me tell
you something, we'd love to see them approve DES again,
because the next thing you know, they'll be after Synovex too."

Indeed, although Carl Cooper may not be aware of it, the
FDA has already issued a Notice of Opportunity for Hearing
on Synovex, to give critics and researchers a chance to submit
findings and review the data on the possible hazards of implanting cattle with estradiol. (The FDA ultimately not only
withdrew this challenge, allowing Synovex to continue to be
marketed, but also canceled a sixty-day withdrawal time, enabling cattlemen to implant their animals right up to the day
of slaughter.)

"I've been feeding cattle for thirty-two years. For twenty-
five of those years I've been using DES, and I haven't seen
any problems whatsoever," interjects a handsome man in his
late fifties who turns out to be Carl Stevenson, owner of the
twenty-thousand-head-capacity Red Rock Feeding Company
in Red Rock, Arizona. "From my way of looking at it, DES is
just a wonderful drug for improving the efficiency of an animal, and it makes me real mad to see the government ban it."

"What is it about DES that makes it work so well?" I ask
Stevenson.

"I'm not quite sure I can tell you," he demurs, his tanned
face breaking into a smile.

"DES is a synthetic hormone," says Cooper, coming to the

rescue. Then he, too, seems to lose explanatory momentum. "Actually," he continues after a pause, "when you get right down to the front line of it, I can't exactly tell you how it works. It just does!"

Stevenson nods in wordless agreement.

"Shit," says Carl Cooper, putting out a fresh half gallon of Scotch, several quarts of soft drinks and a bucket of ice on a makeshift bar as a few more guests arrive. "Folks down here are real steamed up over this thing. Just a moment ago, right outside this door, there was this cattleman who was just about to take a punch at this other guy. He must have been with the government or something." The others in the room laugh knowingly.

"You could talk to anyone here at the Texas Cattle Feeders' Association," continues Stevenson. "They'd put an implant in a steer today and eat it tomorrow. Most of your consumers are just afraid of DES because that's what they hear from the press. But it's my belief that American cattle are the cleanest, finest and most disease-free animals in the world and that our industry is one of the most efficient. Just look at the relatively low cost of food in this country!

"I think this whole organic food business is the dumbest thing I ever heard of," he adds, changing his focus suddenly. "Most of that food is just bought at the supermarket like anything else. Then they punch a few worm holes in it, call it organic and sell it at a higher price. They're just merchandising off the ignorance and fear of consumers.

"If the FDA believed DES was so goddamned dangerous that they had to ban it, how come they never recalled it? I mean, where did they think it would all go? I quit using DES not because I think it's bad," says Stevenson, accepting another free drink from Cooper, "but simply because I didn't want to deal with the consequences.

"My son, who manages our lot, said that he wanted to go

on and use it after the ban. I said to him, 'Dan, I'm not going to do it. I don't want the goddamn government on our backs!' I just didn't want the hassle!

"I wasn't against DES. In fact we bought twenty thousand doses just before the sale cutoff date in July and used them right until the ban on further implantation went into effect in November. We followed the letter of the law. We'd had enough environmental crap already and didn't want to have to fight on this one too, because you just can't win.

"Everything is so regulated that a lot of these cattlemen just get the attitude, 'If the government's gonna screw us, we'll just give 'em a good screwing right back.'"

Although most of the other cattlemen have by now left the Syntex hospitality room to join the cocktail social hour in the lobby, Carl Stevenson is still going strong. "I think we have a vindictive government," he says. "I feel that the government tries to hurt us when it can. Cattlemen are a very conservative group. We don't believe in the government or their liberal philosophy, and that puts us on their shit list."

"What people don't realize," adds Carl Cooper from behind the bar, "is that the cattle industry is a depressed one right now. Fuel costs are up. It's impossible to get loans. There are a bunch of feedlots operating at fifty-five percent capacity. And now this DES thing. All these factors are going to put some of them under." He shakes his head, seemingly depressed by his own prognosis.

"If there were no goddamn government regulations, everything would probably be just the same," says Stevenson, brightening a little at the thought. "Well, let me put it this way. Probably seventy-five percent of the regulations are useless," he adds after a moment's consideration. "Did you know that there were seventy-seven thousand pages of new regulations in the Federal Register last year alone? That's several bibles' worth right there. The sorry thing about it is, there is

no other country in the world today that approaches the
United States in the vigor of its agriculture. That's a strength
that most people in America take for granted, and I'd hate to
see the government strangle it."

8

If any drug violations occur in the feedlots of the Texas Panhandle, they come under the jurisdiction of the FDA's Dallas District Office, one of twenty-two such offices spread around the country. Director of Investigation Theodore L. Rotto, a tall, mustachioed man, is in charge here in the Southwest region of finding out who sold and used DES implants after the ban. He is tired, but it is lunch hour now, so Rotto and several colleagues are sitting around a small conference room munching on sandwiches, drinking coffee and chatting.

"Our budget is shot to hell. But we haven't had enough time even to stop and worry about where we're going to get the funds to keep going," says Rotto with a mixture of humor and concern. Three other colleagues from his staff, who are sitting around the table strewn with lists of feedlots, drug distributors and schedules, nod in agreement. In front of them is a large-scale map of Texas bristling with stickpins that mark the sites of offending lots. A sign above it reads, Polish War Room.

Indeed, since executives at Allied Mills first made their unusual disclosure to the FDA in Washington, district offices like this one have pretty much been on a wartime footing. Each staff member here in Dallas has before him a seven-page list labeled "*Hot Item* DES Feedlot Summary as of 3:00 P.M. April 10, 1980," which tallies how many illegally implanted cattle have been counted so far at each offending feedlot, how many of those cattle have been put on hold by the USDA and how many have already been illegally slaughtered and shipped.

I ask Rotto if he and his staff are finding the cattlemen cooperative.

"Yes. By and large," he says. "But right after this whole uproar began, we sent some of our inspectors out around Amarillo. And do you know what they found in one lot? They found a bunch of guys out there still implanting with DES! We just couldn't believe it! I mean, this thing had been on radio, TV, in the papers, and word about the ban had been spread in all the livestock publications for months, and here are these guys still out there using it. I just wondered, where the hell have these guys been?" Rotto throws his hands up in disbelief and then lobs a crumpled potato-chip bag into the wastebasket.

"Some people were honestly just not aware of the ban," interjects Gary Pearce, a supervising investigator for the FDA, as Rotto unenthusiastically picks up an insistently ringing phone. "But I think a lot of those guys at the big lots knew damn well that they were disobeying the law. They just hoped they'd get away with it without being caught."

"Washington has been talking a hard line," says Rotto, hanging up. "Pat Harris is talking about litigating and people going to jail. But I don't think there is anyone . . ." he pauses for a moment and looks around the conference room before continuing, "There isn't a person in this building who really believes that any prosecutions are going to come out of this. And that sort of gives a person a sense of futility about all these costly and complicated investigations we are involved in." He gestures offhandedly at the piles of paper on the table and the stickpinned map of Texas.

I ask Rotto if, to his knowledge, there have been any prosecutions over drug residues in meat in the past.

"If there have been, I'm not aware of them," he replies with a shrug. "I recall one instance out in West Texas some years ago where we had recovered some DES residues from the

livers of cattle that had been held back for testing. This was
the second violation for that particular feedlot, which at the
time was using DES as a feed additive. Well, the FDA wanted
to prosecute, but first we had to get the evidence, so we asked
the USDA to send us the livers, which they had been keeping
frozen. But it turned out that the livers had not been locked
up under bond, so anyone could have switched them around.
Nor were there any worksheets on them. In short, it was impossible to verify which animals these livers had actually come
from, so that if we had tried to use them as evidence, a
defense lawyer would have been able to throw us right out of
court.

"We have this incredible regulatory agency all set up, and
it's fine to go through the motions of banning a drug. But do
you know something? We haven't got the statutory power
that would have allowed us to recall DES when it was banned.
We didn't even have the resources to go out and check up on
what was happening after the cutoff date last November.
Maybe that's why Allied came to the FDA in the first place:
perhaps they figured no matter what they admitted to, we
wouldn't do anything." For a few moments after this comment,
everyone silently concentrates on his sandwich.

"What has the FDA been able to do to rectify the situation?" I ask.

"Well, we've been to all the veterinary supply houses that
were illegally marketing the stuff, and we've been through their
invoices to see whom they sold it to," replies Rotto. "Then
we've been going out to those feedlots, informing the people
that what they were doing is illegal and that if they wanted
to stay out of any further trouble, they better stop implanting
and start explanting their animals.

"There are a couple of lots that we went to because we
knew from the drug distributor's invoices that they had bought
DES after the cutoff date. But sometimes we'd get all the way

out there, and do you know what? They'd tell us they didn't have any DES," says Rotto, rolling his eyes in disbelief.

"One of these places we went to denied they had been using it, until we pointed out that they had put it right into their computers," adds Pearce, laughing.

"Of course, most feedlots have been a lot more cooperative," adds Rotto. "But putting something into your computer and then denying it is a hell of a stupid way to be illegal."

James W. Reaves works under Ted Rotto as an inspector in the FDA's Oklahoma City Resident Inspection Station. When I arrive at his small office at six one morning, eager to see how the smallest gears of the FDA finally mesh with the livestock producers themselves, I find Reaves already at his desk, drinking a cup of coffee, eating a moon pie and pasting milky Polaroid photos of bottles of DES pellets onto a sheet of paper as possible court evidence.

"The phone rings so damn much during office hours, this is the only time I can get any work done," he says after we have shaken hands and he has offered me a cup of coffee. Reaves is a big, bulky, middle-aged man who chain-smokes and looks as if he hasn't run ten consecutive steps in the last ten years. He sits enthroned behind his drab government-issue gray-steel desk in his windowless office at the Federal Building, stomach straining at his short-sleeved blue shirt so that small windows of white undershirt appear between the buttons.

"Maybe it's true that some of the feedlot operators didn't know what was going on, because often the nurse cowboys who treat the sick cattle are the ones who buy all the medications," begins Reaves when I ask him how so many top-level livestockmen could have all ignored the same law so completely. "But I've been working on this thing since day one, and I think most of this stuff you hear about people being confused about the date the ban went into effect is just a lot of bullshit. They all knew the dates just as well as their own names, particularly the drug wholesalers. If they tell you different, they're just a bunch of damn liars."

Reaves goes back to pasting pictures for a few moments. Then he looks up, lights another cigarette, smiles and says, "All the same, sometimes when I get out to one of those lots and see what a mess they've gotten themselves into over this deal, it's hard not to feel a little bit sorry for them. But they did what they did, the law's the law, and that's that."

When Reaves has finished his paperwork, he grabs his Polaroid camera and a clipboard, turns on the answering machine, locks the door of his office and we head out together toward his government car. On his inspection schedule today is a ranch in Konewa that has shown up on the invoices of one Oklahoma City drug distributor, C. E. Swain Co., as having bought DES after November 1.

As we leave the city and head southeast through the red-earth country of Pottawatame County, past a carnage of squashed opposums along the roadside, I ask Reaves how things have been going for him the last few weeks.

"Well, let me give you an example," he says, a smile creeping across his face. "The other day I went out to inspect this lot where I knew they had been buying DES because I had the invoice from a drug distributor. So, I asked the manager out there if he had any cattle which were illegally implanted. He said that he had checked, and about all he could come up with was forty-eight head.

"So, I said, OK, and told him that was fine and that I was glad he wanted to declare them, because they were starting to test for DES residues at the packing plants again, and if any residues showed up in his cattle, he could forget going to market for a good long while. He just kind of looked at me real strange.

"Well, sir. I'm sitting in my office early one Monday morning. The phone rings. It's that guy. I ask him what's up, and he says, 'Oh, by the way. I just found a few more head that have been implanted.' So, I said, 'All right, about how many are we talking?' He said, 'Oh, about three thousand.'

Still curious about the legendary "discontent cowboy," I ask Reaves if he can tell me anything about him.

"Well, what I heard was that he just got pissed when he wasn't promoted down at Coronado in Dalhart, so he sent a registered letter, with return receipt, to the top boys at Allied Mills in Chicago giving them hell. Then at the bottom he just wrote, 'Oh, by the way. Did you know that your manager down here has been illegally implanting all your cattle with DES?' "

For a moment Reaves falls silent, his face smiling with enjoyment at the thought. "Well, shit! What could Allied do?" he finally continues. "They had this cannon loose on the deck. I guess they thought the jig was up and that there was nothing else they could do but confess. So, off they went to Washington."

I am about to ask Reaves if he knows the name of the cowboy, when, as if reading my thoughts, he says, "A lot of people would like to find that boy. All I can say is, I know what I would do if I was him. I'd leave the country, and fast. I believe there's a lot of fellas down there in the Panhandle that still think they're living on the frontier, and I'm sure they could think of a few things they'd like to do to him."

"What's the guy's name?"

Reaves looks at me incredulously for a moment as if I had just asked him to reveal the true identity of the Lone Ranger. "You don't need to know that," he replies with a coy smile.

"Why not?"

"Because it won't do you any good."

"I'd like to talk with him."

For a while Reaves considers this. Then, with a certain reluctance, he says, "His name is something like Robbs."

We pass through Konewa, and Reaves pulls the car into a

gas station to ask directions to River Bend Ranch. As an attendant is approaching, he leans over to my side of the seat and says in a low, conspiratorial voice, "Out here life is cheap. This must be the most antigovernment area of the country. Sometimes when I'm sitting in this official car, I don't even like to stop."

The attendant is not apparently enraged by Reaves's government affiliation and agreeably gives him directions.

The ranch is situated on a lovely bluff overlooking a fork of the Canadian River. Reaves pauses before a No Trespassing sign out on the road and then slowly noses his car up the driveway past several head of Charolais cattle, which graze in a pasture opposite a wood-frame house.

As we pull up to the house, a face appears behind the screen of the back door, and then J. R. Walker, a young man in his twenties who manages this small family ranch, steps outside, eying the gray government car with circumspection. After introductions have been made and Reaves has had a chance to explain his mission, Walker invites us inside.

With gentle coaxing from Reaves, Walker allows that River Bend Ranch has about 120 head of cattle, forty of which he believes have been implanted with DES.

"When did you implant?" asks Reaves solicitously.

"Well, you see our records are all in a safe-deposit box in Konewa, so I don't really . . ."

"Is it possible that you did it before November first?" asks Reaves, wanting to help Walker resolve this matter as easily as possible, but also not unaware that he is making an investigation of an illegal act.

"Well, now, it just might have been. I just don't . . ." replies Walker tentatively.

"You see, what my drift is, is that the cutoff date for using the stuff was November 1 of last year. So if you used it before, you're OK," offers Reaves helpfully, like a quiz-show host coaching a slow guest who is on the verge of going home empty-handed.

"Actually, I think it was around May," says Walker, his perplexed face brightening a little.

"In May. Well, all right," says Reaves, examining the invoice from C. E. Swain and discovering the DES in fact to have been bought after November 1.

"There are a lot of cows tied up because of this crap," says Reaves, in a manner that artfully combines a suggestion of sympathy with a veiled threat. "When we find people have used these little fellas after November, we have to tie up their cattle."

"Well, actually," stammers Walker, evidently grasping the sequential weakness of the scenario he has just begun to sketch, "I don't see how it could have been May. So it must have been September."

"You remember September," says Reaves, so that it is unclear whether he is asking a question or making a statement. "You're sure it wasn't after November?"

"Oh, I don't reckon," says Walker in that vague manner people often affect when they wish to avoid making a too-definite response to a question.

Reaves sighs, evidently unwilling to continue pressing the still-unresolved inconsistency, and commences to fill out a form on his clipboard.

"And where is the DES now?" asks Reaves when he finishes.

Walker disappears out the back door and reappears a few minutes later with a small bottle half-full of 15-mg pellets of DES, each of which is no larger than a saccharine pill. He hands the bottle to Reaves, who holds it up to the light to examine its contents.

"Well," he says, setting it on a tabletop and readying his Polaroid camera for a photo, "I ain't about to count those little devils."

He snaps a picture, and then, since the FDA has no con-
fiscatory powers, as Rotto explained, he hands the bottle back
to Walker, who receives it with the look of a surprised criminal
who has just had his gun returned by an arresting officer.
Actually the whole "investigation" here at River Bend Ranch
has been a curious one, for nothing has actually been accomplished except the filling out of a form, the taking of one
Polaroid photo, and deliverance of an admonition to Walker.

Driving away from the house, Reaves shakes his head like
an athlete leaving the field after a game that has left him feeling discontent. "Ah, hell. He's a small-time operator," he mut-
ters. "What can you do except fill out a few forms just to show
that someone has been out here?"

As we leave, I turn around for one last look at River Bend
Ranch. J. R. Walker is still standing in the parking area beside the house watching our departure. He holds the bottle of
DES implants in one hand and a copy of the form Reaves has
just filled out in the other. He wears a perplexed look on his
face.

9

Leaving Reaves, I head west across Oklahoma back toward the Texas Panhandle, the straight road stretching monotonously away in front of my headlights. After stopping for a few hours at a roadside motel to get some sleep, I reach Dalhart by noon the next day, feeling both the anticipation and the apprehension of a pilgrim at the end of his journey.

Although Dalhart could hardly be described as a place of spiritual resonance (its main raison d'être is the several railroad lines that intersect in its midst and carry cattle to the far corners of the country), it has, at least for me, acquired a deep significance in my quest. In fact, no sooner have I bounced across one set of these tracks within the town limits than I spot a large electrically lit billboard in a parking lot. It reads, "Coronado Feeders. Custom Cattle Feeding. 12 Miles On FM 297.

The ruler-straight road out to Coronado passes through miles and miles of cropland. The only vertical relief on this horizontal landscape is man-made: power poles, an occasional road sign, pesticide or herbicide storage tanks, or one of the many spidery center-pivot irrigation systems that circumambulate these flat fields in the summertime, leaving huge holes of green punched out of the otherwise dull, buff-colored landscape.

For twenty minutes or so my car seems to float along the unrelieved flatness of the land in constant pursuit of unreachable mirages, which shimmer on the horizon ahead. Then, coming over a slight rise, I spot several derricklike towers affixed on top of a large green structure. Steam is being released from one of them into the cloudless blue sky, so that the entire facility looks like it might belong to a refinery or possibly be part of a remote NASA space-launch facility.

Spreading out around it almost as far as the eye can see, like a vast tweed-colored patchwork quilt, are the thirty-five thousand head of cattle of Coronado Feeders. This living venire of animals that covers the land before me is so awesome that I pull off on the shoulder of the road for a few minutes to drink it in. The balmy wind makes no more than a barely audible sigh as it blows across the plains. The animals, moving about slowly in the distant pens, form shifting patterns of browns, grays and blacks.

In one corner of this tableau, small puffs of dust rise up into the air as miniature figures on horseback move cows from one pen to another. Once the symbol of the open western range, cattle here at Coronado are ordered into neat pens as square as the blocks of Manhattan. In fact, the only feature of the landscape before me that has not been regimented by right angles is a large lagoon for rainwater and manure runoff that lies beyond the feedlot in the distance. The scene before me is so vast that the idea of DES implants no bigger than medium-size seeds seems almost preposterous in comparison. Here, where everything is written large, it is somewhat easier to understand why a cattleman might remain unimpressed by residues that cannot be seen with the naked eye and that can only be measured by sophisticated laboratory equipment in parts per million or billion.

Getting back into the car, I drive up to the feedlot's main gate and stop in front of the office as trucks rumble past on their unending rounds to keep the miles of cement feed bunks filled with grain, alfalfa and silage. I do not know the name of Coronado's manager, the man who so enraged Lester Crawford when he was here. But I have decided that the only possible way to make contact with him is simply to walk in the door and ask head-on for the manager rather than trying to prearrange a meeting.

As soon as I step into the lobby, I feel as if I have been transported to another world. The room is paneled in imitation wormwood, the floor is covered with a thick shag carpeting. Oil paintings depicting western scenes hang on the walls. The coolness of the air conditioning and the sound of soft music wafting from a back office all conspire to create a mood more akin to suburbia than the remote high plains of Texas. Approaching the receptionist, I ask if I can see the general manager.

"Do you mean Leo Vermedahl?" she asks politely.

"Yes, Mr. Vermedahl," I reply, trying to sound as if I had not just heard his name for the first time.

"Do you have an appointment?"

"No."

"What is it that you are here in regard to?" she asks.

"I am a journalist and hoped to have a chance to chat with Mr. Vermedahl for a few minutes," I respond.

The receptionist now has a distinctly dubious look on her face. "I'm very doubtful Mr. Vermedahl is available," she says and then, leaving her desk, vanishes down a corridor. I settle in a lobby chair to browse through a brochure entitled "Meet Coronado Feeders, A Cattleman's Company." The cover shows a color photo of a cowboy on horseback in one of Coronado's cattle pens, the towers of the feed mill silhouetted in the background.

"Allied Mills has a rich heritage in knowledge of animal nutrition and health control," claims the glossy sixteen-page brochure. "Allied has its own team of nutrition and veterinary scientists for developing fundamental approaches to more profitable livestock production. . . . All this technology matched with the knowledgeable management team at Coronado means . . . faster, safer application of more profitable feeding practices. . . ."

As I am flipping through the pages, the receptionist returns to inform me coolly, "Mr. Vermedahl does not want to talk with 'reporters' at this time."

"Would you please ask him if he would be willing just to tell me a little about Coronado Feeders, then," I remonstrate. Without enthusiasm she once again disappears down the back corridor.

Returning to the Coronado brochure, I find that one page has a large color photo of Vermedahl himself. He is standing in front of one of the feedlot pens. His blondish hair is neatly parted, and he is looking with studied confidence into the lens of the camera. The caption above his head reads, "Personalized Service, Dedication."

Suddenly feeling a presence in the room, I glance up from the photo to see Vermedahl himself standing in the doorway. He looks paler and less self-assured than his picture. He says nothing. For a moment I wonder if he isn't just going to have a look at me and then turn around and disappear again. He does not, however, retreat. In fact, he walks over and introduces himself, perhaps drawn out into the lobby to check me out by the same sort of curiosity that has impelled me all the way from coastal America to this remote heartland to find him.

I ask him if he would be willing to talk for a few minutes. He looks at me with unsmiling eyes and then finally says, "I'll answer your questions about the feedlot operation, and that's it."

I follow Vermedahl into his back office, where he sits down with an air of weary fatalism behind a large desk shaped like a half-moon, which has piles of computer printout heaped on top. I cannot look at the orderly piles of paper without wondering whether or not they are the same ones with which Vermedahl plied Crawford when he was here.

"We call ourselves a 'custom' lot, which means that we care for other people's cattle on contract until they are ready for slaughter," begins Vermedahl without much luster in his voice. "Since we've automated the lot, we can take care of approximately forty thousand head of cattle with only thirty-five employees. But right now, we're not running at full capacity. I don't know what it is, but people just aren't eating as much beef as they used to. Things aren't exactly rosy out here."

I wonder out loud if incidents like the present one involving DES might not have some influence on people's eagerness to eat beef.

For a few moments, Vermedahl silently considers this point. "Usually people overreact to things like this," he finally says. "I don't think the consumer activists have been telling it like it is, and that can hurt us a lot."

I ask him what other drugs he uses here at Coronado for growth promotion besides hormonal implants.

He avoids my glance by looking down at his desktop. "We use low levels of Aureomycin when the cattle first get here," he replies. "After that we switch them over to Rumensin [a feed additive that alters the microflora in a cow's rumen to promote increased nutritional absorption]. If we lost all the antibiotics and hormonal implants, we'd be looking at a loss of about four to five dollars per hundredweight. That's our profit margin. With that gone, we'd be out of the game."

"Was Crawford's visit the first time a director of the Bureau of Veterinary Medicine visited Coronado?" I ask, hoping to elicit some response from Vermedahl about the present situation.

"Yeah. He was out here on some program to . . . I don't know," he replies without enthusiasm.

Feeling that our chat is really getting nowhere, I decide, in spite of Vermedahl's caveat against discussing the DES affair, to plunge to the heart of the matter. "What made you decide to go on using DES?" I ask point-blank.

At first Vermedahl seems a little surprised by the bluntness of my question. Then he seems on the verge of answering, as if he actually yearned for the chance to tell the world his side of the story. But soon the look of surprise is eclipsed by one of gravity, and he replies curtly, "No comment."

"Then perhaps you can tell me who the cowboy was who wrote the letter to Allied?"

"I won't respond to that either," replies Vermedahl, his face now chilled with anger. "I've been advised to get my own legal counsel, and I don't think I have anything more to say."

"What has been the reaction of Allied Mills to this brouhaha?" I ask as Vermedahl is about to squire me from his office.

"Well, you'll just have to ask Merle Brinnegar, the vice-president in charge, about that yourself," he replies with a bitter smile.

As I leave, I ask Vermedahl if I can look around the lot this afternoon after lunch. He surprises me by agreeing and then bids adieu with the same coolness with which he greeted me.

10

On the outskirts of Dalhart, I pull in to a café to call Allied Mills in Chicago. After explaining briefly to a secretary why I want to talk with Merle Brinnegar (who, she tells me, is vice-president in charge of the Livestock Products Division), I suddenly find Brinneger himself on the line. No sooner have I uttered "DES" than Brinnegar snaps back, "Whatever you're writing about is just fine, but I'm not going to discuss the matter with you."

When I tell Brinnegar that I am down in Dalhart, there is a long silence, a deep sigh and then, in a much more accommodating tone, he adds, "Well, let me just say that as a company we have no desire to use drugs not sanctioned by the FDA. In this case, our local manager took it on himself to use this drug, and he is no longer part of the company. That's the end of that, that's our philosophy and that's where I'll stop talking."

When I inform Brinnegar that I have just returned from Coronado Feeders, where I actually talked with Leo Verme-dahl right in the manager's office, I hear a noise that sounds like a hand being clapped over the end of the receiver, and a muffled voice. Only after a long hiatus does Brinnegar come back on the line.

"Mr. Schell, let me just say that in no way do I condone what this man or the industry has done," he says, speaking now with a weary sternness.

"Did you know that DES was being used in your lot before your disgruntled employee wrote to you?" I continue.

"I can tell you right now that . . . I know you're writing an article, but I'm just not going to talk about this matter anymore. I don't think there is any object in a journalist going in and—"

"Do you think that this is a story without significance?"

"The trouble is that the press is entrusted to report on things they don't know anything about," retorts Brinnegar. "This year the press is making people afraid of DES. The next year they'll make them afraid of something else by putting a little more fear or hate into it." In spite of his repeated protestations that he does not want to discuss the matter further, Brinnegar seems unable to resist replying to each new question.

"Do you think the FDA and USDA are overreacting by demanding that all cattle be explanted and held for a number of weeks before slaughter?"

"No, no, no!" replies Brinnegar, with obvious irritation in his voice. "That's their job. When people do something illegal, they have no choice. One can disagree with the law, but not disobey it. And generally speaking, I don't think American people cheat. Our company hires knowledgeable people. But obviously you can't be on top of them everyday. When we heard what was happening down there, we went right to the FDA on our own."

"What do you think accounts for the fact that these violations were committed on such a broad scale?" I ask.

"I think you'd have to say that the FDA goofed as much on this thing as anyone else," replies Brinnegar, taking the offensive. "People were very confused about the ban, and that helped them break the law.

"What you have to remember is that DES was used for a long time, first as a feed additive and then as an implant before this ban," continues Brinnegar, a complaining whine beginning to creep into his voice. "Most people were just using up supplies on hand. What's a couple more months when we've been using the stuff for twenty years already?"

"In your estimation has the livestock industry become over-reliant on drugs and chemicals such as DES?" I ask.

"We have meat as inexpensive as we do today because we use drugs and chemicals," he replies. "In any industry there is a risk-benefit trade-off on these new technologies, which can be very difficult for a government agency to manage. But I don't think the livestock industry relies on drugs any more than the consumer does."

"Who was the cowboy who wrote you the letter after he failed to be promoted? I'd like to talk with him."

Another weary sigh comes over the phone. "Mr. Schell, I'm just not going to say anything more about this. As you know, the FDA is looking into legal action, and I think it would be better just to stop here."

Thanking Brinnegar for his time, I take a seat at the café's counter to order lunch. To my dismay, the whole room is filled with suffocating, greasy smoke from a deep-fat fryer. Next to me is a truck driver eating an enormous platter of french fries drenched in ketchup and one of the largest individual portions of chicken-fried steak I have ever seen. The man himself is a colossus so large that the space between our stools is almost inadequate to keep our two bodies from touching. In fact, from the rear it is impossible even to see the top of the stool on which he sits, because it is engulfed by his huge posterior, which sags down around it on all sides like a blob of plastic that has been heated to its melting point.

While I wait to order, I browse through a copy of an Amarillo newspaper that I find on the countertop. Under bold black headlines, a front-page article reports that new FDA figures for illegally implanted cattle have now jumped over the four-hundred-thousand mark. I am halfway through the article when the waitress, a stout woman almost six feet tall (who looks as if she had been raised on hormonal growth promotants herself) approaches with a pad and pencil. Forgetting for a moment that I am in the Texas Panhandle, which kills over three million head of beef cattle each year in its seventeen processing plants, I ask for a salad.

The waitress looks at me as if I had just ordered bean curd.

"We don't offer it," she says sourly and thrusts the plastic embossed menu forward for me to review again.

"How about a hamburger with lettuce and tomato?" I counter, feeling a need today to insinuate as much roughage as possible into my meal.

"No lettuce," says the waitress bluntly, her pencil hand, which has heretofore been poised over her order pad, suddenly dropping hostilely to her side.

"Tomato?"

"Lemme check."

She moves over to my neighbor (who has just lit up a cigarette in the middle of his steak dinner) to give his giant-size paper cup of Dr Pepper a refill.

When my burger arrives, it is anointed with one thin persimmon-colored slice of tomato. Clearly, Dalhart affords no refuge for vegetarians, which I am not. But here, even the suggestion that one likes edible greenery seems almost un-American. I eat quickly, finding myself lamenting anew how difficult it is—even with all the new technology—to get a simple, decent meal in the food-producing heartland of America.

11

I leave the café and head back toward Coronado, glad to be out on the open road again, with the wind blowing the greasy smell of french fries out of my hair. I arrive at the feedlot, park and set off down one of the long asphalt access roads that divide the cattle pens. All around me is a sea of beef. Acres of Angus, Hereford, Brangus, Charolais, Simentel, Limoisin and assorted other breeds and half-breeds, which watch my progress curiously from the surrounding pens as I pass by. The only sound other than the distant hiss of steam from the feed mill and the occasional roar of a faraway truck is the coughing and wheezing of thirty-five thousand cows, an endemic problem in feedlots such as this one, where dust is a fact of life during the dry months, and respiratory disease is often hard to control, even with the regular use of antibiotics.

I pass one of Coronado's four "hospitals," white steel structures spread around the lot where sick cattle can be isolated and treated. As I approach a processing building, where new cattle are unloaded, branded, vaccinated, deloused, implanted and otherwise medicated before going into the lot, I hear the sound of someone operating a hydraulic squeeze-shoot (a mechanical stanchion that traps an animal's head and squeezes its body hydraulically so that it can be worked on).

Walking over, I find a man in his fifties, wearing a bloody apron over his jeans and western shirt, unlit cigar clenched between his teeth, working cows beside a rack of branding irons. A file of cattle are lined up behind the squeeze in a long curving alley, its whitewashed surfaces so splattered with manure and blood that they look like Jackson Pollock frescoes.

As I draw nearer, I see that the man is holding a stainless-steel surgical scalpel in one hand. And having secured a steer in the shoot, he grabs its ear and begins scraping the furry surface until a thin jet of blood spurts out. The animal gives a bellow and unsuccessfully tries to free itself from the chute with a clanging of hooves on steel. The man scrapes several more times with his scalpel, then, seeing me, reaches down and holds up a tiny white kernel between his bloody thumb and forefinger and announces, "That's it. That's what one of them little DES buggers looks like when they come out."

Having successfully explanted one more illegally implanted animal, he flicks the partially absorbed DES pellet down onto the ground and takes several consecutive drags on his soggy cigar to see if he can revive it.

I introduce myself and ask him his name. As the chute opens, and the steer lunges noisily forward to freedom, I am surprised to hear what I think is the name Robbs.*

After a new animal has come crashing into the chute, I ask in disbelief, "Did you say your name was Robbs?"

"Yep. Robbs. Derryl Robbs," he says, grabbing the ear of the new animal and feeling around its surface for the telltale lump.

For a moment I am rendered speechless. Is this the legendary Robbs who wrote the infamous letter to Allied Mills and whose name James Reaves had so reluctantly given me?

"We've already done nine thousand head," Robbs reports, scraping away at the next ear, oblivious of my state of shock. "I'm getting pretty good at it now. But these babies are ready to go to market soon, and if we've got to keep them another month or two, that's going to cost someone a bundle."

* The name has been changed to protect the identity of the cowboy.

As I am trying to figure out how tactfully to ask if the Robbs before me is *the Robbs* (I have no first name), another steer charges into the chute. "Feel here. That's it. At least what's left of it," Robbs says with a cheerful innocence that makes me wonder how he could possibly be the man I am looking for. I reach out and feel the ear. Just beneath the skin is a bump that feels like a BB. Robbs starts scraping and a moment later flicks the remains of another only partially absorbed DES implant to the ground.

"I don't know what the big deal about gettin' these things out now is," says Robbs, scraping away. "Hell, in the past they always sent 'em to market with no-never-mind if the stuff was still in their ears or not."

"Boy! This DES thing has sure gotten a lot of publicity," I finally venture, curious to see if Robbs's face will register any sensitivity to the subject.

"Yep," he says, without apparent concern.

"Does that guy who wrote the letter still work here?" I ask after allowing what I hope is a decent interval of time to elapse between my prying questions, while Robbs is scraping intently on the ear of a new steer.

"Nope," he finally says, removing himself from the list of suspects. "His wife does, though. She runs the computer."

12

I leave Derryl Robbs to continue his seemingly endless task of explanting cattle, and I drive into Dalhart once again to find a phone. Calling back out to Coronado, I ask the receptionist for Mrs. Robbs.

"I'm sorry, she's not in today. I believe she must be home in Channing," the receptionist obligingly replies. Checking the phone book for Channing, a small town south of Dalhart, I find a listing for a Martin Robbs.

The road between Dalhart and Channing shoots straight out across the barren high plains where Channing—a cluster of houses, a store, two cafés and a gas station—stands like an island.

I stop at the Matador Café and ask a man inside if he can direct me to the house of Martin Robbs. He looks at me and shakes his head. Across the street in the general store, I get some vague directions that send me off down an unpaved road that branches out from the main highway and runs a little way until it hits the edge of the desert plains and then stops as if it had run right up against the ocean. A few children play in the roadway, unbothered by traffic and sheltered from the noonday sun by shade trees.

Several grand old wood-frame houses with broad front porches are mixed in with inexpensive tract homes, rundown shacks and trailers. The only thing they share in common are aluminum TV antennas, which sprout skyward, straining to catch the signals from Amarillo sixty-five miles away.

Martin Robbs and his family live in a small white house

with several bales of hay stacked up in the dusty front yard to feed the two colts, which run loose in a makeshift paddock behind.

When I get out of my car, two children run away and hide. Through the screen door I can hear the sounds of a television set. I knock. Wait. Knock again. Finally a pleasant-looking man in jeans, a western shirt, cowboy boots and hat emerges from the kitchen into the living room.

"Howdy," he says noncommittally through the closed screen door. "What can I do you for?"

As I explain that I am a journalist who is investigating the DES affair, he looks at me with a mixture of wariness and amused disbelief, flabbergasted, I suppose, that someone should have come so far to track him down in this out-of-the-way town. When I mention to him that I have just talked with Leo Vermedahl, his otherwise-cheerful eyes narrow for a moment, and he says, "Well, I've got nothing to hide. So if you want to, you might as well come on in.

"I've been in cattle all my life," begins Robbs, sitting down in an old leather chair in his living room, which shows the disordering effect of his small children. "I'd been at Coronado as head cowboy for four years, and when the job of yard boss opened up, well, I thought that I . . . it just seemed to me that the fair thing for the feedlot to do would have been to appoint one of their own people. But that's not what Vermedahl wanted to do. He brought some other guy in from another feedlot, and I just plain couldn't see that, or how I could continue to get along with him. So I quit."

Robbs leans back in his chair and puts his feet up on the coffee table in front of him, which is littered with kids' toys, unwashed dishes and several old newspapers, and gives a smile that does not quite come into full bloom because of the wad of chewing tobacco that is stuffed inside his left cheek.

I ask Robbs what role he played in exposing the illegal use of DES.

"Well, the story you hear around these parts now is that some cowboy turned Coronado in to the FDA. But that's not true," replies Robbs, his voice tinged with defensiveness. "Allied Mills turned itself in. All I did was to write a letter up there to Chicago. I would never have turned Coronado in to the FDA myself.

"I felt like I had been done an injustice by not being hired, and I felt like Allied Mills needed to know what was going on, so I told them. I also mentioned that they had all their cattle down here implanted illegally with DES. Now there may have been some guys at Coronado who just did what they were told and didn't know legal from illegal. But I figured that at least up in Chicago they could tell the difference. And I reckon they could, because when they got my letter, this guy Brinnegar wanted to know right off what the hell was happening down here. And when he found out, he got himself over to the FDA just about as fast as he could." Robbs reaches for an empty number-ten tin can that sits on the floor next to a saddle and spits a jet of tobacco juice into it.

I ask Robbs if before the incident the FDA came around the feedlot much.

"Not before this," he says with a closed-lip laugh. "There are supposed to be inspectors, but I don't guess I ever saw an FDA guy . . . that is not until this whole thing blew up anyway." For a moment Robbs turns toward the TV, which is showing footage of demonstrating students in Iran. "I just know my mind, and I didn't think it was right for that guy Vermedahl to put himself ahead of the law," continues Robbs as events in Iran fade into a beer commercial. "Vermedahl was just after power. He likes folks to kiss his rear end. I'd whup it, but I wouldn't kiss it," Robbs gives another one of his closed-lip smiles.

"What I still don't understand is why Vermedahl would want to jeopardize a whole business over DES when there are other alternatives," says Robbs, shaking his head. "Sure I'm getting the business for all of this, but I still think it's good that they're catching this deal now. As long as the cattle people could get DES, they would have continued to use it."

I ask Robbs if he thinks people like Vermedahl should go to jail. He ponders the question while he packs a new pinch of tobacco into his cheek.

"Well, if you rob a bank and they catch you, they're going to arrest you, because it's against the law. Right? And that's what these guys did, didn't they? They broke the law. And if they're not going to enforce a law, why have it?"

One of Robbs's children begins to cry outside. He gets up to see what has happened. "I'm no scientist and can't judge about whether this DES is good or bad," he says as he sits down again. "But they say it's not good for you. So, it really shocked me when I learned how many lots were still using it and how many distributors were still selling it."

Robbs relieves himself of another jet of tobacco juice into the number-ten can. "I guess the FDA can be an awful damn pain in the neck sometimes," he continues philosophically. "But if we didn't have it, we'd be in trouble, wouldn't we? Just look at all these medications we've got. People could just go out and put any damn thing they wanted into animals if no one was looking after the situation. From my way of thinking, that would be kind of a bad deal.

"When you go to the supermarket for some meat, a person doesn't have any idea what might be in it. This whole affair sort of makes me wonder. Stuff in the meat might not affect us adults, but if you've got kids coming along . . ." His voice trails off. He stares out the door where two of his children are now playing happily.

Evening is drawing near. As I thank Robbs and get up to leave, he adds wistfully, "Actually I hate to see all this happen. It's no good for anyone. Right now I'm out of a job, and just hanging around breaking a few young horses. I'll be glad when it all passes."

13

By the time the FDA made their final tally of violators in the late spring of 1980, they had found that forty-nine drug-distributing companies had illegally sold DES after the July 13, 1979, cutoff date for sale and that 318 different feedlots in twenty states had illegally implanted 427,275 head of cattle with DES after the November 1, 1979, deadline against further use. They also reported that at least 25,400 head of illegally implanted cattle had been sold and slaughtered before they could be quarantined.

Commenting on the accuracy of these figures, *Feedlot Management* magazine noted, "One thing seems certain: there were far more cattle implanted with DES than ever detected."

While the full magnitude of violations was still being uncovered, many regulatory officials, including Secretary of Health, Education and Welfare Patricia Harris, spoke with outrage about the need for prosecutions and possibly jail sentences for offenders. Their thinking seemed to be that if no penalties were exacted for such flagrant violations of the law in this case, drug users would have even less incentive to adhere to FDA regulations in the future.

And yet when I checked back with the FDA in February 1983, almost three years later, I found that no cases against DES violators had yet gone to court. "Does this mean that there will never be any prosecutions of these DES violators?" I asked William Rados in the FDA's Public Information Office, who had replaced Wayne Pines under the Reagan administration.

"Well, these things are up in the air," he replied. "But as I understand it, the feedlot managers have been told that they will not be prosecuted because of mitigating circumstances. The only cases still under consideration are those involving the firms that illegally sold DES."

"Can these people ultimately expect to be prosecuted?" I asked Rados.

"I just don't know," he replied.

As the incident began finally to pass into oblivion, FDA officials were clearly relieved. Once again they began to act as if DES was at last a drug of the past. But as I continued to travel around the country and talk with veterinarians and cattlemen, I learned otherwise. While it is true that most of the large feedlots were not about to risk having their cattle impounded again, I discovered that numerous smaller ranches and cow-calf operations continued to implant their animals with DES just as before.

But it was not until February 1983, when FDA officials themselves discovered another series of cases where DES had been illegally used, that the subject again surfaced publicly. This time, almost fifteen hundred fancy-grade veal calves from five different farms in upstate New York were discovered with residues of DES in their systems. The drug itself had apparently been illegally sold to farmers by a Canadian called Gustaaf VanGenechten, who had been traveling around upstate New York peddling plastic bags of a white powder that he claimed was "effective for weight gain in animals."

When I call E. Pitt Smith, Buffalo district director of the Food and Drug Administration, to ask him about the violations, he tells me that "what was unusual about these cases was the fact that the farmers were injecting their calves with DES along with penicillin. I have never heard of that before.

I guess they were not implanting them because the meat in-spectors at the slaughterhouse would be able to detect the pellets in their ears."

I ask Smith if any of the DES-treated meat had made its way to market before the violations were discovered.

"Well, let's put it this way," replies Smith after a pause. "The USDA did just condemn ninety-three carcasses from these farms that were already in cold storage down in New York City."

"Had any other contaminated carcasses already been eaten?"

"We just don't know."

And what about the future? Was this most recent illegal use of DES limited just to five farms in New York State?

"No," Smith replies quickly. "In fact, just yesterday I got a line on a farm that isn't even in New York. The five farms are just what we know about. I am sure there are others."

14

When diethylstilbestrol was finally banned in 1979, those cattlemen who did not continue to use it illegally were compelled to turn to one of the other brands of growth-promoting sex hormones still on the market. Although the alternatives were somewhat more expensive than DES, cattlemen have found a wide variety to choose from.

Ralgro, manufactured by the International Minerals and Chemicals Corp., and Ralabol, manufactured by Brae Laboratories, contain an anabolic agent with a similar chemical configuration to estrogens called zeranol, which is derived from the fungal mycotoxin zearalenone, a natural metabolite of the mold *Gibberella zeae*.

Steer-oid, manufactured by Anchor Animal Health, contains a combination of estradiol and another hormone produced by females, progresterone.

Compudose, manufactured by Eli Lily & Co., contains the estrogen estradiol. MGA, manufactured by the Upjohn Co., is a hormonal feed additive containing a synthetic progestogen.

Synovex-H (for heifers) and Synovex-S (for steers), manufactured by Syntex Agribusiness, Inc., a division of the Syntex Corporation, contain, respectively, combinations of estradiol and testosterone, and estradiol and progesterone.

The market for growth-promoting hormones, particularly in pellet form, is extremely lucrative, since an estimated 99 percent of all commercially raised feedlot cattle are implanted. As Gary Kuhl, extension livestock specialist at Kansas State

University, told a 1983 Kansas Cattlemen's Day audience, "I don't think that there is a producer that can afford not to use implanting as a management tool. If you can increase that rascal [cow] by thirty to forty pounds with a two-dollar bill, there isn't a banker in the world who wouldn't trade places with you for that kind of deal, because that's a ten-dollar return for every dollar invested."

The Syntex Corporation, which manufactures birth control pills and therapeutic hormonal products, as well as various kinds of diagnostic equipment and ophthalmic, dental- and beauty-care products, has garnered the largest share of the hormonal-implant market with its product Synovex. For the 1981 fiscal year, Syntex reported net corporate sales of $710.9 million.

"We have a well-defined goal, to be a one-billion-dollar company by 1984 or 5," President and Chief Executive Officer Albert Bowers told *The New York Times* that year. For fiscal 1982, Syntex net sales jumped to $813.3 million.

Synovex, Syntex's first animal-health product, was introduced in 1956 and, since the ban on DES, has done "extremely well" in the words of one company spokesman. Although the company refuses to divulge sales figures, it does note in a Synovex brochure that over 50 percent of feedlot cattle raised in the United States today are implanted with its product. The implants consist of eight orange-colored pellets, each no bigger than a piece of bird shot, which lie like peas in a pod inside an inch-and-a-half-long white plastic cartridge.

When the pellets are subcutaneously inserted in the ear (chosen as the implantation site because of the unlikelihood that cow ears will ultimately be eaten by humans), the hormones begin to be slowly released into the animal's bloodstream and to promote faster growth. Cost to the cattleman, including handling the animals, is approximately $6 per head.

Contrary to popular mythology about hormonal growth promotants, implants like Synovex conclusively seem to increase rather than decrease the proportion of lean to fat meat in a beef carcass. In a company-distributed "Synovex Performance Report," Syntex management states, "The effect of such a change in body composition can be quite startling. Based on an increase of 8.4 pounds of protein and 22 million fat cattle marketed, the use of Synovex could result in 185 million pounds of additional beef protein a year with no additional protein input."

"Synovex Implants Can Make You More Money," claims a banner headline in a full-page color ad that Syntex places in livestock magazines.

How much money?

One company-sponsored field trial claims that cows at pasture gained between forty and fifty-five pounds at an approximate saving of $28.00 to $38.50 per head.

In forty-eight-day trials on feedlot cattle, Syntex research showed average improvements of 17.3 percent in daily weight gain and 9.4 percent increase in feed efficiency compared to a nonimplanted control group.

"Even if other implants were free, you could be money ahead buying Synovex implants," says a fortune-cookie-like admonition at the bottom of each page of a sheaf of Syntex field-trial results that are given out to cattlemen for promotional purposes.

And, if these commercial entreaties for their product are not sufficient inducement for cattlemen to buy Synovex, the Syntex Corporation also offers free caps in which a customer can parade around the slogan, "Nothing Satisfies Like Beef."

Wanting to know more about this best-selling growth promotant, I stop in at the Syntex headquarters in Palo Alto to talk with Dr. Howard J. Ringold, senior vice-president in charge of basic research, and Dr. Richard A. Edgren, director of scientific affairs.

The Syntex Corporation's headquarters is adjacent to Stanford University and is itself very suggestive of a campus. Its low, modern buildings with red-tile Spanish-style roofs are scattered across 105 tastefully landscaped acres. Occasional joggers can be seen trotting down the asphalt pathways, past groves of trees, well-cultivated beds of flowers, fountains, and white-smocked lab technicians on their way to lunch or a cup of coffee in the company's handsome Food Services Building. There is a corporate art museum (today displaying a collection of antique cans and containers). Outdoor modern sculptures are discreetly placed around the grounds. Bulletin boards announce company-sponsored lectures, events and club activities. There is a feeling of benevolent order, prosperity and decorum here in this corporate preserve, which makes the nation's dusty, sprawling, fly-plagued feedlots—to which Synovex implants are ultimately destined—seem remote indeed.

Ringold is a dark-haired man in his fifties who wears a three-piece tan suit. His office, like almost everything else here at Syntex, is a tasteful room with modern furnishings. The only intervening noise is the rush of the air conditioning.

Edgren is a tall, lanky, middle-aged man who wears glasses and a business suit, and sports a perfectly trimmed, flat-top haircut.

As we sit around a small conference table sipping decaf coffee, I ask the two men how Synovex implants work.

"The actual mechanism of how estrogen stimulates growth is not really known," replies Ringold with a smile. "It is believed, however, that it triggers the release of growth hormones [somatrophin, produced by the pituitary gland], which naturally cause an animal to grow faster. But this is just a theory that has not yet been proven."

"Would a consumer eating a piece of beef from a Synovex-implanted animal be liable to ingest any harmful estradiol residues?" I ask.

"The amount of residue would be infinitely less than the amount your own body produces itself each day," replies

Ringold emphatically. "The residues should be no higher than the low parts per trillion, an insignificant toxicological amount.

"For example, if you assume that the average American eats one hundred and fifty grams of meat a day, and if all of that were beef from implanted animals, the residue level would be less than one one-thousandth of what a prepubertal child (who produces practically no estrogen) would have in his or her system.

"Then, if you consider that these natural hormones are not well-absorbed by the oral route (unlike DES)—only about ten percent is actually taken up into the body—then the amount a human would be getting from such beef would be no more than one ten-thousandth of a human's lowest daily production."

"The other thing to remember is that these hormones have specific target sites in a cow, such as the hypothalamus, the pituitary gland, the uterus or the vagina, where they are picked up by special estrogen-sensitive receptors and sequestered," says Richard Edgren, chiming in at last. "The presence of estradiol in muscle tissue is vastly diluted compared with what ends up in target organs and tissues that are not ones the consumer normally eats."

"To put it more concretely," adds Ringold, driving the point home, "a small child drinking milk every day would receive about four hundred and fifty times more natural estrogen from that milk than from his one hundred and fifty grams of implanted meat.

"We're not saying that the amount of estrogen released into an animal from a growth-promoting implant is necessarily less than the amount the animal produces itself," continues Ringold somewhat hastily, as if he did not want to leave the false impression that the dose received by the animal from Syntex's product was inconsequential. "It may or may not be less, depending on the species and sex of the animal, and if it's a female, what point its estrus cycle is at. There is tremendous variation. A steer, for instance, which normally produces very little estrogen, will get more from one of our implants than it produces itself, while a heifer that is in heat will get considerably less."

"In either case it will be an inconsequential amount, particularly when you compare it with the quantity of estradiol in a woman's system during ovulation, or after she gets pregnant, when her estrogen level will go up four or five hundred times," says Edgren.

One thing that still confuses me as I talk with Ringold and Edgren is this: It may be true that residue levels of estradiol in meat are theoretically very low from Synovex implants, but how is it actually possible for a USDA meat inspector or FDA lab technician to distinguish between the quantity of estradiol in a steak, for example, that was put there endogenously by the cow's own endocrine system and the quantity that may have been added exogenously by a hormonal implant?

"You can't tell the difference," says Ringold with a smile when I pose the question to him. "Well, I shouldn't say that you can't. What I mean is that you can't distinguish the difference from a tissue sample taken at a slaughterhouse. Only in a lab, by tagging the exogenous estradiol molecules with radioactive material and then later making an assay, can we distinguish the difference."

"If by some fluke or error—let's say if a farmer puts several implants right into the edible tissue of an animal and the estradiol levels become very high just before slaughter—how would an inspector be able to detect the problem?" I persist.

"We don't believe that could happen," replies Ringold with an expression of a teacher who has just been asked a question that is possibly intelligent but irrelevant to the point he has repeatedly been trying to impart to his students.

The question of increasing residues of substances that are naturally occurring in those foods, but also possibly dangerous in large or prolonged dosages, is an extremely thorny one. It is also one that has had the FDA moving in contrary directions over the past decade. Although both DES and estradiol are estrogenic in activity and are both lumped into the category of being suspected carcinogens, DES at least had the virtue (for regulators) of being a synthetic compound that does not occur naturally in plants or animals and that, under the Delaney Clause, or general safety clauses of the Federal Food, Drug and Cosmetic Act, could be banned if it began showing up in residue form. But what was the correct line for carcinogens like estradiol and other sex hormones that are naturally occurring? How could the FDA say that no detectable residues of these compounds were permissible when, in effect, God had put them there in the first place?

Originally wary of adding to the human burden of estrogen from exogenous sources, such as implants, the FDA used to require that all animals fattened on Synovex be held back from slaughter until at least sixty days after implantation. The regulation was clear enough, but actually neither the FDA (which must establish permissible drug residues) nor the USDA (which must inspect carcasses for these residues) had any practical means of testing for compliance.

So, in 1979, the FDA reopened the case file on Synovex. Referring to the drug as a carcinogen, they issued a Notice of Opportunity for Hearing in the Federal Register, soliciting further documentation and comment on the drug's continued use, methods of detecting residues and the potential danger of those residues.

In 1983, almost four years later under the Reagan administration's new policy of trying to speed up action on drug-use applications, and after the Syntex Corporation had resubmitted volumes of new data and affidavits from experts in the field supporting the company's contention that Synovex left neither large nor harmful residues, the FDA vacated the notice. Moreover, in a second action, they remanded the sixty-day withdrawal time between implantation and slaughter. For the first time in the twenty-seven years that Synovex had been on the market, cattlemen could now use these implants right up until the day a cow was slaughtered.

These actions appeared to represent more than a softening of position toward the Syntex Corporation. The FDA seemed to have decided that it was time to take a much less restrictive policy in general against implants that contained naturally occurring hormones.

In February 1983 at an Office International des Epizooties symposium, "Sanitary Aspects Concerning the Control and Use of Anabolics in Animal Production," held in Paris, France, Dr. Lester Crawford, director of the FDA's Bureau of Veterinary Medicine, and Dr. Theodore Farber, director of the BVM's Toxicology Staff, proposed that the United States allow all naturally occurring hormones such as estradiol, testosterone and progesterone to be used essentially without regulation in animals. There was one stipulation. They told the Paris symposium that sex hormones should be considered to be under safe conditions of use if they did not show up in meat residue levels that exceeded 1 percent of the daily production of prepubertal boys and girls.

"If higher levels are anticipated from endogenous anabolic agents, these compounds should be subjected to the same series of tests required for synthetic anabolics," stated Crawford. "This approach embraces the proper level of concern for public health while at the same time recognizing the practical necessity of using anabolics [steroidal hormones] in rearing livestock."

It would have been hard to design a set of regulations calculated to please companies like the Syntex Corporation more, even if they had been drafted by their own staff. The presumption seemed to be that since the drug industry's own laboratory tests with radioactively marked molecules of estradiol had not shown large residues, no such residues could or would occur and thus no further concern with these hormonal implants was warranted.

What these proposals seemed to be advocating was that implants containing natural sex hormones be, in effect, removed from the regulation system of meat inspection and residue monitoring, which, at least theoretically, examines and subjects meat to periodic testing. Wondering if this was an accurate assessment of the new proposed FDA position, I called up Theodore Farber at his Washington, D.C., office.

"We are privy to information sent to us by Syntex that shows that they have developed new methods for detecting estradiol residues by radio-immune assay," replies Farber. "And according to these, even with an implant right behind the cow's ear at the time of slaughter, the levels of estradiol in the muscle tissue don't get up that high."

"Does this mean that no measures will be taken to assure that estradiol does not exceed prescribed one-percent levels for prepubertal children in meat?"

"That's right," replies Farber. "Syntex has demonstrated a research method to us—one that would probably take too long for the USDA to use in the field—that has assured us that there should be no concern over using the preparation in animals, even under an abuse sort of situation where a cow might get loaded with several pellets at once."

"What if someone implanted the muscle tissue itself with several pellets?"

"Well, I don't know about that," replies Farber. "I don't have any data in regard to a pellet being put into muscle tissue itself."

Back at Syntex, I ask Ringold and Edgren their views on the carcinogenicity of estradiol and other estrogens.

"Natural estrogens like estradiol may be co-carcinogens [meaning that they may act synergistically with other compounds to cause cancer], but you cannot trigger cancer with estrogen alone," Ringold tells me. "The mechanism of estrogen involvement in a tumor is by hyperproliferation [enlarge-ment] of a given target organ or tissue, such as the uterus or breast. When a tissue is bombarded with estrogen over a long period of time, it may become disposed to cancer, so that if there is a virus, toxic chemical, or other mutagen present, it is possible for a tumor to develop."

"If estrogens are not dangerous at these low levels, why was DES banned?" I ask.

"First of all, DES residues are more persistent, particularly in the liver," replies Ringold. "Because of their unique chem-ical structure, there is a possibility that DES can react directly with cellular DNA. This may give it the capability of becoming a direct carcinogen. This has nothing to do with its direct estrogenic activity, however. And, in my view, this is the major reason to be concerned about DES but not estradiol.

"The second thing you must remember about the use of sex hormones in meat animals is that you must have enough of a residue to have a biological effect before you can point the cancer finger," continues Ringold. "I think most biologists would agree that in general you need at least a substantial portion of your body's own daily rate of production of a hor-mone before you get such an effect and can even talk about carcinogenicity."

Looking through the general conclusions on sex hormones of the International Agency on Cancer Research's definitive volume on these compounds, I find the following: "In humans, endogenous hormones are important in the initiation and pro-gression of tumors. The incidence of tumors in humans could be altered by exposure to various exogenous hormones singly or in combination."

The authors of this monograph go on, however, to explain, as Ringold just has, that, "For an administered estrogen seri-ously to influence the human hormonal environment, it must be equal to or greater than the amount of estrogen produced endogenously."

But in a section subtitled "Animal Data," while the authors concede that, "in the majority of experiments in which animals were treated with estrogens and which resulted in carcinogenesis, high dose levels were used," they go on to caution that, "information currently available is, however, inadequate to indicate the minimum doses required to produce carcinogenesis, and these could be much lower than those commonly employed in animal studies."

I ask Ringold how he views such statements, which claim that we do not yet know what a cancer-causing dose of estrogen is.

"What can I say, except to go back and intelligently examine a statement like that by taking a person's daily production rate of a sex hormone and see how significant the added increment is by comparison?" he replies with a sigh of exasperation. "I mean, let's look at reality! A person's production of estrogen or testosterone may naturally undergo a doubling in a matter of hours all by itself, so I don't see how anyone can rationally argue that having your daily production rate increased by one one-thousandth or one ten-thousandth from elsewhere can cause any harmful biological effect."

"Then why are perfectly reputable scientists so cautious?"

"Well, it's not rational in my view," replies Ringold, laughing and tilting back in his chair. "I mean, good heavens! If you're sitting looking out the window and you happen to see a scantily dressed woman with a nice figure walk by, your own production of testosterone may increase by fifty percent in a matter of seconds. Now, is that something you're going to get worried about?"

"So you are not afraid that the use of naturally occurring hormones in meat animals may turn out with a bad ending as in the case of DES?" I ask.

"No, I am not," he replies. "But since I am in drug development myself, I know that although you can get a lot of valuable data from animal studies, there is still no substitute for human data. There will always be the possibility that effects that do not show up in test animals will later appear in human beings."

Ringold reaches for his cup of now-tepid coffee and takes a sip. Then, looking distantly toward the window, he adds, "The question of DES is a hard one for me to be objective about." He went on to explain that a close relative is a DES daughter. "What happened was a terribly unfortunate thing."

Silence falls over the room for a moment. Then, his voice regaining some of its earlier forcefulness, Ringold adds, "I am not saying that growth-promoting hormones are dangerous, and I believe most scientists familiar with the subject would concur with that assessment. But we live in a world of risks. And while I do not believe in placing people in jeopardy, I think we always have to be willing to acknowledge this risk if we wish to continue moving scientifically forward."

15

The operation is a common and relatively simple one. A veterinarian will make a surgical slit in the sheath of skin that encloses a bull's flaccid penis and will then reroute his member through the side.

Of course, when the "sidewinder" or "teaser bull" identifies a cow in estrus (heat), he naturally becomes aroused and wants to mount and impregnate her. But with his erection skewed off to the side, he will not actually be able to penetrate her vagina. He will, however, inadvertently succeed in leaving a daub of color from a marker hung around his chin on her rump as he clamors for consummation. In doing so, he will accomplish his purpose, namely, to mark cows in heat so that a cattleman can tell which of his animals are ready to be bred, either naturally by a bull or by means of artificial insemination (AI).

Particularly if a cattleman is going to "AI" his herd, heat detection can be a laborious and costly procedure. The problem is that his cows will all come into heat at different times, making the marking process a critical one and also necessitating many trips by the technician who is actually performing the artificial insemination.

But now all this has changed. "Teaser bulls" and the once-cumbersome technique of "heat detection" have been rendered obsolete by a new group of commercial, hormone-like compounds known as estrus synchronizers. With one or two injections, every animal in a large herd of cows can now be chemically induced to come into heat on exactly the same day, like so many alarm clocks all set to go off at once.

The thirty-two-page color supplement ("Breeding Management for Building Profit") that the Upjohn Co. put into *Beef Magazine*'s 1983 National Cattlemen's Association Annual Convention issue represents an unusually aggressive ad campaign. But Upjohn, a pioneer in the field of estrus synchronization, has a new product out that they believe is a winner, and they appear to be sparing few costs to promote it. The product is called Lutalyse. When I ask James Randall, its product manager at Upjohn in Kalamazoo, Michigan, about it, his voice reflects the kind of optimistic buoyancy about a product that every sales chief dreams of.

"We've had antibiotics, hormones, bacterins, serums, but now as we move forward into this new group of compounds that promote estrus synchronization, I think you'd have to say that animal science is in one of its most exciting periods of development," he tells me over the phone. "These compounds have the potential to revolutionize the industry. When we began, our goal was to sell twice as much our second year as our first year. We achieved that goal, selling somewheres between two and three million doses. It's hot . . . well, let's not call it 'hot,' " he says, not wanting to sound too much like a booster for an athletic team. "Let's just say that we think it's a promising product."

Lutalyse is a naturally occurring prostaglandin, a group of endocrine compounds that work similarly to hormones, although they usually exert no more than a localized effect on the tissue in which they are produced.

When properly stimulated, most tissues in the mammalian body produce one prostaglandin or another. Minute amounts of these very potent chemicals affect almost every biological function, including respiration, blood clotting, digestion, circulation, nerve response and reproduction. Researchers who have begun studying prostaglandins have commented on their "awesome" and "bewildering" diversity.

In human medicine, doctors have started to use prostaglandins instead of dilatation and curettage or saline injection to abort fetuses in the second trimester of pregnancy. Prostaglandins are also being used on women who miss their periods as a form of menstrual induction. Certain kinds of prostaglandins that relax the muscles surrounding blood vessels are being experimented with on patients with heart and vascular problems, while still others that condition the size of air passageways in the lungs are being experimentally used to treat asthmatics.

The field of prostaglandin research is a new and very complex one. Its significance was underlined when the 1982 Nobel Prize for medicine was awarded to three key prostaglandin researchers—John Vance of the Wellcome Foundation Ltd. in England and Sune Bergström and Bengt Samuelsson of the Karolinska Institute in Sweden.

I ask Randall which prostaglandin Lutalyse contains and how it affects the reproductive cycle of cows?

"We believe that dinoprost promethamine, the active chemical compound in Lutalyse, is produced somewhere in the reproductive tract, although we are not quite sure where," he explains. "What we do know is that it plays a very important role in stimulating the reproductive system of mammals back into a cycling mode after ovulation if fertilization does not occur. It is this characteristic that makes it interesting to us as an estrus synchronizer."

Normally what happens in the twenty-one-day bovine reproductive cycle is that approximately five days after ovulation, a cluster of cells, called the corpus luteum, begins to form around the empty egg follicle on the ovary and to produce the hormone progesterone. It is the progesterone that puts the reproductive system on hold and prevents ovulation from taking place again until the first egg has had a reasonable period of time to be fertilized and implanted in the uterus wall. If conception does not take place by the sixteenth day, the gears of the cow's reproductive cycle begin to advance once more. The corpus luteum begins to regress (to "lutalyse"), suppressing the production of progesterone, which in turn allows the ovary to begin producing a new egg.

As an Upjohn product brochure describes it, Lutalyse "resets the animal's biological clock," causing its corpus luteum to regress prematurely, and the production of progesterone to subside so that a new egg follicle can develop. If a cattle breeder does not want to wait out the natural cycle of each of his cows, all he has to do is inject 25 mg of dinoprost promethamine intramuscularly into each animal at an approximate cost of five dollars a head. (The motto Upjohn has aptly given Lutalyse is "You Call the Shots.") In a matter of hours the cows' reproductive systems will have raced toward ovulation like tapes put on Fast Forward.

The ability to bring a whole herd of cows around into reproductive concordance not only enables a cattleman to get rid of his arcane "sidewinder" bull, but also to breed all his animals in one fell swoop, and to schedule his calving season to coincide with good weather and optimal pasture conditions. A piece of promotional literature from Upjohn immodestly describes this new chemical technology as heralding the "Dawn of a New Era in Cattle Breeding Management."

"One thing we're always telling our clients is that Lutalyse won't make a cow any more fertile," insists Jim Randall. "People who think that they can substitute our product for good management are going to be disappointed. We encourage our people to adopt Lutalyse only as a part of a whole program of good management. We really could have put on a medicine show with this stuff and done one hell of a business the first year," Randall adds cautionarily. "But we're just not out to sell Lutalyse like Rubik's Cube."

Just as the Roman god Saturn, after he was banished from

the heavens, gave Janus the gift of double knowledge so that he could know the future as well as the past, so nature has imbued Lutalyse with the power to inhibit the process of conception and birth as well as to promote it. Not only has Lutalyse been approved by the FDA to synchronize estrus in cows, but it has also been approved as an abortifacient, for use in making pregnant feedlot heifers miscarry.

"Open your feedlot heifers to a more productive future," proclaims a glossy advertisement that Upjohn places in livestock trade journals. "Now there's a way to abort heifers as they're processed into your feedlot. . . . The entire process takes place in such a gentle and quiet manner that these heifers are likely to stay on feed while abortion occurs. . . . Don't let pregnant heifers drain your feedlot's profitability!"

"Actually it is pretty ironic that Lutalyse works so effectively to promote efficient breeding *and* to terminate unwanted pregnancies," says Randall, emphasizing the word "and" with a chuckle. "But the mechanics are the same. If there is a calf in the cow's stomach, our product just kicks that old estrus cycle into gear by prematurely causing the corpus luteum to regress. When that happens, a new egg starts developing, and the fetus is naturally expelled."

And why would a cattleman want to abort a heifer? Because once in a feedlot, the job of a cow is gaining pounds as rapidly as possible, not reproduction. An animal that is expending energy developing a fetus may be a big eater, but she will also be a slow gainer. And since occasional herds have as many as 30 percent of all new heifers accidentally bred, some feedlot operators automatically inject each heifer with Lutalyse as they come into the lot off the trucks for their final three-month fattening period.

Although Upjohn's Lutalyse was the first estrus synchronizer and abortifacient approved for commercial use in cattle by the FDA, several other companies have now entered this lucrative market with competing products. Ceva Laboratories,

Inc., manufactures a product called Syncro-Mate B.; Cutter Laboratories' Haver-Lockhart Division has recently come out with a product called Estrumate; and the Syntex Corporation has just introduced a new synthetic prostaglandin and abortifacient called Bovilene.

Research for new and profitable ways to manipulate the reproductive systems of animals have not stopped with estrus synchronizers and abortifacients. Almost yearly, new commercially viable products are being discovered and tested. For instance, in 1983, animal scientists at the University of Maryland reported that they had come up with a new synthetic luteinizing hormone-releasing hormone (LHRH) that blocked the production of testosterone and could be injected into young piglets to castrate them chemically without surgery.

A little overwhelmed by Upjohn's encomiums to Lutalyse, I ask Randall if the drug is known to leave any residues in meat. After very insistently reminding me that dinoprost promethamine is a "naturally occurring substance in all mammals," Randall explains, "After one pass through an animal's lung, ninety percent of it is converted into inactive metabolites. By the end of twenty-four hours, virtually all of the drug is cleared from an animal's system."

Noting that the red-white-and-black bottle in which Lutalyse comes is inscribed at the bottom with the warnings "Caution: Federal (USA) law restricts this drug to use by or on order of a licensed veterinarian," and that Upjohn's technical bulletin warns, "Not for human use. Women of child-bearing age . . . should exercise *extreme caution* when handling this product," I ask Randall how hazardous Lutalyse can be to humans.

"We recommend that people handle it carefully," says Randall without his earlier ebullience. "Our label does have a warning for pregnant women to keep away. But the thing to remember on your pregnant women is that Lutalyse is dose-specific and species-specific. There has been a whole lot of stuff published by people who do not have the whole book of information. But what you have to keep in mind is that the prostaglandins that cause abortions in women are a whole different class than the ones we find in cattle. Nonetheless, we've put a warning right there on the package just in case."

In point of fact, the active ingredient of Lutalyse, Fa_2 (PGF_2a), has the same effect on the reproductive tract of human females as bovines. As Ronald Mackey, a veterinarian who has a monthly question-and-answer column in *Beef Magazine* cautioned his readers,

> Lutalyse . . . [does have] some undesirable side effects when handled by humans, especially women. In fact, it is stated on the label that pregnant women should not even handle the bottles as they could cause abortion and changes in the menstrual cycle . . . just from absorption through the skin.
>
> I don't believe that these things can be stressed enough, especially now that we have licensed female veterinary technicians working in feedlots and handling these products.

16

―――

"Thanks to MGA It's Been Another Quiet Day," proclaims the headline in a full-page color ad in *Feedlot Management* magazine. The ad shows a photo of several cows lounging peacefully against a corral fence and silhouetted by the setting sun.

"That easygoing calm when heifers are on rations containing MGA is unmistakable," reads the blurb below. "There is no bawling, no riding, no restless milling around. It's not surprising that experienced cattle feeders can tell immediately when a pen is on MGA. It's the only additive that keeps heifers out of heat—and at the feed bunks."

Melengesterol acetate (MGA) is a synthetic progestogen (a steroidal female hormone) that is manufactured as a feed additive by the Tuco Agricultural Division of the Upjohn Co. to promote growth by preventing feedlot heifers from coming into heat. The reason why cattlemen do not want heifers to come into heat while they are being fattened is not because they fear they will be bred (there are rarely any bulls around in a feedlot), but because during those several days when a cow is in estrus, it tends to get very restless and rambunctious. Instead of placidly eating and putting on pounds, it is likely to be trying to mount or "bull" its pen mates, not only disturbing them, but also raising clouds of dust that can lead to respiratory problems for the whole herd.

For these reasons heifers have traditionally not been a particularly profitable prospect for feedlot operators. But by mixing 0.25 to 0.50 mg per head of MGA in liquid or powdered form into daily feed rations, Tuco/Upjohn believes that they have made the feeding of heifers a money-making proposition. "For More Profits and Fewer Problems, Feed MGA," an Upjohn promotion exhorts farmers. "MGA Fed Heifers can make you more money than any heifer you've ever fed."

What kinds of increased profits can a farmer expect? A 10.3 percent improvement in weight gain and a 6.5 percent improvement in feed conversion. "This pencils out to an improvement in net profit of $3.00 to $10.00 per head. . . . And that's above the cost of MGA," claims an industry flyer.

Interested to find out more about MGA, I call up James W. Lauderdale, Ph.D., who is a soft-spoken staff scientist with a branch of Tuco's Animal Health Research and Development Department called Performance Development. I ask him how much of MGA's growth-promoting effect is due to its "tranquilizing" effect.

"Well, frankly, I would prefer not to use that kind of terminology, because the animal is not 'tranquilized' in any sense of the word," Lauderdale replies, with a suggestion of irritation in his voice. "Yes, MGA quiets heifers down by blocking estrus. That does keep them from riding each other, and at the feed bunks eating. But we also think it stimulates their own production of estrogen, which has its own growth-promoting effect."

MGA stops an animal's estrus cycle by hormonally blocking ovulation. However, it allows the ovarian follicle to develop to just under ovulatory size. And since the follicle is one of the main production sites of estradiol, the cow's endocrine system continues to secrete levels of estrogen as high as a pre-estrus animal. Why is this important? Because, as the manufacturers of Synovex, Compudose and Steer-oid implants know, estradiol promotes growth.

"I think what is important to remember about hormones is that they don't really start up anything new in an animal's body," continues Lauderdale philosophically. "They simply change the rate of what normally goes on. I don't know if a car is a very good analogy, but rather than shifting a car from neutral to first, you might say that hormones shift an animal from first to second . . . they just speed things up a bit."

Since MGA is a synthetic hormone like DES, I ask Lauderdale if there have been any "problems" with it.

"I honestly can't identify any for you," he replies. "We have a large technical service staff that deals with use-problems under field conditions. But since we started selling it in 1968, we've accumulated quite an extensive use-history, and I'm reasonably comfortable it does what we say it will."

What I had intended to ask Lauderdale was whether or not there were any human risks associated with the use of MGA. But concerned as he is with "performance development," he has replied to my question as if I were a livestock producer asking whether or not MGA were an effective growth promotant.

In fact, in talking about antimicrobial and hormonal products used in livestock production, I have repeatedly noticed the tendency of drug company officials and their promotional literature to avoid discussions of what these compounds are, how they biologically work and how they can affect those people who come in contact with them. It is not that research is unavailable, or that the people in question are ignorant about this information, but rather that in focusing on a drug's efficacy, these other considerations seem quite irrelevant.

Rephrasing the question, I ask Lauderdale what dangers, if any, MGA may pose to humans.

"We are talking about a progestogen that is being fed at very low levels," replies Lauderdale, now with a suggestion of defensiveness in his voice. "There is no incentive for the cattleman to feed more, because it won't do any good, and there is a lot of incentive to stay on the low side to save money.

"Anyway, a human being cannot ingest—is physically incapable of ingesting—sufficient quantities of meat products to elicit a biological effect from MGA. You would have to eat several hundred pounds of meat a day to even begin to see a biological effect at the normal residue level of ten to twenty-five ppb. So if you're talking about residues in meat, we don't see any problem."

I ask Lauderdale what would happen if a person ingested or inhaled periodic quantities of MGA—while working around a feed mill, for instance.

"Well, MGA is a progesterone. We have not found any problems with it for men," answers Lauderdale. "It was investigated several years ago as a birth control agent for women and is in fact in some contraceptive pills right now. As such, it certainly will inhibit menses if administered at high-enough doses. I suppose someone might be foolish enough to eat soybean-meal feed in which it is mixed, but it wouldn't be very tasty." Lauderdale dismisses the subject with a laugh.

The Feed Additives Compendium, put out each year by the Miller Publishing Company in Minneapolis to keep farmers and feed-mill operators abreast of the changing rules and regulations that relate to feed-additive drugs, cautions that MGA "should be used only as directed. Excessive contact with skin should be avoided. Destroy empty container. Do not re-use." It also reminds users of the FDA-required forty-eight-hour withdrawal time.

On a trip to eastern Colorado, I visited two feedlots that use MGA and discovered that the withdrawal times for the drug, like many others, often go unobserved. At one of these feedlots I asked a young employee who was in charge of mixing feed about procedures for taking cattle off MGA two days before shipment to market. "There isn't hardly any procedures," he replied with a snort of laughter, hastening to add that "his ass would be grass" if I quoted him or named the feedlot where he works.

"We had one foreman in here a while back who tried to do

things pretty straight, but he gave up," he continued. "The problem with this MGA stuff is that often we wouldn't be shipping a whole pen of animals at the same time, and it was a pain in the ass to separate out the ones that was going to get shipped and put them on special clean feed. The boss didn't want the hassle. So he just told us to keep mixing the stuff right into the ration for all of them until the time they put the cows on the trucks."

The other alternative to separating cattle is to take the whole pen of heifers off the drug two days before those that are ready to go to market leave. When I posed this as a possibility, this particular feedlot hand gave another contemptuous laugh and rejoined, "Yeah. Fat chance! Two days after the cows stop eating this stuff, they start getting crazy again. You know, they come into heat and start trying to hump each other, raise hell and kick a lot of dust up in the air. The owners need that like a second asshole. The folks who run this place just can't be bothered worrying about a bunch of withdrawal times. Anyway, they know that the chances of getting caught are just about zilch. [In 1981 the USDA only took 327 tissue samples to test for violative residues of MGA. In 1982, the number fell to 281.] The attitude around here is just to feed 'em up, ship 'em out and hope that nothing goes wrong with the inspectors."

In fact, not much appears to "go wrong with the inspectors" from the perspective of feedlots like this one. I am unaware of a single carcass that has recently failed to reach market because of residues of exogenously introduced hormones. This is not to say that harmful residues of MGA are regularly contaminating the meat we eat. (In fact, the last limited USDA sample that was done showed no recent violations.) However, neither does this preclude the possibility that they do occur from time to time. What especially concerns some researchers is that although MGA is not known to react directly with DNA to produce cancer, it is suspected, like other progestogens, of being a cocarcinogen.

17

During the spring and summer of 1982, San Juan newspapers ran daily articles about the increasing number of Puerto Rican children who were showing signs of premature sexual development. The cause was uncertain, but appeared to be related to their contamination with some kind of estrogenic compound.

"*Histeria Con El Estrogeno*" trumpeted a Spanish-language paper in a bold headline. "Premature Puberty in Puerto Rico Put at Epidemic Levels" and "Estrogen in Food Linked to Ovarian Cysts in Tots," proclaimed headlines in the English-language San Juan *Star*.

I had first become aware of the situation in the spring of 1982, when I chanced to read two short letters to the editor of the British medical journal *The Lancet*. In these letters, three pediatric endocrinologists from Puerto Rico were replying to an earlier *Lancet* editorial that generally commended the World Health Organization's Food and Agriculture Organization for a report they had issued on the use of hormonal growth promotants for meat animals. The position of the FAO had been that when used properly, these compounds could provide significant benefits to society with minimal risk.

"We are very worried about this practice of using hormones on livestock," wrote pediatric endocrinologists Dr. Carmen A. Saenz de Rodriguez and Dr. Maria A. Toro-Sola, both from De Diego Hospital in San Juan. "It has been allowed by the World Health Organization, but the necessary controls will not be strictly enforced in many countries. In Puerto Rico, such products as diethylstilbestrol (DES) and zeranol (an estrogenic nonsteroidal growth promotant derived from zearalenone, a natural product of fungal origin) are sold over the counter without a veterinary prescription. We have been investigating this matter because of an alarming incidence of premature thelarche (prepubertal development of the breasts) in Puerto Rico.

"During the past ten years, 375 patients with premature thelarche have been observed in our practice: 85 percent were seen during the years 1979–81. We found a high incidence of ovarian cysts in sixty-one patients (16 percent aged 8 months to 6 years)," continued Dr. Saenz's letter. "We urge WHO to review its position on the use of anabolic steroids such as DES and zeranol in meat production."

"Premature sexual development has become a serious public-health problem in Puerto Rico," wrote Dr. Adolpho Perez-Comas, associate professor of pediatrics at Ponce Medical School and a practicing pediatrician across the island in Mayagüez, in the second letter. "In the western region of the island we have evaluated 272 such cases in children under eight years of age during the past ten years, and physicians in other areas have had similar experiences. . . . 81 percent of the patients with premature thelarche and 90 percent of the patients with precocious puberty presented increased estrogen levels."

In October, after arriving in Puerto Rico myself to investigate the situation, I went immediately to De Diego Hospital, a tall high-rise building in the Santurce section of San Juan, to talk with Dr. Saenz de Rodriguez, who is director of pediatrics. After a crowded ride on a sluggish elevator, I arrived at the pediatric floor and found Dr. Saenz, a spirited middle-aged woman with brown eyes, blond hair and a serious but warm smile.

"For years I have been encountering periodic cases of precocious puberty," Dr. Saenz tells me when she is finished seeing the last of that morning's small patients. "But in 1980, when I started finding one or two children like this in my waiting room every day, I knew that something quite serious was wrong. From the symptoms they were exhibiting, I was sure that they are being contaminated with some kind of estrogen."

I ask Dr. Saenz to describe the symptoms. Without replying, she picks up a handful of Polaroid photos from the top of her desk and hands them to me. Each shows the small body of a naked young girl. As I slowly thumb through them, Dr. Saenz gives me a case-by-case commentary in a tone of voice that matches the expression on her face—a mixture of outrage, sadness and determination.

In the first photo, a four-and-a-half-year-old girl with delicate coffee-colored skin, doelike brown eyes and almost fully developed breasts lies on an examining table. She smiles with a sweet innocence at the camera, seemingly unaware of the dramatic changes that have gone on in her body.

"She had an ovarian cyst," says Dr. Saenz tersely.

A twelve-year-old boy stands against a white wall looking with blank bewilderment into the camera. He wears a silver crucifix around his neck, which dangles down between two grossly swollen breasts.

"We've had to schedule him for surgery," says Dr. Saenz matter-of-factly. "The emotional stress on him is incredible."

A one-year-old girl, whose teeth have not even completely come in, lies on the examining table with a ruler stretched across her chest to measure the diameter of her enlarged breasts. She has a pacifier in one of her hands. Dr. Saenz says nothing. She just shakes her head.

A five-year-old girl, looking wild-eyed into the camera as if a weapon were being aimed at her, lies on the examining table. Her breasts are as large and well-developed as a fourteen-year-old's Her mons veneris is covered with a scraggly tangle of pubic hair.

"This one had a well-developed uterus and had begun to have some vaginal bleeding," says Dr. Saenz. "These are developments that we would not usually expect until eight or nine years of age at the very earliest."

Dr. Saenz has photographed these damaged children in every angle of repose. The most haunting ones are those that, like inversions of prison mug shots, have the heads (and legs) cropped out, so that all that remains is a delicate child's torso incongruously encumbered with the misplaced sexual attributes of an adult. There is about this stack of milky and artlessly composed Polaroid pictures a kind of tawdry obscenity that suggests the merchandise from an adult bookstore except for the fact that they are of medically abnormal children and do not convey even the slightest sense of eroticism.

"By the time some of these children get to us, they have gone so far into puberty that we cannot arrest the process," says Dr. Saenz somberly. "For about eight percent of the children there is nothing we can do." It's a frightening thing to see a very little girl advancing into puberty and not know what you can do to stop it.

"I have seen hundreds of children like this, and I am certain that there are thousands more going undiagnosed because this problem has become so widespread that even many doctors are no longer getting alarmed about it. But I think these children are being contaminated with large amounts of estrogen from someplace."

Opening the door from her office to her examining room, she extracts some medical records from a cardboard filing box. "This little girl came to me at age one-and-a-half," she says, scanning one of the records. "She had enlarged breasts, and

we discovered an ovarian cyst that we had to operate on.
Two-and-a-half years later she was back. She had advanced
thelarche, pubic hair and another ovarian cyst. She looked
eleven years old. We took that cyst out and sent it off for an
assay. The results showed an enormous amount of estrogen
in it, as much as in a twenty-year-old woman. A little girl is
hardly supposed to produce any estrogen at all. Now she is
five-and-a-half and going quite fast into puberty."

The phone rings. Dr. Saenz answers it, speaking in Spanish.
When she hangs up, she sits quietly behind her desk for a
few moments before speaking again and then declares, "Estrogens are carcinogenic. Everywhere in the medical literature
one is cautioned to treat estrogens with great care, not only
because of their profound biological activity on the reproductive system, but also because they cause cancer. The Commonwealth Health Department's statistics on uterine and ovarian
cancer show a much higher incidence of cancer in exactly those
towns and areas here in Puerto Rico from which we are getting
the most children with signs of thelarche and precocious
puberty."

When we have finished talking, I follow Dr. Saenz to the
pediatric ward to visit one of her young patients, a cute little
girl of five years with shiny black hair and limpid brown eyes.
Her parents are in her room, readying to take her home after
three days under observation in the hospital. As we enter, the
small girl looks up from her coloring book like an animal
startled while grazing.

"I would show you the child's symptoms, but the parents
would be embarrassed," Dr. Saenz says to me softly in English.
"She is well advanced with pubic hair and enlarged breasts.
We gave her a sonogram, which showed the uterus quite
prematurely developed. Normally you're not supposed to even
see these organs on a child her age."

Speaking in Spanish, Dr. Saenz asks the father, a short,

sleek man with a black mustache and ruffled, Spanish-style
shirt, how they first became aware their daughter was developing abnormally.

"Well, we just began to notice that our daughter's breasts
were swelling up. But when we first went to the doctor, he
said he didn't think anything much was wrong. After we
began to notice pubic hair, we decided to bring her here,"
says the father as Dr. Saenz translates. He speaks shyly and
almost inaudibly, as if the matter were a painful one for him
to discuss in public. As he talks, he puts his arm around the
shoulder of his daughter, who cuddles in beside him, her
enlarged areolas and nipples making small dark protuberances
through her thin cotton nightgown.

"Her ovaries and vagina are so well developed, I wouldn't
be surprised if she started menstruating in a year or two,"
says Dr. Saenz to me. "But her bone structure, which also
should be influenced by prolonged dosages of estrogen, is
normal, which suggests that she has received more of a
sudden shock of estrogen than a prolonged exposure."

Back in her office, I ask Dr. Saenz why adults are not being
affected by whatever source of estrogen is causing premature
thelarche and precocious puberty in children.

"Adults are larger, and since they naturally produce greater
quantities of estrogen than children, they are less sensitive.
But there may be long-range effects we can't see yet, such as
high incidence of uterine and cervical cancer in women.
Thirteen percent of these girls have ovarian cysts. So I am
concerned over the long run about the whole population."

"The detailed analysis of histories on all of our patients
discards their use of medications or creams containing estrogens [as a cause], and none had neurological or other adrenal
disorders," wrote Dr. Saenz in the *Journal of the Puerto Rican
Medical Association* in February 1982. "It was clearly observed in 97 percent of the cases that the appearance of abnormal breast tissue was probably related to the weaning

from a formula to local whole milk in the infant group. At a later age, a dietary history of a greater consumption of local whole milk, poultry and beef was referred by the parents."

I ask Dr. Saenz how she can be so sure that the children are being contaminated with estrogen from meat and milk rather than another source. (There are of course a variety of plants, such as certain clovers, high in estrogen and a number of other chemical compounds that have estrogenic activity. Moreover, here in Puerto Rico there are also an unusually large number of pharmaceutical companies that manufacture birth control pills.)

"When we take our patients off meat and fresh milk, their symptoms usually regress," replies Dr. Saenz simply. Then she reaches down beside her desk and takes several bottles and boxes of pharmaceuticals out of a briefcase. With a smiling defiance, she hands them to me.

"When we started suspecting that the contamination might be coming from meat or dairy products, we hired a detective and sent him around to the various veterinary supply houses," says Dr. Saenz as I examine the drugs. "He went to about twenty different outlets and told the clerks that he had a very skinny cow that he wanted to fatten quickly. They gave him these and told him to put three implants into his cow at once." She points to one of the bottles.

"Stilbestrol Implants - 250 Pellets. For Veterinary Use Only, Anchor Serum Co.," says a black-and-white label on the bottle, which is filled with minuscule white pellets of DES.

A second bottle, filled with a clear, yellowish liquid, is labeled, "ECP - Estradiol Cypionate. The Upjohn Co."

ECP is an injectable estrogen that is used to bring recalcitrant cows into heat. It is also used to expel dead fetuses or placentas from the wombs of cows after parturition. As I subsequently learned from a Puerto Rican farmer who keeps dairy cows, ECP is also sometimes used illegally on the island in the hopes that a few shots will quickly fatten up an underweight animal destined for the slaughterhouse or help a refractory dairy cow increase milk production.

The final drug that Dr. Saenz's detective has procured is a cylinder of Ralgro, a growth-promoting implant that she had mentioned in her letter to *The Lancet* as a possible cause, along with DES, of the endocrine disorders she was observing.

"One of the most obvious problems with all these hormonally active animal drugs is that most medical doctors are unaware that they exist," says Dr. Saenz, shaking her head. "I mean, I had really no idea what was out there being used until I started looking into it. So it is perfectly possible that there have been other such cases of human contamination, but that no one has thought to try to trace the symptoms back to drugs for animal use."

Wanting to corroborate all that Dr. Saenz has told me, I go over to the San Juan *Star* to chat with Robert Friedman, the reporter who first broke this story in Puerto Rico.

"I was completely ignorant about this whole problem myself until a member of my own family began to get swollen breasts," Friedman, an affable middle-aged man, tells me over a cup of coffee in the *Star*'s cafeteria. "We were of course concerned and went to see a doctor. He took one look at her and sent us over to Dr. Saenz. She recommended that we take her off of local fresh milk and meat, which we did. Now, I'm not a scientist, but I can tell you that her symptoms have disappeared." Friedman smiles with a look of pleased bewilderment.

"Once I was involved in this issue through our child, I of course spoke to Dr. Saenz about writing an article," continues Friedman. "Initially she was very reluctant and wanted to persevere through the Commonwealth Health Department. It was only after they repeatedly failed to do anything to find out what was happening that she agreed to let me do a story.

"When Dr. Saenz was quoted in print as suggesting that there might be estrogen contaminating the local food supply,

and people began to stop drinking local milk and eating local
meat, it created a hell of a sensation," continues Friedman.
"Things really went crazy. Industry started getting all up in
arms and began giving Dr. Saenz all kinds of hell, because
with a twenty-two-percent unemployment rate the Puerto
Rican economy is very vulnerable."

For a while, the estrogen scare caused an undetermined
slump in the sale of local beef, a 5.5 percent slump in the sale
of local milk and a 30 percent drop in the sale of chicken.
Dr. Saenz and her husband—who were as closely identified
as anyone with efforts to investigate the problem—were
threatened on several occasions. In one instance, someone
fired a shot into their home.

"Possibly it is not the local food supply that is causing the
problem, we don't know," concludes Friedman. "But the impression the bureaucrats at the Health Department, FDA and
Center for Disease Control have created is one of being more
interested in protecting business and themselves than public
health. They just don't want to accept the fact that something
abnormal is happening. The local Health Department operates
just like Lenny Bruce used to say, 'When you've been cheating
on your wife, even if she's got pictures, deny it.'" Friedman
laughs.

"'The FDA representative here went on TV, paid for by To-
Ricos, a company that produces poultry, and said it was OK
to eat chickens because he had personally inspected them.
But how could he know?" asks Dr. Saenz, throwing up her
hands in exasperation when I mention to her what Friedman
has said. "You just can't tell if a piece of meat has estrogen
residues in it by looking at it.

"When you're trying to get to the bottom of something like
this that involves the health of children, and the government
authorities tell you you are crazy or just trying to be political,
and when people are attacking you, it is very frustrating." Dr.
Saenz sighs.

Curious about whether the statistics on premature thelarche and precocious puberty here in Puerto Rico represent an unusually high percentage of such cases for a population of approximately 3.2 million people, I call up Dr. Alfred Bongiavanni, a pediatric endocrinologist who is a professor of pediatrics, obstetrics and gynecology at the University of Pennsylvania School of Medicine and former director of Children's Hospital in Philadelphia. He is also a former professor of Dr. Saenz.

"I find the figures are quite startling," he replies without hesitation, when I ask him if he is concerned by the number of reported cases of thelarche and precocious puberty in Puerto Rico. "Let me just give you an unscientific comparison. Philadelphia is an area of about seven million people. Here at the School of Medicine we see no more than three or four cases each year. In Puerto Rico there are hundreds each year, and I suspect those who are brought in for treatment are only the tip of the iceberg."

And what does Dr. Bongiavanni think about Dr. Saenz's lonely battle against Puerto Rican health authorities?

"I think the public-health authorities see Dr. Saenz as a nuisance whom they would rather not be bothered by," he says. "I could imagine the same thing happening in other states as well . . . you know, a hundred kids pop up with big breasts, and the secretary of health tries to brush it off because he has other things to think about. But I am quite familiar with the situation down there, having been at Ponce Medical College, and I don't find her presumption that some kind of estrogenic substance is getting into the food supply outrageous at all. In fact, I think she ought to be commended rather than attacked for her heroic efforts to bring attention to it."

In April 1982, the Commonwealth Health Department, the Food and Drug Administration and the Center for Disease Control (CDC) finally cooperated by collecting and sending seventeen samples of meat and milk to an FDA lab for testing.

For four and a half months no results were announced. Then, on August 11, 1982, the San Juan *Star* obtained a memo sent by Patricia A. McQueen, consumer safety officer in the FDA's Bureau of Veterinary Medicine, to its San Juan branch office saying that FDA labs had been "able to detect elevated estrogen levels in two poultry samples," one of which was locally raised by To-Ricos, owned by ConAgra, America's largest poultry producer, the other an import from the mainland produced by the Mississippi company Rogers Royal.

A week later, on August 18, however, after the contents of the memo had been published, federal officials began downplaying the "significance" of these findings, saying that although they had detected some "estrogenic activity" in two samples, the finding was of little significance, since they had not actually been able to chemically isolate any estrogen itself by gas chromatography in later assays of the same tissue samples.

Gerald Guest, deputy director of the FDA's Bureau of Veterinary Medicine, claimed that the initial tests "could mean nothing. . . . Just to go into the supermarket and take random samples off the shelves and test them doesn't lead anywhere."

"How can they say that there is no contamination down here after they only took seventeen samples of red meat, milk and poultry from the whole island?" angrily asks Dr. Perez-Comas, who had written one of the initial letters to *The Lancet*, when I speak to him in his Mayagüez office after the FDA statements. "Seventeen samples isn't even enough to tell the story of one village, or even one factory, much less an island this size."

Suspicious of the slow and incomplete way in which the FDA and CDC seemed to be probing the problem—they had, for instance, never contacted either Dr. Saenz or Dr. Perez-Comas to examine their medical records—Dr. Saenz felt discouraged and abandoned. She also knew that any tissue samples that the FDA might take in the future would probably not be very revealing, since by now any contaminators would have been scared off by all the publicity and mended their ways. But, anticipating just this problem, she had had the foresight months ago, before all the publicity had begun, to collect and freeze samples of meat, milk and poultry herself. She now sent these to her colleague, Professor Alfred Bongiavanni, for independent analysis.

Bongiavanni first ran Saenz's samples through a gas chromatographer to test for DES, estradiol and zeranol, the compounds that her detective had purchased freely at Puerto Rican veterinary supply houses. He found no significant residues. I ask Bongiavanni if these results surprised him.

"No," he replies without hesitation. "I was not really surprised. What you must remember is that we only had fourteen samples, and we were only testing for three out of many different kinds of estrogen."

Since the cost of continuing assays by gas chromatography for any other possible estrogenic contaminants was prohibitively expensive and time-consuming, and still not convinced the samples were uncontaminated, Bongiavanni decided to approach Dr. Saenz's Puerto Rican samples another way, through a testing technique called Estrogen Cytosol Receptor Assay. This method of assaying tissues for residues would be able to tell him if there were any estrogenic substances in general in the samples, although it would not be able to pinpoint the specific nature of the compounds should some samples come up positive.

An Estrogen Cytosol Receptor Assay involves the use of a special preparation of prepubertal-rabbit uterine cells that have been purified so that the only hormone receptors they contain are those that are capable of recognizing and taking up estrogens. The cells contain radioactively marked estradiol, which is displaced when they are put in proximity with a substance that contains any other kind of estrogen. By measuring the amount of displaced radioactive estradiol, researchers are thus able to determine the levels of estrogen that exist in the samples being tested.

But before he would know whether or not the levels of estrogen he might find in the Puerto Rican samples were relatively high or not, Bongiavanni had to establish a comparative baseline of normal residue levels in other meat. To do this, he purchased random samples of beef, pork, poultry and milk at several local Philadelphia markets and submitted these to the same assay procedures as the samples sent by Dr. Saenz.

His results were telling. Although the milk samples from Puerto Rico and Philadelphia showed similarly low levels of estrogens, one Puerto Rican pork sample and several chicken samples showed much higher levels than the Philadelphia samples. (Whereas the Philadelphia samples showed a low of 3 ng [nanograms] of displaced estradiol per kg, and a high of 532 ng, the Puerto Rican samples showed a low of 58 and a high of 7,750 ng/kg displaced estradiol.) One of the chicken samples again came from To-Ricos.

"What we found was a significant amount of estrogen," says Dr. Bongiavanni, emphasizing the word *significant* when I ask him to appraise his test results. "We are not sure what kind of estrogens we are dealing with, or even whether it is weak or strong estrogen. But what we found is cause for concern, not only because of the immediate problems that children like Dr. Saenz's patients are showing, but because we really do not know what the implications of high, long-term exposures to estrogen over the next twenty years will mean for these children in terms of cancer. Now that we have at least some evidence of a problem, I just hope that the CDC and the FDA will get going soon and find out what is happening."

In March 1983, almost a year after the CDC had finally taken its first seventeen samples from Puerto Rico and sent them to the FDA for testing, I call Dr. Jose Corderro, a staff scientist at the Bureau of Toxicology and Birth Defects at the CDC, to find out what progress has been made on the case.

"We still have not come up with anything conclusive," he tells me. "Just last week we had a meeting of experts on estrogens in the environment to try to sort out what steps should be taken next."

I ask him if he has any suspicions about what has been causing the problem. He notes that since the initial seventeen samples, the CDC collected another eighty-three samples of meat and poultry. When they were subjected to mouse-uterine bio-assay in FDA labs, they showed no sign of estrogenic activity.

"The number of possibilities of what might be going on is immense," he replies noncommittally. "It could be some kind of estrogen in the food, or water, pesticides that have estrogen-like effects, plants that are high in estrogenic substances. Or possibly it's coming from some other environmental source. We're just not sure yet."

Well aware that Dr. Saenz and Dr. Perez-Comas have criticized the FDA and CDC for being slow in responding to what they consider to be a serious public-health problem, I ask Corderro if he feels that there has been any official foot dragging or inclination just to ignore the problem in the hope that it would go away in time.

"We have only been looking at this problem for a little over a year," replies Corderro coolly. "Legionnaires' disease took several years to resolve. Toxic shock has been getting looked at for three or four years. I don't think it's fair to say that this case has been 'dragging on.' It happens to be a complex matter, and, like it or not, we are just not rich enough to do a fast million-dollar workup with all the necessary tests to find out what's going on. All we can do is to be systematic, and that's what we're trying to do."

I ask Corderro if he has any reason to suspect that the estrogen is coming from meat.

"I think it would be unfair to try to say that it was one

thing or another," he replies. "At this point we really don't have evidence to point in any one direction."

Six months after I first met her in San Juan, I call up Dr. Saenz to see if she has had any new revelations. She acknowledges that the CDC have finally collected a whole new batch of meat samples, and that they have all proved negative when tested for estrogenic activity. I ask her if in view of this finding she is still convinced that meat and/or dairy products are the source of the problems she has been observing in her practice.

"Yes," she replies emphatically, as if the answer to my question were self-evident. "I would bet my neck on it."

I ask her why, then, have the recent government samples all come up negative when tested for estrogenic activity?

"I think that whoever was using this estrogen has stopped," she replies. "Since December 1982 the number of cases of children coming through my office has dropped dramatically. My suspicion is that chicken has been the source of contamination."

I ask Dr. Saenz why she suspects chicken.

"I recently learned that last year, over a half million pounds of local chicken were sold to the school lunch program," she replies. "The chickens all weighed about three and a half to four pounds. Then a curious thing happened. I learned from a friend of one of my patients who worked as a distributor, that locally produced chickens suddenly began to go to the market weighing between one and one and a half pounds less than previously. This made me wonder if the publicity hadn't scared the growers from adding to their feed whatever it was they were using.

"When I checked with the chicken industry, they sent a delegation to my office with all their records trying to explain the discrepancy by saying that now they had started to kill their chickens at forty-eight days of age rather than fifty-six. But that seemed very strange to me. Why would they want to do that? And what I would like to know is, how could a chicken gain a pound and a half in eight days anyway?"

When I check back again with Dr. Alfred Bongiavanni, he, too, expresses suspicion about the curious manner in which local chickens had shrunk in size since the publicity surrounding the cases of premature thelarche and precocious puberty. When I ask him if he is still convinced that the problems are being caused by meat or milk, he pauses for a moment's reflection and then says, "Of course, I have not had an opportunity to do any field work in Puerto Rico. But based on what I know and the information I have received from Dr. Saenz, I think that it is very likely that she is right."

18

Diagnosing humans who have been contaminated with estrogens is difficult, not only because the symptoms are easily attributed to other causes—dysfunctions of the person's own endocrine system, for instance—but also because, as Dr. Saenz pointed out, should the offending drug be used in livestock production, most doctors would more than likely be completely unaware of it. As a result, even if they were to encounter patients with evident endocrine imbalances, it might not occur to them, as it finally did to Dr. Saenz and Dr. Perez-Comas, to investigate the possibility of contamination from animal drugs. In fact, the cases of premature thelarche and precocious puberty found among the children of Puerto Rico, whatever their cause, are rather unusual because the symptoms of estrogen contamination were so pronounced that they could not easily be overlooked.

There are of course other, far-subtler effects that researchers are still groping to understand. For instance, studies have suggested that elevated levels of estrogen in young women taking birth control pills may lead to an increased incidence of thromboembolism (a disorder caused by the formation of blood clots that can lead to a stroke) and melanoma (a form of skin cancer that is often untreatable). Another study has suggested that high levels of estradiol may be responsible for heart attacks in men. However, a third study found that women over forty who receive estrogen therapy have a lower rate of heart disease than those who do not. The data on these hormonal effects are still so incomplete and so conflicting that it is impossible to draw any general conclusions at all about either their safety or their danger.

But the most controversial and least understood effect of sex hormones on humans is their potential to cause cancer. The International Agency for Research on Cancer's (IARC) *Evaluation of the Carcinogenic Risk of Chemicals to Humans* states,

> The administration of estrogens to adult women is causally associated with an increased incidence of endometrial cancer. There is also a possibility that the risk of breast cancer is increased by such therapy, but the evidence is inconclusive. . . . At present, the specific role of endogenous hormones in the development of breast cancer is unclear.

About the synthetic estrogen DES, the monograph states,

> Evidence strongly suggests that the administration of estrogens [to humans] . . . is causally related to an increased incidence of endometrial cancer; diethylstilbestrol is no different from other estrogens in this respect.

About androgens (such as testosterone, also used widely in growth-promoting implants for cattle) the monograph says,

> Prolonged androgen therapy may be associated with an increased risk of hepatocellular [cells of the liver] tumors [in humans], but the evidence is not conclusive. . . . There is, however, sufficient evidence for the carcinogenicity of testosterone in mice and rats.

About progestins (like the synthetic progestogen MGA, fed to heifers to promote growth), the monograph states that evidence is inconclusive, noting only that, "there is no adequate data to assess whether progestins used as contraceptives [many birth control pills contain progestinal agents] alter the risk of developing cancer."

A 1983 CDC study seemed to confirm these findings, concluding, moreover, that birth control pills not only failed to increase the risk of cancer, but helped protect women against cancer of the ovaries and uterus. However, two other 1983 studies, one published in *The Lancet* and the other in the *American Journal of Epidemiology*, concluded that women taking hormonal birth control pills containing progestogen did have a substantially higher risk of developing breast and cervical cancer.

Are progestins cancer-causing? Like so many of the studies on other sex hormones, the data are bewildering and inconclusive.

After taking over five hundred pages to survey the literature on the subject, the IARC monograph concludes that while there is both adequate human and animal data causally connecting sex hormones to cancer, "the mechanism(s) by which hormones act in the induction of cancer is not understood."

Other growth-promoting drugs, like zeranol (contained in Ralgro and Ralabol), which have estrogen-like action, are also arousing suspicion. R. Shoental, with the Department of Pathology at the Royal Veterinary College, London, has been doing research on the carcinogenicity of both zeranol and zearalenone. In a letter to me he noted that "Both preparations induce tumors of the sex organs, when rats were exposed to them at the perinatal period . . . It is regrettable that in the USA, the long-term effects of *Fusarium* mycotoxins (zearalenone) have not been adequately studied."

Where so little is known with any certainty, there is quite naturally plenty of room for debate. The strongest proponents of the continued use of hormones in the production of livestock are quite naturally those scientists who have developed the drugs and are on the staffs of the drug companies who market them.

"These hormones, like any drug or technology, can be dangerous if improperly handled," acknowledges Syntex's Dr. Howard Ringold. "But I suspect that the only time there ever was even a possibility that meat animals were contributing a hormonal burden to humans was back when chickens were being injected or implanted with DES to caponize them. But I believe that the amounts of estrogens that our present products are adding to the human burden through meat are negligible. In my view, people are unrealistically afraid of their cancer-causing potential. And I don't believe in this danger from meat any more than I believe in poltergeists, psychics or flying saucers."

"I think that you have to remember that just the subject of sex hormones in food is a very emotional one," says Dr. Theodore Farber, director of the BVM's Toxicology Staff. "People are afraid of what these hormones might do to them and they are afraid of cancer, but their fears are not based on scientific knowledge. I think it was Shakespeare in *Henry the Fifth* who said something to the effect of, 'Of all the passions, fear be the most accursed.'

"I am not denying that if you give enough hormonal material to an experimental animal, you will produce cancer in that animal. There is no question about that. But I think if people were aware of the triviality of hormonal residues that are left in meat, and the much larger amounts of hormones they take in from natural foods like milk, eggs and grains, then they would be less fearful."

Roy Hertz, M.D., director of the National Cancer Institute's Endocrinology Branch for twenty-eight years and now research professor in the Department of Pharmacology at George Washington University Medical Center, views sex hormones, particularly estrogens and their potential dangers, much differently than Farber and Ringold. In a paper for a symposium held at the Cold Spring Harbor Institute in 1978 entitled "The Origins of Human Cancer," Hertz rigorously defended what he calls the estrogen-cancer hypothesis, namely that "both exogenous and endogenous estrogens and their metabolites play a significant and possibly etiologic [disease causing] role in the pathogenesis of cancer in estrogen-responsive tissues of man and animal." He noted, "In general, it would seem that chronic elevation above the level of endogenous estrogen production [that amount the body produces naturally by itself] would qualify as a potential carcinogenic dose."

After Hertz had presented his paper, he was questioned by Dr. J. D. Watson, the noted biologist who received the Nobel Prize for his pioneering discovery of DNA. "I have always been prejudiced against DES," said Watson, "but I haven't heard any quantitative statement from Dr. Hertz of the probability that the amount taken in [by humans] from meat will do any damage. It seems to me that is something which should be settled."

"I would say that given ideal conditions of control, [in] agricultural practice, and the proper supervision and surveillance of exposure to the public, the risk would be substantially reduced to almost zero," replied Hertz. "However, just consider our experience with respect to radiation exposure when it was found that so many X-ray machines all over the country were pouring out more radiation than we had expected. Similary, consider the accidental exposure to stilbestral experienced by patients, feed handlers and industrial pharmaceutical workers. Then you begin to appreciate that when we're talking about distribution of an agent that has a biological effect in parts per trillion, one of the best ways to control its accidental distribution is not to have it in the environment, unless there's a very strong reason. . . . My feeling is that the present

reasons for having it in meat production are so insignificant as
not to warrant that risk."

When pressed by a colleague to be more specific about the
levels of exogenous estrogen that must exist in meat before a
risk of cancer to the consumer becomes really meaningful,
Hertz replied simply, "The answer to your question is that we
do not know."

When I have an opportunity to speak with Hertz myself, I
ask him why he is so cautious about estrogens.

"What has to be remembered is that the endocrine system
is extremely delicate," he tells me. "The total amounts of
hormones involved in normal functions are just trace amounts
to begin with. To add any increment of hormones over and
above this is simply not justifiable in my view.

"I know that industry people say that the amount of estrogens they are adding to an animal's system are far below
levels that naturally occur after conception. But my response
to them is, 'Fine. But why add more?' The natural surges of
hormones are already enough of a biological burden on the
body. We know that these endogenous hormones already
play a vital role in the development of malignancies in the
female genital tracts and in the breast. So, just because these
chemicals are present in the body doesn't justify burdening
it with even more, particularly when the amounts that are
effective are in microgram quantities."

I ask Hertz to comment on the FDA's recent cancellation of
all withdrawal times for hormonal implants containing naturally occurring hormones.

"I think it is fallacious," he replies bluntly. "These drugs
were already in so many hands that it was difficult enough to
control them. Why make the situation worse?"

When I ask Hertz if he feels the FDA and the USDA have
been successful in regulating agricultural hormones in a safe
manner, he replies almost curtly, "My view is that we are

confronting technologies that are really beyond our means of effective control."

Wondering about Hertz's views on other sources of estrogen, I ask him if he looks on birth control pills with the same circumspection as hormonal growth implants.

"There are two conditions that make the circumstances very different," he replies. "The first is that contraceptives are taken under the supervision of a doctor. The second is that when a consumer decides to take them, she is making a free choice, presumably with full knowledge of the alternatives and the possible adverse effects. But in the case of hormonal food additives, the consumer has no idea that he or she is ingesting them. And I simply don't see any reason why a person should be involuntarily exposed to them. I simply take a purist view about these kinds of food additives," Hertz continues. "Unless there is a compelling need—in the case of famine, for instance —I don't think the actual, or even potential, risk can be justified. For drug companies to present these compounds as being without risk . . . is completely out of order, since we don't really know what their long-term cancer-causing consequences will be."

Those researchers, regulators and industry spokespeople who maintain that the risks of using more and more hormones in the production of livestock are negligible base their evaluation on the presumption that they will not be widely misused. For instance, in a recent 1982 report, "Hormones in Animal Production," the UN's Food and Agriculture Organization came up with the following evaluation: "It is clear that in most cases the contribution [of hormones to humans] from meat of treated animals is insignificant when hormones have been properly used, and therefore must be considered biologically without impact."

There are of course many scientists who are not yet quite so ready to acknowledge that agricultural hormones such as

we have described are "biologically without impact" on
humans even when they are "properly used." But even if we
were to assume that they are, as the FAO report and most
drug company spokespeople do, we are still left with an incomplete assessment. What is the impact of these drugs when
they are not "properly used"? For if the previous chapters
show anything, they show that agricultural drugs are often
used improperly and illegally. What is the effect of this improper and illegal use? It is virtually impossible to say.

IV

INSPECTION

"You see that discoloration there? Well, that's caused by pneumonia, and I can't pass a lung like that," says Dr. Thomas Harris, a meat inspector with the USDA's Meat and Poultry Inspection Program who works at the McDermott Meat Co., a slaughterhouse in Berkeley, California. "A lung like that is OK for dogs, but first it's got to be sterilized," adds Harris, slicing into its blotchy surface with a razor-sharp knife and then lobbing it into a plastic drum marked "Dog Food."

Turning back to a stainless-steel tray where other internal organs—a heart, two kidneys, a liver and assorted lymph nodes—still steam in the cold morning air from the warmth of a freshly killed steer's body cavity, Harris adds parenthetically, "We've got to at least cook these things even if they are for dogs, because, you want to know something? There are a lot of poor people out there who eat canned dog food."

Harris is one of approximately 5,500 inspectors who are required by federal law (the first meat inspection legislation was passed in 1906 after Upton Sinclair's classic *The Jungle* exposed unsanitary conditions in the nation's slaughterhouses) to inspect every animal carcass destined for human consumption.

Harris, who works here on the line at the McDermott Meat Co. deciding which bovine carcasses and internal organs are fit for entry into the meat markets of America, making judgments like St. Peter at the Pearly Gates, is a handsome man

with a black mustache, a hard hat and a rubber apron over a
white smock. Earphone-type sound mufflers help mute the
deafening cacophony of high-pressure steam used for cleaning, the clanging of steel on steel as carcasses move down the
slaughter line, the whine of the hide and tallow removers and
the snarling of a large chain saw used to split carcasses into
sides of beef here on the killing-room floor.

Harris stands in the middle of this noisy room wearing a
wooden scabbard of cutlery slung around his waist. Beside
him is a clipboard covered with a plastic flap to keep blood
and water from splattering on a tally sheet of the day's problems. "Flukes," "Granuloma," "Pneumonia," "Cervical Abscess,"
"Contamination," "Antibiotics," "Arthritis," "Liver." Clumps of
check marks have been placed after several of the headings
indicating the maladies that Harris has found on the inspection
line since he came to work at three-thirty this morning.

The killing room around Harris is filled with animals, minus
their hooves, heads, tails and skins, which hang down from
an overhead track and slowly snake their way past the various
stations of the various slaughterhouse workers like macabre
piñatas. Unlike a normal assembly line where workers and
machines labor to put together a manufactured product, here
in the slaughterhouse the process is reversed. Whole animals
are herded in from outside pens to be killed and then slowly
disassembled, their constituent parts systematically removed
and sorted into barrels, hampers and onto racks, as if an industrial film were being run in reverse.

The animals begin this process of demolition when their
throats are slit, and then—with tongues hanging limply out of
their mouths—their bodies are unceremoniously hooked behind the tendons of their rear legs and are swung up into the
air onto the overhead track, which moves them through the
killing room like bags of clothes on a dry cleaner's motorized
rack. Once bled, their hooves are clipped off with a gigantic
pair of hydraulic pincers. They are then beheaded, skinned,

trimmed of excess back fat and finally eviscerated just as they
reach the position where Harris waits to perform his modern-
day auguries over trays of internal organs.

Just as Harris finishes with one batch of organs and makes
a quick inspection of the hanging carcass from which they
have come, a burly meat cutter with tattooed arms wheels up
another cartful.

Harris reaches out to palpate some lymph nodes and then
deftly slices them open with one of the sharp knives at his
side. "If you see any blood or discoloration here, that's a
definite sign to start looking for pathology or other kinds of
toxicity," he proclaims. "The lymph nodes are like a filtering
system. Sometimes we'll find cancer. If the tumor is benign,
we will pass it. But if it is malignant and has spread, out it
goes." He sticks up his bloodied right thumb and makes a
gesture like an umpire calling a runner out at home plate.

"Actually, it's been a pretty good day," he says cheerfully.
"But sometimes we'll get batches of bad animals. The feedlots will just ship 'em out and hope they'll get through even
though they're sick and have been recently medicated. Last
Thursday, out of one load of sixteen cows I had to reject four.
They were hospital cattle someone just decided to shoot up
and get rid of. It was obvious." He steps over to a small sink
and rinses off his hands and knife.

"Some of the slaughterhouses out there are just killing shit,"
he continues. "They don't care. They buy junk cows at ten
cents a pound and sell them at ten times that amount. What
the hell! They can afford to have a few carcasses condemned.

"Actually, we're just a medium-size plant here," says Harris
as the next carcass swings around toward him. "We get by
here with one USDA vet inspector, namely me. But you go
into one of these houses where they're killing three hundred
an hour, they will have a lot of inspectors who just work
under the supervision of a vet [called the inspector-in-charge].
If they see something strange, well, then they have to stop the

whole line and call the vet. I've been in some of those houses where they're killing a lot of old cows, and they have trouble with almost every single animal. Here we're killing mostly top-of-the-line animals, and we still have to keep on our toes."

Like a samurai, Harris gracefully slices into the bile duct of a large gelatinous liver before him and then holds his butcher knife aloft. On the end of it are several small, flat, brown nematodes, which look like pieces of a whole-wheat noodle. "We're looking for a lot of things. But one of the biggest problems we have is liver flukes. There is no FDA-approved drug for them now, and they are very common." He scrapes the flukes off his knife and onto the floor and then slices a tic-tac-toe grid in the flat surface of the purple organ before him.

"If I'm rejecting an organ for human use but it can be used for dog food, I put a grid on it. If I reject it completely, I put Xs on it. That means it can only be ground up for fertilizer."

The organs of the next animal are wheeled over for Harris's inspection. He passes them as fit for human consumption and places them on a rack to one side, where they hang on hooks in neat rows, looking like deformed boxing gloves. "You can generally tell the state of an animal's health from the internal organs," says Harris, pausing for a moment. "After a while the sick ones really jump out at you.

"You can also tell a lot about meat by looking at the color of the fat. For instance, grass-fed beef is yellower. When you put them in a feedlot and grain them out, the fat will whiten up. These haven't been in a feedlot long enough," he says, pointing at the advancing row of brackish-colored carcasses.

Sharpening his knife, Harris strides over to another rack where the skinned and detongued heads of the cattle hang on hooks with their eyes bulging out, like so many Georgia O'Keeffe still-life subjects. He grabs a head with a steadying hook, and slices a few pieces of flesh off each cheek. "There is one stage of the tapeworm that will encyst here," he says, stabbing at the cheek area with his knife. "You eat it, you get it." He winks.

Then he walks over to check a carcass just as it moves down the line to be sawed in half. He steps around it the way a connoisseur of art might circumambulate a piece of free-standing sculpture in order better to appreciate it from all angles.

"What I'm looking for is lesions. They tell me if an animal has been injected recently with some sort of drug that might leave a residue and require me to send some tissue samples off to the lab. The problem is that it takes quite a while for me to get the results back. By that time, the meat is in the stores, and about all I can do is keep an eye on the next batch of cattle from that lot, if I can identify them."

Not only must Harris check for diseased cattle, and carcasses that show signs of drug or chemical residues, he must also take periodic tissue samples as part of an overall monitoring system, the National Residue Program, run by the USDA's Residue Evaluation and Surveillance Division (recently changed to the Residue Evaluation and Planning Division), a branch of the Food Safety and Inspection Service. This involves sampling animals for fifty to sixty different compounds on a random basis.

"Residues in food can present a hidden but serious threat to the public health," notes a circular on the National Residue Program put out by the Food Safety and Inspection Service.

> Because residues generally cannot be seen, smelled or tasted, they are difficult to detect. However, high doses of some of these chemical residues have been linked to such serious conditions as cancer, liver and kidney disorders, birth defects, and allergic responses. Therefore the monitoring of raw meat and poultry for drugs and chemicals is necessary to assure that approved compounds are not being misused, and are not presenting a danger to consumers.

Each year the Residue Evaluation and Planning Division feeds the previous year's toxicological data into a USDA computer and comes up with a program that instructs the meat inspectors on how many tissue samples to take from each kind of animal. The samples are then sent off to various federal, state and private labs for assay. When this random monitoring program uncovers a problem, the Food Safety and Inspection Service then orders the Meat and Poultry Inspection Program to begin what it calls a "surveillance program," a more intensive look aimed at specific kinds of animals, residues or even the livestock of certain producers.

"One of the problems with these surveillance situations is that often they will preempt our random monitoring," Dr. John Spaulding, the Residue Evaluation and Planning Division's director tells me one day on the phone. "Sometimes our labs will really get jammed up with samples from our chronic troublemakers (antibiotics, sulfa drugs, DES) and throw things out of kilter for a while."

When DES was finally banned in 1979, Spaulding's Residue Evaluation and Surveillance Division began to phase out its regular DES monitoring program. It was a compound they were glad not to have to continue to test for, because in Spaulding's words, "It was an extremely difficult and expensive drug to pick up through random monitoring."

I ask Spaulding if his division still tests for DES and whether or not they are concerned about residue from the other kinds of hormonal implants that are now being used in its place.

"We did some monitoring of DES last year, and I think we'll be doing some more this year," he replies. (In 1981 the USDA monitored only 62 carcasses for DES. In 1982 the number rose to 138.) "But on the other kinds of implants . . . well, we've kind of been in and out of the deal over the years. Most of them contain natural estrogens, and the FDA has now concluded, after looking at the changes of estrogen levels in

the tissues of implanted cattle, that the increases are too small
to worry about. So we haven't been doing any checking."

Is Spaulding's division concerned with the possibility of
residues from the various prostaglandins, such as Lutalyse?

"We don't test for them at all, because these compounds are
so short-lived," he replies.

And what about MGA?

"This is a popular one, and we have been monitoring it as
well as putting it on a semisurveillance-type program," replies
Spaulding. "But it is only used in heifers, and we have found
no violative residues. The only ones we have encountered have
been in what I call the 'chatter area' and are not real significant."

When I ask Spaulding if he feels the USDA's residue-
detection program is an effective one for shielding the consumer from unwholesome meat, he responds without hesitation. "Yes, I think we are on top of things."

Curiously, when I had interviewed him for the first time,
two years earlier in 1980, he had impressed me as much less
sanguine about the efficacy of the National Residue Program.
"Our problem is that we're at the wrong end of the chain,"
he had told me with exasperation in his voice at that time. "I
mean, we aren't a police system. We have no powers to
inspect on farms. No one tells us that an animal has been
double-dosed on some drug before being shipped. Controls
on exposure to toxic substances and drug residues at the
source just don't exist. It's all voluntary. And all that we can
do here is to monitor and survey. We can only tell after something has gone wrong. We have no program for prevention.
The animal has usually gone to the stores and been eaten by
the time our tests come back from the labs."

"Well," replies Spaulding, mixing a laugh with a sigh after
I remind him of his earlier words, "I guess I feel much better
now than I did a few years ago. We have moved away from

just chasing people who are violators to what we call 'residue-avoidance concept.' We are working with the companies who make these compounds and with the agricultural community in general on educational programs to try to assure that residues—which harm everyone—are controlled at the source. In fact, our agency went to Congress and got some money to fund various agricultural extension schools around the country to start working with farmers to inform them how to get this sort of avoidance into their management program."

While Dr. Spaulding now waxes with an apparently new-found optimism about the residue-detection ability of his division and the newfound "cooperation" between producers and regulators, others are more pessimistic. Carol Tucker Foreman, who was assistant secretary of agriculture under President Carter and was at that time in charge of meat inspection, bluntly labels this "cooperation" as "collusion" and a diversion of funds away from the much more important task of sampling and regulating.

I ask Spaulding about this assessment.

"About the only problem we haven't cleaned up is antibiotics and sulfa drugs in baby veal calves," Spaulding finally replies, almost buoyantly. "These young calves are under a lot of stress. [They are raised in the dark on iron-deprived diets, which make them anemic so that their meat will be white rather than red.] Oftentimes a producer will treat them with sulfa drugs and antibiotics before they are shipped so that they will make it to slaughter OK. And this has been a problem."

The problems of drug residue in meat are, however, not quite as simple as Spaulding suggests. Quite apart from the fact that the ingestion of antibiotic residues by humans contributes to the overall pool of resistant organisms—in the same manner as low levels of antibiotics fed to cattle subtherapeutically—residues may have another more immediate consequence. Humans who are allergic to drugs like penicillin can

have life-threatening hypersensitive reactions, such as going
into anaphylactic shock (in which the smooth muscles contract
and capillaries dialate) which can lead to death. Other kinds
of allergic reactions can be induced by the ingestion of miniscule amounts of sulpha drugs, which are not only widely and
massively used in veal calves in which levels of up to one
hundred times the permissible amount have been found, but
also in swine. During 1984, for instance, violative levels of
sulpha were found in more than 6% of all hogs tested. In the
mid-seventies, levels rose to as high as 12% in swine and 16%
in calves.

Another kind of dangerous residue in meat comes from the
use of injectable worming agents, and pour-on grubicides and
dipping agents which are used to control such parasites as
lice and ticks. All of these chemical compounds are legal,
although each has a required withdrawal time, a period of
days or weeks before slaughter time when the farmer must
cease using the chemical to avoid harmful residues in the meat.

Unfortunately, these withdrawal times are frequently not
observed, which means that animals get shipped to slaughter
houses before residues in their systems have been completely
metabolized. The result is that consumers end up eating meat
containing violative levels of active chemical compounds. And
since such carcasses show no outward sign of such residues,
inspectors are rarely able to detect the problem and impound
the meat.

Quite apart from the legal drugs which may leave harmful
residues in meat because they are overused or misused, there
is another whole category of drugs which are cause for concern when used "extra-labelly," or in a manner unapproved by
the FDA. For instance, the antibiotic spectinomycin has been
approved for swine, but is often used illegally to treat cattle.
Dimetridazole, cleared for use in turkeys, is illegally used in
swine. But perhaps the most alarming case of "extra-label"
use is that of chloramphenicol, a broad spectrum antibiotic

which has been banned from use in meat animals since 1968, when it was found to cause bone marrow depression or aplastic anemia in many human beings after very low and short-lived periods of exposure. In 1984, the death of one Kansas farmer was circumstantially attributed to his having absorbed a miniscule amount of the drug through an open wound on his hand while treating his animals.

What makes chloramphenicol so interesting to livestock producers is its effectiveness against pathogenic bacteria which have become resistant to other approved antibiotics such as oenicillin and tetracycline. So important had the illegal use of chloramphenicol become to the meat industry that by 1984, 95% percent of the vets surveyed by the magazine *Animal Health and Nutrition* admitted to using the drug. A third of this number admitted having used it for the past ten years. But even without a veterinary prescription, livestockmen found the drug easy to obtain in almost any animal drug supply house.

"We are receiving reports almost daily from persons across the U.S. who are concerned with the flagrant disregard that some of these animal drug dealers have for state and federal laws," Dr. William Bixler of the FDA's Bureau of Veterinary Medicine told the Association of Veterinary Drug Distributors during the summer of 1984, as the FDA launched an effort to crack down on the "extra-label" use of drugs such as chloramphenicol in meat animals. But so overdue was their effort that it did as much to underscore the agency's helplessness to control the misuse of animal drugs as to reassure the public that the government could still be counted on to protect the food supply from contamination with illegal compounds.

I ask Spaulding if he thinks hormonal compounds used in beef production present any dangers to humans.

"I would say that from the residue angle, things look pretty good," he responds. "I guess you might want to look at the people who handle some of the drugs. They are the ones who are likely to be getting much higher exposure to these things. It all depends on the conditions under which they are working."

There are, however, a growing number of meat inspectors in the field who are not quite as positive as the latter-day Spaulding about the USDA's ability to certify the wholesomeness of meat. While it may be true that some producers are becoming more aware of ways to prevent residues because of programs initiated by Spaulding's office, many inspectors on the line appear to have less and less confidence in the Food Safety and Inspection Service's commitment rigorously to inspect and select out those animals whose carcasses are contaminated.

In her 1983 report, "Return to the Jungle," on the USDA's meat-inspection system, Kathleen Hughes from the Center for Responsive Law, in Washington, D.C., interviewed a number of inspectors. She found that many were concerned that their effectiveness was being eroded by budget cuts and policy changes, which had been initiated by officials whom President Reagan had appointed to top-level positions in the USDA. She noted that several of these new officials had come to government directly from the meat industry itself.

For example, John Block, the secretary of agriculture, is an Indiana hog farmer. Richard Lyng, former head of the American Meat Institute (the most visible meat-industry lobbying group in Washington) is now deputy secretary of agriculture. C. W. McMillan (with whom I spoke during the DES affair), formerly executive vice-president for government affairs in the National Cattlemen's Washington office, is now assistant secretary of agriculture and serves as Block's main spokesman on meat-inspection policy. John McClung, formerly Washington bureau chief for the feed industry's weekly trade journal, *Feedstuffs*, is now director of information and legislative affairs for the Food Safety and Inspection Service.

The appointment of such men to top USDA positions has

had an at-once-subtle but important impact on how field inspectors go about their jobs.

"Lax enforcement allows contaminated products bearing the mark of inspection to be sold all over the world and at home," Hughes quotes Dr. Carl Telleen, a federal meat inspector, as telling a hearing before the House Agriculture Committee. After a twenty-two-year career as an inspector, Telleen claimed that the Reagan administration has "sold out the American meat consumer."

The Federal Veterinarian, put out by the National Association of Federal Veterinarians, published a letter in 1982 in which its Arkansas chapter also criticized the government's new policies toward meat inspection:

> Field veterinarians in the Meat and Poultry Inspection Program are becoming increasingly frustrated, and even humiliated, by the manner in which our responsibility and authority for implementing the Agency mission . . . has been undermined and circumvented by higher levels of Meat and Poultry Inspection management, as they apparently respond to pressure exerted by Washington politicians on behalf of the meat and poultry industry.

Like Thomas Harris, often the meat inspector will be the only government employee in a slaughterhouse or packing plant. Each day he must go to work side by side with the company's workers and deal with its management. He shares coffee breaks and lunch hours with them and will sometimes fraternize with them after work. He knows the financial problems of the company and the fears of his fellow workers that if the plant does not do well, it will be closed. All these factors can exert considerable pressure on an inspector, often making it difficult for him repeatedly to reject carcasses, or even to slow down a processing line while he makes a detailed but time-consuming and costly inspection.

Not only has there been a change in personnel and attitude

in Washington, but policies and regulations have also undergone a significant shift over the past few years. In October 1981, for instance, the USDA approved regulations that allowed production lines in hog-slaughtering plants to be speeded up. Kathleen Hughes reports that whereas previously a team of three inspectors would have been expected to examine approximately 337 hogs per hour, now they suddenly found themselves responsible for 506. The Food Safety and Inspection Service (FSIS) claims that "new procedures" have enabled them to increase efficiency with "no significant difference in reliability."

New regulations approving speedups in slaughterhouses killing cattle were also proposed. USDA officials contend that these were justified by lower incidences of disease and residue contamination, which they feel is due to better animal breeding and health care. But critics are concerned lest the statistics on which the speedups are based are not in themselves just the result of less rigorous inspection procedures. As of February 1983, the FSIS had not yet adopted new cattle-line speed requirements.

According to Hughes, another rule change (which was heavily lobbied for by the American Meat Institute) obligates an inspector to seek out his inspector-in-charge when he spots what he thinks is a problem carcass before he can actually stop the line for a more detailed look. As one inspector told Hughes, this changed procedure "acts as a disincentive to carefully examine questionable carcasses," for the simple reason that by the time the line can be stopped, the carcass in question will have inconveniently worked its way down past the inspection station.

Asked what the justification for such a revision in procedure was, Assistant Secretary of Agriculture (and a former vice-president of the National Cattlemen's Association) C. W. McMillan told Hughes that inspectors had been "abusing their authority to stop lines." When Hughes queried him about why they would want to "abuse their authority," she reported McMillan as replying, "Who knows? Maybe he [the inspector] had a fight with his wife that morning."

The question of whether or not the USDA's Meat and Poultry Inspection Program still stands as an effective bulwark between the consumer and "unwholesome" meat was raised by the Government Accounting Office in 1981, before Reagan even took office. After GAO inspectors had visited sixty-two meat-packing plants, they reported that they had found a "high incidence of unacceptable ratings" and a "large number of deficiencies," and they made a number of recommendations for improvement.

As of 1983, not only had none of the GAO recommendations been implemented, but the board of inspectors of the Program Review Branch (which evaluates the work of USDA inspectors in slaughterhouses and meat-processing plants) was slated to have the number of routine inspections it made each year cut. Before 1983, this panel of inspectors had rated plants on a numerical scale from one to four and put the management of companies receiving the lowest ratings on six-month probations either to clean up or to have their names publicized in local papers. At the request of the meat industry, the Reagan administration discontinued both practices.

These actions came on the heels of a 1982 report in which Program Review Branch inspectors had found the "potential" for unwholesome meat to slip past inspectors in approximately 71 percent of the plants they visited.

Perhaps the most debilitating blow to the meat-inspection service, however, has been the government's refusal to hire the full complement of inspectors that were authorized by Congress. As of November 1982, some 584 positions, out of an authorized 5,995, remained unfilled, and this 7 percent vacancy rate continued approximately the same through 1983, with the FSIS claiming that vacancies are "filled by other qualified inspection personnel on an interim basis." But Hughes reports that whereas in 1978 a slaughterhouse meat inspector only examined an average of 11.3 million pounds of meat a year, by 1981 the figure had risen to 12.7 million pounds, causing inspectors to begin complaining, like overworked air-traffic controllers, of fatigue and burnout because of growing work loads and longer hours.

According to Hughes, these changes in procedure and attitude have caused some veterans of the meat-inspection trade to doubt the efficacy of their own system and have made them reluctant to lend their official stamp of approval ("USDA Inspected and Passed") to meat destined for the consumer, which they know they have not had an opportunity to examine thoroughly.

"There is a good chance that the American public consumes meat with violative residues of carcinogenic and teratogenic [causing abnormal fetal development] chemical residues with some regularity," Carol Tucker Foreman recently told a congressional committee.

She added, in a later interview with *The New York Times*, that the National Residue Program was never designed to prevent contaminated meat from reaching the public, but that, in her words, "It merely monitors the incidence of violations and tries to prevent recurrences. I have always made the assumption that we are missing a good part of the contamination."

"Sometimes it can get real nasty being an inspector," admits Thomas Harris back on the killing-room floor of the McDermott Meat Co., months before the effects of most of these changes even began to be felt in the slaughterhouses around the country. "In some plants, an inspector is constantly up against management pressure to pass questionable carcasses on through. If you have to condemn a few head, you begin to get into some big money."

When Harris speaks of "big money," he is speaking of millions of dollars. For instance, in the fiscal year 1982, meat and poultry inspectors condemned 122,745,184 carcasses (e.g., 121,350 cattle, 37,788 calves, 247,858 swine, 1,224 goats, 57,109 sheep and 43,305,362 poultry, or less than half of one percent).

Not infrequently, however, contaminated and unwholesome meat slips completely through the inspection process and is sold to consumers as fit for consumption. Between September 1981 and January 1982, for example, the USDA's Program Review Branch of the Food Safety and Inspection Service found that adulterated or misbranded meat was leaving one out of five U.S. packing plants. In January 1983, John Coplin, a former Main Station Supervisor for the USDA's meat grading program, filed a complaint with the Office of Special Counsel of the Merit System Protection Board calling for an investigation of what he called "massive illegality, mismanagement, abuse of authority and substantial and specific dangers to public health and safety" in the USDA's meat-inspection program.

He claimed that as a grader he had personally witnessed the repeated over-pumping of cured meats with fluid to increase their weight; the use of spoiled meats to make frankfurters and baloney; and the transporting and slaughter of sick, crippled and diseased livestock, "some so bad that they had to be given shots to get them up on their feet."

In 1983, for instance, the USDA discovered through a televised NBC report that the Cattle King Packing Co. in Colorado, which had a $20 million contract to supply beef to the nation's school cafeterias, had been slaughtering diseased and even dead cattle, some of which were reported to have been contaminated with salmonella bacteria.

Also in 1983, Leonard Koppel, President of the Fort Plain Packing Co. in New York, was convicted of felony charges of slaughtering dying and diseased cattle, and of harassing USDA meat inspectors assigned to his plant. (He received a one-year suspended sentence, three years of probation and a $10,000 fine).

In 1984, a federal grand jury in Philadelphia returned a thirty-one count indictment against the Summit Beef Co. and the Taylor Pet Food Co. in Pennsylvania, claiming that between 1980 and 1984 the two companies had conspired to buy dead, dying and disabled animals (many heavily and illegally medicated) as pet food, only to resell them as human food destined for hospital patients, school children and air force personnel.

"What are you going to do," asks Harris, shrugging and smiling wryly. "We're here to inspect meat, and we're all that stands between the meat-eating public and the wild blue yonder." Harris slashes an *X* on a condemned liver and lobs it into the dog-food barrel.

Just then a loud buzzer rings on the killing-room floor, signaling morning coffee break. I follow Harris down a windowless corridor to a battered green door displaying a sign that reads, "USDA Field Operations, Meat and Poultry Inspection Program."

The small, dingy room beyond the door is the meat inspector's office, a symbolic representation of the tenuousness with which government authority is exercised in the middle of a privately owned plant. Inside, Harris sits down, takes his stocking feet out of his rubber boots and puts them up on his narrow desktop.

"When I first get here in the morning, I'll go out into the pens to inspect the cattle that have been trucked in the night before," he says, drinking coffee out of a Styrofoam cup and munching on a glazed doughnut. "If I see a sick-looking animal or one that shows any sign of contamination, I'll tag it. Then, when its carcass arrives at my station, I'll probably take a tissue sample. You know, it could be a drug, a pesticide or something completely unrelated to agriculture, like the PCBs that sometimes get into feed.

"Antibiotics are a big problem," continues Harris. "We're not so much worried about the resistance problem here as actual residues that show up, particularly in old dairy cows, which are injected before being slaughtered for meat. Whenever I see an injection lesion, I'll run a STOP test just to see what I come up with."

I ask Harris what a STOP test is. He puts down his half-eaten doughnut, gets up and opens the door of a small, square stainless-steel contraption beside his desk that looks something like a microwave oven.

"This is an incubator for bacterial cultures," he says, as he extracts a glass petri dish from inside. "These dishes are covered with special bacteria. Now, when I find a carcass which I suspect of having an antibiotic residue, I take a swab from the kidney, daub it on one of these petri dishes, and then place the whole thing in the incubator to see if the growth of the bacterial culture becomes inhibited in any way. This is what we call a STOP test, or Swab Test On Premises."

On the surface of the agar-gell mixture that covers the bottom of the petri dish in Harris's hand I can just make out a velveteen covering of bacteria growing like a lawn of microscopic grass. The growth covers the whole surface of the gell except for one circular area right in the middle.

"You see that blank spot?" asks Harris, pointing with his half-eaten doughnut at the bacterial clearing. "That's caused by the microbial-inhibition effect of the antibiotic still in the animal's system. If a ring of bacteria dies around the swabs, I know I've got a problem, because it means residue.

"If I get a positive like this, I'll try to find out which feedlot the animal came from, although we don't always have a surefire way of tracing an animal back to its place of origin. But I like to know who the chronic offenders are. And if I think we have a shyster, I'll try to identify him and in the future run tests on the cows from that lot just to check," adds Harris.

As we head back to the killing room after our coffee break, Harris detours into a large, dimly lit, walk-in cooler, where sides of beef hang in long rows. Doing slalom around three or four sides, he finally stops. Examining the hindquarters of one side carefully, he points at a greenish, discolored area in the fat surrounding an almost imperceptible puncture mark and says, "OK, you see that? That's probably the site of a tetracycline injection. I did a STOP test on this animal and got a positive. But before I can officially reject the carcass, I have to send a sample off to the FDA lab in San Francisco for further testing. That'll take about a week, and then we can decide whether or not to condemn the meat. But in the meanwhile, at least I have grounds for impounding this carcass now and not just letting it slip on down the line like we usually have to do."

Harris gives the haunch of the offending side of beef a reassuring slap with the palm of one hand and then walks over to a cagelike structure. Inside, there are a variety of plastic bags hung on hooks filled with various internal organs.

"We've got to test those too," says Harris, pointing at a liver in a large Baggie. "Sometimes they're bad even though the meat's OK. We've got to lock 'em up. That's the rules. Somebody might try to escape with the evidence." Harris gives a mock-conspiratorial smile.

"I'd like to think we do a pretty good job," says Harris with professional pride as we walk back toward the killing room. "We work hard. But I was a feedlot practitioner for five years back in Nebraska before I came to California, and I've seen what they put into some of those animals before they ship them. I do worry about all the antibiotics and stuff they use. I mean, let's face it, we've only had these drugs around in large quantities for thirty years or so, and we really don't know what their sustained use will finally mean."

V

CONCLUSION

Over the past several decades, the ways in which livestock are produced in the industrialized world have undergone a dramatic transformation. Antibiotics, new feed technologies and hormones have all played a major role in this transformation. While the short-term benefits in the form of greater efficiency in mass production and thus lower meat costs to consumers are undeniable, assessing the long-term risks has been a much more elusive undertaking. In many instances drugs and chemicals have been approved before the long-range consequences of their use are completely understood. Frequently the studies that might have helped establish the degree of such risk have not been done, or have only been done incompletely because of the immense costs they entail. But just as often it has been impossible to do conclusive testing because the state of our scientific knowledge has not been sufficiently advanced. Instead, we have often allayed our fears with short-term studies that, though important, are too incomplete to tell us all we need to know. It is true that each time a hog consumes a subtherapeutic dose of tetracycline, a cow ingests a small quantity of printer's ink or insecticide, or a steer is implanted with a hormonal pellet the consequences to humans is probably negligible. But when the use of these compounds is extended over millions of such episodes and continued for decades, the cumulative effects may present a whole different magnitude of effect.

As Dr. Saenz discovered in Puerto Rico, even those animal

drugs that are illegal, or that are supposedly restricted by federal law to use "by or on the order of a licensed veterinarian" can be bought without prescription through the mail, at feed stores, pet shops and even some supermarkets. They frequently fall into the hands of people with little experience in using them and no understanding about the effects of misusing them.

Almost anyone familiar with farmlife or the livestock industry has witnessed instances of carelessness and misuse of animal drugs and chemicals. Livestock may be treated right up to slaughter time with no observance of federally required withdrawal times. Drugs approved for only one species of animal may be used on an "extra label basis" for another. Large overdoses may be given on the assumption that if a little is good, a lot is better.

Many of those who handle animal drugs, veterinarians included, are carelessly exposing themselves and their fellow workers to contamination. Their cavalier attitude is frequently startling. On one occasion, for instance, I witnessed a Texas cowboy pick up a syringe as if it were a water pistol and shoot a co-worker in the face with estradiol cypionate, an injectable estrogen (which Dr. Saenz's detective had succeeded in illegally purchasing) used to abort animals or induce them to expel mummified fetuses. On another occasion, I witnessed an experienced cattlewoman repeatedly douse her hands and arms with the highly toxic grubicide Coumaphos (an organophosphate) while pouring it on the backs of cattle, where it kills the grubs of heel flies and lice by being dermally absorbed into the animal's system.

Many cattlemen seem almost to cultivate a disregard for caution around potentially dangerous drugs and chemicals, as if prudence might be misinterpreted as timidity or unmanliness. A corollary of this kind of machismo is the cattleman's often-haughty disregard for government inspectors, who are viewed not as protectors of the public health but as bothersome fuddy-duddies, sent forth from the disdained, and possibly socialistic, world of "big government" to spy and intrude on private enterprise.

Cattlemen are people of a practical rather than scientific bent. They are more concerned to know *if* a drug is effective rather than *how* it is effective. And, working outside as they do where the wind blows free across vast open spaces and where there are relatively few signs of man's encroachment on the environment, minuscule amounts of anything can easily seem trivial, and the consequences of carelessness insignificant.

Habitual carelessness easily turns into lawlessness. And as we have seen in the case of DES, not only is the potential for the lawless use of animal drugs real, but government regulatory agencies are often ill equipped to handle it when it does occur.

After the 1983 DES violations in upstate New York, Lester Crawford lamented to me, "Although livestock producers have traditionally been among the most law-abiding citizens you'd ever hope to find, there has been a breakdown of this sense of law and order. I think you'd have to say that recently we have seen an epidemic of people using drugs in a careless and lawless manner."

Although there are many areas in which it would behoove us all to be wary of blindly accepting the ever-increasing use of drugs and chemicals in the husbandry of meat animals, it also behooves us to remember that a fearful concern that leads to the rejection of all of these new livestock technologies will be as blind as one that leads to embracing them indiscriminately. Certain feed-additive antibiotics—such as those that are not used for human therapy, or those few that curiously do not generate R plasmids—can be a great asset to livestockmen if used judiciously. Certain hormones, such as those prostaglandins that are very short-lived, and even certain growth-promoting hormonal implants ultimately may prove not to pose unreasonable risks to humans when used properly in meat animals. And when the shock of thinking about cows eating ethylene and propylene pellets wears off, we may actually wish to applaud such new technologies as Dr. Erle Bartley's amazing plastic hay.

But in those cases where the consequences of continued widespread use are still not yet clearly known, or where reputable scientists have provided evidence that continued use may prove injurious to us or to our environment, we will be ill advised to blunder wrecklessly on, business-as-usual.

The use of penicillin and tetracycline feed additives, which we once believed we could feed to animals with no ill consequences to humans, now appears to be compounding a serious problem by decreasing the efficacy of these very drugs for human use. Like the air we breathe, the water we drink and the food we eat, we find that bacteria are not the exclusive province of any one country, any one part of the body, any one person or even any one species of animal. They are more like an unseen matrix connecting all forms of life. The discovery of the specific mechanisms by which resistance to antibiotics is transferred between living things reminds us that in spite of our biological diversity we are all, in the last analysis, inextricably joined.

"The vulnerability of microorganisms to antibiotics is a kind of commons—a resource, which, as we consume it by the use of antibiotics for nonmedical purposes in animals, is now diminished in man," noted Donald Kennedy, a biologist who is president of Stanford University and was commissioner of the FDA under President Carter when that agency last attempted to regulate the use of penicillin and tetracycline for feed-additive use. "The benefit of using these drugs routinely as over-the-counter products to help animals grow faster, or in prophylactic programs, does not outweigh the potential risks posed to people."

The sex hormones with which almost all beef cattle are now raised in this country may not pose such a well-documented and clear-cut danger as penicillin and tetracycline feed additives. In their case, it is not so much what we already know about them but what we do not yet know about their widespread and often indiscreet use that gives cause for concern.

"One can easily appear Luddite about the use of hormones in meat animals," says Samuel S. Epstein, M.D., professor of occupational and environmental health at the School of Public Health, University of Illinois Medical Center in Chicago. "Even though the consequences of their use are unclear, one can still look at them by way of analogy to our experiences with other hazardous drugs and chemicals. Over the last forty years we have paid such a terrible price for refusing intelligently to assess the risks of new technologies before leaping into them. We have too often perturbed natural systems for short-term gains, but with disastrous long-term consequences. And quite apart from science, I feel instinctively that it is a terrible mistake to interfere with anything as delicately poised as the endocrine system, with so little information about where it is leading us."

"When it comes to using drugs and chemicals in meat animals, we find ourselves in a situation in which our problems are well ahead of our answers," says Dr. Jere Goyan, dean of the Pharmacy School at the University of California in San Francisco, reflecting on his tenure as commissioner of the FDA after Donald Kennedy. "We just have not yet developed the science to back up reasonable regulations and safeguards in advance of their use. And until that time, if we are going to err, it would seem wise to me to err on the side of safety."

INDEX

ABOUT THE AUTHOR

ORVILLE SCHELL's interest in the subject of livestock technology came out of his own experience as a working rancher in California. A journalist and China scholar whose articles have appeared in *The New Yorker, Life, Rolling Stone* and many other publications, he is a former Alicia Patterson Foundation Fellow. He is the author of *In the People's Republic, Brown* and *"Watch Out for Foreign Guests!"*